MARTHA W. GRIFFITHS

Emily George, R.S.M.

UNIVERSITY
PRESS OF
AMERICA

LANHAM • NEW YORK • LONDON

Copyright © 1982 by

University Press of America,™ Inc.

4720 Boston Way
Lanham, MD 20706

3 Henrietta Street
London WC2E 8LU England

All rights reserved
Printed in the United States of America

Library of Congress Cataloging in Publication Data

George, Emily.
   Martha W. Griffiths.

   Bibliography: p.
   Includes index.
   1. Griffiths, Martha Wright, 1912–   . 2. United
States. Congress. House–Biography. 3. Legislators–
United States–Biography. I. Title.
E748.G876G46   328.73'092'4 [B]   81–40922
ISBN 0–8191–2347–1   AACR2
ISBN 0–8191–2348–X (pbk.)

E
748
G876
G46
1982

CONTENTS

Preface	. . . .	v - vi
Chapter I:	Pre-Congressional Years . .	1 - 34
Chapter II:	Congress, 1955-1960 . . .	35 - 66
Chapter III:	Ways and Means and Joint . . Economic Committees	67 - 142
Chapter IV:	Women's Rights	143 - 210
Chapter V:	Welfare Study	211 - 264
Chapter VI:	Retirement	265 - 276
Bibliographic Essay	. . . . . .	277 - 282
Index	. . . .	283 - 295

PREFACE

Martha W. Griffiths is a Congressional biography of Martha Wright Griffiths, Michigan Democrat, who served in the United States House of Representatives from 1955 to 1975. Griffiths became well known in 1972 when she maneuvered the Equal Rights Amendment out of the House Judiciary Committee where it had been bottled up for nearly fifty years. But to Griffiths, the ERA was just one achievement and perhaps not even her most important. In her twenty years in Congress she worked in a fundamental way toward substantive policy changes in the areas of social security, pensions, welfare, and taxes. Further, she consistently championed equal rights legislation affecting both men and women. Chapters III, IV, and V treat of these matters and comprise the heart of the biography. Chapter I introduces the reader to Griffiths' pre-Congressional years; Chapter II tells of her struggles as a junior member of Congress; and Chapter VI provides a wrap-up of her service on Capitol Hill.

There is a way in which *Martha W. Griffiths* tends toward semi-autobiography. A good deal of time was spent with Martha Griffiths and her husband Hicks, as well as in interviewing persons significant to the Griffiths' story. Additionally, ample use was made of rather voluminous papers among Griffiths' personal holdings and in the University of Michigan Bentley Historical Library. The size and currency of these data allow the facts to speak for themselves. The reader will find, therefore, a biography more descriptive in orientation than interpretive.

The author is indebted to the Sisters of Mercy for allowing her time to pull this study together and for supporting her by grants from the Mercy Action Fund and the Sister Mary Raymund O'Leary Ministry Fund. She is grateful to an anonymous donor for supplementary income. Dr. Robert M. Warner, former Director of the Bentley Library in Ann Arbor, and his staff were particularly helpful to her and must be thanked. So, too, the library staffs at Mercy College of Detroit and the Benton Harbor (Michigan) Public Library. There were many others who assisted through the ups and downs of constructing a biography, but special credit must be given to Elizabeth LaForest, R.S.M., for meticulously editing the text and to Dr. Doris B. McLaughlin, Associate Research Scientist of the Institute of Labor and Industrial Relations, University of Michigan (Ann Arbor) and Wayne State University (Detroit), for offering insightful corrections and a bit of wit. Dr. Mary Lou Callahan, Professor of Political Science, Mercy College of Detroit, also reviewed the chapters concerned with public policy formation. Jane Mackowiak, R.S.M., Eileen M. Colquitt, and Bernadette Sykes, SNDdeN, heroically typed and retyped until every word was in place. They are friends indeed. Finally the author is grateful to her mother, Martha George, who lived her last years while the manuscript was in progress and who kept the author going by her encouragement and prayer.

CHAPTER I

On January 28, 1928, future member of Congress Martha Wright Griffiths wrote in her diary: "Today is my last day of fifteen. One more year of life has gone. What have I accomplished? . . . I must be, I will be successful in something if it is merely in washing dishes." "But," she had confided to her journal a few weeks before, "I truly wish to be a journalist." And as though to inspire herself to this attainment she had penned a double adage: "'Reliability is the keystone in the arch of success. Neglect is the mother of ignorance.'" To sleep less and not "end up in the poor house because of a wasted youth" had been her final admonition to check what she considered her adolescent waywardness.[1]

The diary of a sixteen-year-old can reveal something of the future adult. Martha Wright would continue to prod and excel, being graduated as valedictorian of her class. But Pierce City, Missouri, was provincial and the Great Depression so deep by the time she finished high school, there seemed no way out for a small-town girl. That she found a way can be credited to her parents and to her husband, Hicks George Griffiths.

The Missouri Ozarks was where it all began for Martha Griffiths.[2] The first large band of pioneers had come to this midwestern outpost in the 1830s. The next migrated some forty years later with the opening of the southwestern branch of the Pacific Railroad. The Irish, who numbered among the builders of the transcontinentals, were followed by the Germans and the Poles, many of whom settled in what was then known as Peirce, named after Pacific's vice-president. In 1970, Pierce City, as it was now called, was incorporated as a village and seven years later was large enough to qualify as a small city. From the outset, the predominantly white settlers determined cooperatively to farm the surrounding apple and pear orchards and to mine the highlands rich in lead, zinc, and iron. Before the turn of the century, Pierce City had a post office and a hotel, electric lights and a telephone system, several churches and schools, a lyceum where philosophy and Greek were taught —even an opera house and a literary club. The only major establishment missing from this list of achievements was a permanent library, which, to Griffiths' youthful disappointment, was not built until 1933. By this time she was at the University of Missouri.

While Griffiths was growing up, Pierce City's vigor was already on the wane. Any hope of recovery came to a decisive halt when the Pacific Railroad closed down because of declining migration to the Ozarks. As a result, the local residents slipped from a peak population of 2500 to 1500. The bright side of this demise was that on into the twentieth century, Pierce City retained a small-town atmosphere, a character greatly enhanced by the plethora of trees which lined every street. Occupying the frame house on the shaded corner of Elm and Pierce were the Wrights—(Charles) Elbridge Wright, Nelle Sullinger Wright, and their two children, Martha and her brother Orville Edward, who was four years her senior. The Wrights moved to Pierce City in 1921 when their farm located just outside the city limits burned to the ground. Martha was nine at the time.

The Wright and Sullinger families had been identified with southwestern Missouri since 1850, their forebears having first migrated to the Ozarks during the Jacksonian Era. These long-term settlements contributed to building a permanent subculture held fast by mores and sanctions and providing little room for anonymity and innovation. Even in the twentieth century change was not encouraged.

Fortunately for Martha Wright, her paternal grandmother, Jeannettie Hinds Wright, broke through these ancestoral barriers. After the death of her husband she learned to be a seamstress and, by sewing, clerking, and managing a hotel, put three sons through high school in an era when few children went beyond eighth grade. She was also an ardent suffragette: first in the voting line and numbered among those who championed a woman president.[3] Martha's father inherited his mother's grit and liberal ideas. During the isolationist, business-dominated 20s he advocated free trade and social experimentation. Elbridge Wright was a Democrat, and his daughter not only had a special affection for her father but was drawn to his political leanings. The latter can be gleaned from her diary entry on the occasion of Herbert Hoover's inauguration: "I hate to think of looking at his picture for four years," she wrote.[4]

Had better times prevailed, Elbridge Wright might have made a name for himself. As it was, he was fortunate to be able to provide for his family as a letter carrier, hoping all the while his two children would have opportunities for the social and economic mobility he did not have. Both seemed destined for college until the Depression when Wright thought that, to provide for Orville, Martha would have to forego a higher education. The stately 5-foot-10 Nelle Sullinger Wright objected. Far-sighted and liberated for her times, she believed a woman had to be prepared for the future, and she took an active role in life around her. During World War I she worked outside the home as a substitute postal carrier. A proponent of practical concern for one's neighbor, she was always engaged in raising money for the sick and poor of the area. Nelle Wright was also an exceptional homemaker and a very fine cook—skills she passed on to a willing and capable daughter. She was ingenious in making the home a place of both work and play and, because of her, there was always something interesting to do in the Wright family. In 1930 she decided that the most interesting thing that could happen would be for her eighteen-year-old daughter to go to the University of Missouri and study literature. To make it possible, she took in boarders.[5]

Martha Wright was delighted with the new base of activity the University afforded her. She joined the debating team and did volunteer work for the campus radio. This small-town girl who read every book she could get her hands on became a familiar face to the campus librarians. In fact, within twenty-four hours of paying her tuition, she ran up a $2.65 fine for removing Goethe's _Faust_ from the stacks. She quickly established a rigorous reading schedule which she faithfully kept. In the morning and evening she read in her rooming house, reviewed current periodicals in the library between classes, and at lunch-time caught up on back issues. On weekends she scoured the Columbia public library for books the University did not have— three being her customary consumption over a weekend. As a result of this near obsession with books Griffiths quickly acquired rapid reading skills. She further became committed to the cause of education, particularly the need for libraries; and she built a vast reservoir of knowledge from which she later drew as a legislator and a speaker.[6]

In Martha's sophomore year, twenty-one-year-old Hicks George Griffiths left Union College in his home state of New York to pursue political science at the University of Missouri. The following year, the bright, witty Easterner was paired with Martha Wright on the debating team. A courtship followed and on December 28, 1933, Hicks and Martha were married. Hicks often quipped that from then on everything was "Wright."[7]

Martha Griffiths favorably impressed her in-laws. One described her as having a pleasing physical appearance; as "very good looking though no classic beauty . . . about 5 feet 5 inches tall, not heavy and yet not skinny . . . [having] nice eyes and lovely teeth." She likewise dressed to their liking—properly but not extravagantly—was a good cook, and seemed "very modest in her demands." She and Hicks Griffiths were obviously devoted to each other.[8]

And devoted they were. For the "Mother of ERA," as she is sometimes called, to admit that by herself she would never have had the temerity to become a public servant may seem a contradiction; but, she explained, "it really was not."[9] Although her husband could not give her a wedding ring when they married, he gifted her with confidence in her abilities and did whatever he could to draw them forth throughout their married lives. He persuaded her to become a law student and insisted that she enter politics. He ran her initial campaigns and was her chief political adviser. They built together. In the early years of their marriage, they helped each other become established professionally and worked as a team to revitalize the Michigan Democratic Party. During the twenty years from 1955 to 1975 when Martha was in Washington and Hicks was in Detroit, they supported one another through their mutual belief that what each was doing was worth the sacrifice of separation. Such cooperation convinced Martha Griffiths that if every man were like her husband there would be no need for an equal rights amendment, and she would not have to work so hard on behalf of women. She hoped some day a monument would be erected to her spouse bearing the inscription: "He always thought women were human."[10]

In 1934 the Griffiths moved from Columbia to the University of Michigan Law School in Ann Arbor. Although Hicks had been accepted at Harvard, he chose the midwestern campus because it admitted women. From the outset Hicks determined that Martha would have a professional career so that if anything would happen to him she would be respectably independent. Initially she had not planned to go into law but succumbed to Hicks' urging.

Marriage and higher education proved to be a happy combination for both although they had few economic resources. Hicks took a job in the law library and Martha was part of the clerical staff on the Michigan Law Review. During the summer she worked as a secretary at the university hospital. While the struggle for economic survival left them little time for campus social life, they broke their work-study routine by playing bridge on Saturday nights and occasionally by entertaining their classmates at Sunday breakfast.[11]

Upon graduation in 1940—the law school's first married couple—the Griffiths went to work for the American Automobile Insurance Company—Martha at ten dollars a week less than Hicks. With the outbreak of World War II, Hicks joined the legal staff of the Michigan Office of Price Administration (OPA) and later became Chief Price Attorney for Michigan and Utility Counsel to the National OPA Office on matters affecting Michigan. Martha meanwhile was hired as the first woman contract negotiator with the Army Ordnance Department in Detroit, a position that did more to prepare her for the future than she realized at the time. As an attorney she was put to work writing contract changes, first with munition manufacturers, and later with vehicle producers. Since the government bought quantities of wartime goods amounting to millions of dollars, she dealt with corporate vice presidents. This experience not only put her in contact with significant persons but taught her how big business functioned from the inside out.

In April 1946, Martha established a law practice which Hicks joined in August upon completing his stint with the OPA. G. Mennen ("Soapy") Williams, another University of Michigan law school graduate and former deputy director of the Michigan OPA, became partner to the Griffiths the following February. By that time, Martha already had had her first taste of politics as an unsuccessful candidate for the Michigan Legislature.

This initial bid for office was a woman's idea. One day Griffiths received a telephone call from Phoebe Munnecke, who had been with her at a gathering of women lawyers. Munnecke, a long-time suffragette, urged Griffiths to run for the legislature and, though she was a Republican, she promised Griffiths her personal support. "I refused," recalled Griffiths, "but my husband said, 'You run.'" And she did, only later to admit that she was "not a completely reluctant candidate." In retrospect, she also laughed at her naivete. "I had captained the debate team in high school and college. With hardly any trouble, I could see myself swaying vast audiences, doing great good, changing the whole course of the world."[12] This rather romantic notion did not stand her in good stead in 1946. With only 27 candidates to be elected for Wayne County, including 21 for Detroit, she garnered 8,882 votes in the primary, running eightieth in a field of ninety-two.[13] If she could take comfort in loss, it was in knowing she had done as well as she had in a year when Democrats were defeated everywhere. On the positive side, the primary afforded her the opportunity to get public exposure, with the result that in 1947 she was elected as Seventeenth District representative to the Michigan State Central Committee.

The 1946 setback also proved to be a blessing for an emerging group of dissidents gathered around the Griffiths. Doubtful that the regular party could possibly secure a reversal in 1948, they began creating a grassroots movement that they hoped ultimately would supplant the moribund leadership. "We want to build an organization," Hicks told interested listeners; and, if his words did not persuade, the 1947 state party convention did. The jockeying among county organizations for top leadership alienated the more idealistic Democrats.[14] One commentator caught the mood in describing the situation as a "slow case of internal combustion."[15] Martha, meanwhile, went on the Central Committee with the idea of preparing herself for the changeover. She was determined to learn the politics of organization, as well as techniques for raising funds and recruiting women into the party. After several months of testing, the Griffiths and their small band of associates decided it was time to move beyond the regular organization. In broad outline, Martha told about what took place on November 21, 1947: "Some eighteen months ago," she wrote an inquirer, "Mr. Griffiths and I invited sixteen Democratic leaders into our home and formed the Michigan Democratic Club of which Mr. Griffiths is the Executive Secretary. It was the purpose of this organization to foster wider and more active participation in the Democratic Party. We intended to do this by setting up clubs throughout the State, locating candidates and fostering interest in every campaign."[16] Included in what has now been styled as "the famous basement meeting" were Secretary of Labor John W. Gibson; Ann Arbor millionaire businessman Neil Staebler who later succeeded Hicks Griffiths as State Party Chairperson; Mel L. Laliberte, a Flint public relations expert; and several attorneys and businessmen from western Michigan.

In a veiled way Griffiths' statement announced that these mavericks intended to defeat both the Republicans and the regular Democrats in the forthcoming general elections. Dissent was always risky, but in 1947 it was tantamount to rendering the Democrats impotent. Wallace Progressives and Thurmond "Dixiecrats" were soon to break with President Truman, thereby leaving the field wide open for a Republican victory in 1948.[17] In Michigan, the new breed's only hope against further dissention was to hold the line against creating another faction in the splintered party and to wrest the organization from the hands of State Party Chairperson John R. Franco whom they referred to as "Der Fuhrer."[18]

The first thing the reformers decided to do was to discover from select county leaders whether or not Democratic Clubs could be organized at their level. They were convinced that without a network of county organizations their plan would not succeed. Several meetings were called throughout the state to explore this issue, and the results were encouraging. One key member spoke for many when he said that this strategy was "the only way to drum up interest in Democratic candidates."[19] Confident that the counties would go along, in February 1948 the group legitimated itself by incorporating as the Michigan Democratic Club. The Griffiths and Laliberte were designated to draw up a constitution in which they pledged both the restoration of the Party to its former integrity and the administration of justice and social welfare to all citizens of the state. In March the Club authorized Hicks to prepare for the fall primary.[20]

Hicks and his staff had already begun to urge the new rank and file to make themselves available for political office, especially in strongly entrenched Republican counties. This meant, in the language of one of Griffiths' later slogans: a candidate for every position, a worker for every precinct, and a challenger at every poll.[21] According to the strategy, it mattered less how successful these aspiring officeholders were. What was more important was that safe incumbents be challenged, that this be done particularly at the precinct level where the victory ultimately would be won. Outstate Michigan was particularly ripe for these tactics because there disenchantment with Republican Governor Kim Sigler was being strongly voiced by members of his own party.

The new Democrats' ultimate goal was to replace Sigler with their own candidate. They believed Michigan needed a new face—a young face, and a new voice that would speak for the workers, for the poor whites and blacks congregating in the cities, for youths needing educational facilities and staff. Michigan was ready for its own New Deal and so were the unions. The task was to find a candidate who personified this growing desire to bring Michigan into a progressive era.

Since the meeting held in the Griffiths' basement, Griffiths' law partner, Mennen Williams, was identified as a possible prospect. To ascertain Williams' voter appeal, the Griffiths arranged several neighborhood gatherings where the folksy 6-footer could meet people socially but purposefully. Between square dances he spoke about improving labor conditions, including a fair employment practices act. Despite a family fortune and Princeton education, Williams professed "a messianic vision" to dedicate his life "to the service of the underdog."[22] This emphasis went over well with Michigan's large ethnic groups. The political pundits, however, were mixed about Williams' ability to carry the election. The least they could say was that he would present a strong challenge to Sigler. The Griffiths, too, were unsure of the results but were willing to put all they had behind their law partner. In early spring 1948, the Club decided Williams should enter the primary. "Nothing short of a cataclysm will stop me now," Williams wrote Lawrence Farrell, Upper Peninsula Democrat and his former OPA boss.[23]

The enthusiasm, idealism, and planning did not mask the reality that a November victory would be difficult to achieve. By April, Martha was already admitting that the effort had cost dearly. "Between politics and the practice of law" she and Hicks were "exhausted most of the time."[24] The real work, however, the work of winning, had just begun. First there was the primary and then the general election to win—without the money and experience of Franco's organization. "You know, we are amateurs," Hicks Griffiths confessed to Larry Farrell. Whatever advice Farrell had to give would be gratefully received as it was starting at the bottom in learning how to win.[25]

There was no end of work to be done. A University of Michigan voter survey revealed that a new campaign strategy would have to be designed in response to issues significant to the electorate.[26] Winning also meant courting organized labor, a role assigned to Williams and Hicks. The unions were ready. In March the Michigan CIO announced that it was going Democratic and urged all its members to become politically active and get themselves elected as convention delegates. The AFL, less cohesive than the CIO, was also sought out by Williams' supporters. "The A.F.L. is new in Democratic politics," Martha Griffiths informed one of the local chiefs. "The A.F.L. should support the man who can do the most for them."[27] Winning also meant active campaigning.

Martha Griffiths, billed as "an excellent talker," travelled with Hicks throughout the Michigan countryside.[28] Party regulars scorned these efforts as futile, but not the Williams' people. Even before the primary, Martha exuded victory. "This 'Dead Party' had not shown for years as much life as it is now," she wrote India Edwards, Vice-Chairperson of the Democratic National Committee. After listing anticipated gains county by county, she asked Edwards "not [to] count Michigan out, for we are going to do all we can."[29]

By September all the hard work began to pay off when Williams won the primary in a sharply contested race. That he defeated Sigler two months later, at the same time Michigan voted for Republican Presidential Candidate Thomas E. Dewey, attested to the vigor of the new Democrats and demonstrated the potential of organized labor. The Griffiths were elated with the outcome —and their lives were changed. "We elected our partner Governor," Martha wrote a close friend, "and we elected me as a member of the Legislature. Hicks is now the State Chairman of the Democratic Party. We lead a hectic life."[30]

The drive to elect Williams had paved the way in Wayne County for a pro-Williams' legislative slate. In the primary for First District Representative, Griffiths garnered 41,000 votes, enough to secure a November victory. Concentrating primarily on Williams' campaign, she attributed her success to friends. "In the final election I moved up eleven places from my numerical position in the primary," she told an acquaintance of her army contract days. "My only explanation is that all of Ordnance must have voted for me."[31] Actually Hicks had done such an outstanding job with Williams that Martha could not help but reap side benefits. Labor endorsed her as did the influential <u>Civic Searchlight</u>. And people had not forgotten her performance as wartime contract negotiator. In the general election the "youthful, striking Mrs. Griffiths," as the <u>Detroit News</u> called her, received nearly 390,000 votes.[32]

Williams was delighted with Griffiths' election as

she was with his. "There never has or never will be a better representative than you," he told her.[33] Thirty years later, Mildred M. Jeffrey, long-time political activist and labor representative, stated that Williams' advancement was always before anything Martha Griffiths might have wished for herself. Reminiscing on the occasion of Griffiths' retirement from Congress, she wrote: "It seems like yesterday when we urged you to run for the Legislature in 1948. I recall you saying, 'But my first responsibility is to help Mennen.' We said, 'You can help him by being a candidate and running with him.' And that's what you did, not only as a team-mate in the campaign but also in the Legislature."[34]

In 1949 what Williams needed most, and what Griffiths could give—one of two women out of a hundred Representatives—was to challenge the sixty-one Republicans with a whole set of progressive programs. Griffiths expected that the new administration would usher in a "wonderful, if strenuous" year, but agreed with Williams that without a Democratic House "a difficult time [lay] ahead for us."[35] The Legislature had grown set in its ways. One-third of all Representatives in 1949 were over sixty; only 20 percent were under forty. The pay was meagre, and there were no perquisites. At most, the Legislature was a place where the enterprising could come and test their mettle, and then move on. Those who stayed seemed, to the 37-year-old Griffiths, to have been there forever.

During her four years in Lansing Griffiths served on committees dealing with judicial matters, conservation, private corporations, public utilities, and the state constitution. Her initial appointment to the conservation committee particularly pleased her because of her keen interest in the problem of soil erosion. But once she learned that the committee's annual task was solely to discuss hunting and fishing regulations, she felt angry and frustrated.[36]

The Legislature nonetheless provided an arena where she could press for reform. To help Williams redeem his campaign pledge to workers, particularly the urban blacks, Griffiths introduced a fair employment practices bill in 1949. According to Griffiths, the Republicans, objecting to the bill's penalty clause and the independent status of the proposed commission, strove "to put [the] F.E.P.C. on the books, and then prove that it won't work."[37] Not until 1955, when Griffiths was already in Congress, did Williams get the law he wanted.

In addition to her fight for workers' civil rights, Griffiths was active in formulating an enlightened unemployment compensation law that increased benefits substantially, extended the payment period by six weeks, raised the maximum benefit by nearly 50 percent, and provided tax relief to small employers and to other businesses with stable employment records. Moreover, she was known for her consistent support of nutrition bills, highway safety legislation, and laws which required swift and equitable justice throughout the state judicial system.[38]

The Michigan Legislature also served Griffiths as a public forum where she appealed against the prevailing conservatism of her colleagues. She inveighed against gasoline taxes for consumers while corporate profits remained unchallenged, and she decried balanced budgets at the expense of essential human services. "[To] save the people with the wealth and tax the people who can't afford to pay" was a philosophy she could not abide. Nor could she tolerate the "iron curtain" tactics of the Republican-dominated committees. Killing a bill in committee was, in her opinion, "government by trickery." On several occasions she attempted to force legislation on the floor by a discharge petition, a strategy she was to put to dramatic use in Congress.[39]

Griffiths looked upon her fours years in the Michigan Legislature as a time for building her spirit and for learning the dynamics of lawmaking, particularly parliamentary technique. These years also revealed whose side she was on. When Frank X. Martel of the Detroit-Wayne County Federation of Labor asked her to support the prohibition of women bartenders so as not to arouse the criticism of the professional drys, she said she could not be a "traitor" to her sex and would have "to vote for the women."[40] In the main she found her initial venture into politics "interesting, if not financially rewarding."[41] That the Capitol Press Corps commended her as one of Michigan's ten outstanding legislators testifies to a job well done.

Between 1948 and 1952 the Griffiths lived hectic lives. Not only did Martha have her legislative duties, but both she and Hicks had to keep their law practice active to survive financially. The pace might have been less demanding had Hicks been free to devote most of his time to the firm, but his work as head of the Democratic Party, a post he held for a year and a half, consumed a great deal of time and was very difficult.[42] His predecessor, Franco, had left a sizable debt which Hicks determined to pay in a year—and did. Hungry office-seekers, turned down in favor of the new Democrats, clustered around James R. Hoffa's former attorney, George S. Fitzgerald, who was serving on the Democratic National Committee. They warned Williams that if he did not get rid of Hicks the whole party would collapse. Even some less embattled old-timers, including those who supported Williams, thought Griffiths was too uncompromising in his views as to who should constitute the party. Although the Governor discounted the rumbles as "conflicting ideas in our party," there was indication that he differed with his chairperson on party membership. Williams saw the organization as an umbrella under which disparate groups could compromise to achieve party goals, and where organized labor, especially the UAW, had a special role. He also believed he should listen to all professed Democrats; to have, in short, more than "one conduit." Griffiths, on the other hand, held to the idea that the party should devote its efforts: first, to those responsible for the 1948 election; and, second, to those Democrats who subscribed to reform. To invite in other elements was to "throw conscience away."

The estrangement between old and new Democrats peaked during the 1949 Detroit mayoral election. Griffiths and August Scholle, president of the Michigan CIO, put the weight of their respective organizations behind five-term council member George Edwards. Infuriated by party and union support in the supposedly non-partisan contest, the newspapers and the influential Citizens League deserted Edwards. Disenchanted Democrats took this as their cue and joined Republicans in electing the politically inactive City Treasurer, Albert E. Cobo, as mayor. In June 1950 Griffiths stepped down as party chairperson and Williams appointed him a judge of probate.

Griffiths' new job did not free either him or Martha from involvement in the 1950 campaign. Martha's decision to run again for the legislature made it necessary to counteract the bad press that had been building up against Williams and the party. That Williams was to win only by a little more than a thousand votes shows how severe the opposition had become. In May, Martha launched a novel campaign initiative. Inviting twenty women to a Sunday breakfast, she suggested they begin immediately to explain the election issues to Wayne County women on a block-by-block basis. She also planned to enlist two hundred additional women, each to sponsor ten neighborhood parties where all registered women voters could come and hear where the Democrats stood on issues of mutual interest. Griffiths was particularly concerned that unvoiced questions be addressed. She knew from her experiences as a trial lawyer the special importance of answering every inquiry on the minds of the silent courtroom jury. She hoped that in the relaxed atmosphere of their neighbors' homes, the women would speak freely, and she was certain her plan would succeed because the Michigan Legislature had just turned down every appropriation that had to do with children, education, and mental institutions—matters which deeply concerned women.

By summer, the main responsibility for these "Teas for Victory" fell to Griffiths as speakers and hostesses eased themselves out of their assignments. To free herself for the circuit, Griffiths gathered a small core of women to arrange speaking schedules, telephone prospective hostesses, mimeograph invitations, and address envelopes. Hicks joined the effort by raising money for postage and other campaign necessities and, beginning in August, the Governor's wife, Nancy, regularly accompanied Martha to an average of six teas a day. In the last month before the election, they attended more than two hundred such gatherings, the final one held on election eve.

In her "Teas for Victory" Martha Griffiths had tapped a significant source of support not only for Williams but for herself. One party organizer ascribed the reason to greater knowledge of and participation in party affairs. "People _wanted_ to hear. People _wanted_ to know. People _wanted_ to ask questions."[43] Writing to India Edwards some months after the campaign, Griffiths said that her plan had helped take some of the heat off Williams, although it had been more than she had anticipated in effort and less than she had hoped for in converts. "Everyone involved worked hard and long," she noted, "but on the other hand, we enjoyed it. We were sure that we were making a real contribution."[44] What Griffiths had also done was to build a coterie of women attracted to her own political fortunes, women eager and willing to assist her in 1952 when she decided to run for Congress.

The decision to enter national politics in 1952 was built on the endorsements of both the UAW[45] and the Seventeenth District leadership and on the enthusiasm and urging of Hicks who promised to manage her campaign.⁴⁶ The political climate unfortunately was not good for the Democrats. After twenty years of Democratic control, Americans were looking for change. How bad things really were was documented in the spring of 1952 in a survey conducted by the Michigan Democratic Central Committee. The findings were "so damaging" to the party—more voters preferred Eisenhower to all the other candidates combined—that campaign headquarters shared the information only with Williams and senatorial aspirant, Blair Moody.⁴⁷

Groundswell for change further meant that the National Democratic Committee would have little money to spare for Congressional office seekers. The $1,000 earmarked for Griffiths was pumped into the Stevenson-Sparkman television campaign as Democratic prospects worsened. Nor did the State Central Committee have money for national campaigners. Whatever the Griffiths needed had to be raised on their own.⁴⁸

As though nationwide disenchantment with the Democrats and lack of money were not enough, the Seventeenth District offered its own challenges. Before Griffiths' successful election in 1954, the District had never voted Democratic, and the Democrats who had managed to survive there were, in large part, identified with Franco. Twenty years later, Williams remembered the Seventeenth as being "very rambunctious" and said that if he had had to depend solely on its support, he never would have been elected Governor.⁴⁹ Had Griffiths not possessed the pluck of her fellow Missourian, Harry Truman, the Seventeenth District would have been enough to keep her out of the campaign. There were times when she had to face the taunts of the voters.⁵⁰

There was, however, an exhilaration in making a bid for national office. Moreover, there was room for freshness of approach. In 1952 Griffiths introduced a unique campaign strategy: she traveled her district in a trailer, an idea generated by two of her associates. One, unsuccessful in finding a store-front office for her in the district, suggested she rent a trailer; the other pictured the trailer as a roving caravan where her constituents, especially the women, might come, enjoy a glass of juice, and discuss election issues. Griffiths objected but surrendered to the pleading of her friends. Why not give it a try?

At first the trailer received a mixed reaction, including its share of hecklers. Soon, however, many acknowledged that Griffiths had "a secret weapon" in the vehicle she carted around the district "like a Good Humor man." She had found a way, the <u>Detroit News</u> observed, "to get to her constituents, let them ask questions about government, and answer them on the spot." Voters could meet her face to face, a contact which she discovered was as important to her as to them. Griffiths recalled later that without the trailer she probably would have remained unknown to most women.[51]

But driving the trailer up and down the district from June until November was no unmitigated pleasure. Griffiths, her staff, and whoever they could enlist were out in the neighborhoods by 9 each morning, Griffiths personally canvassing the bars to meet the patrons. At 5 in the afternoon she had to be off to campaign coffee parties, so it was often not until 11 o'clock that she and Hicks had their supper. There was also the sheer physical exertion of hauling the 40-foot van through the narrow streets. Hicks insisted that part of voter appeal would be in seeing her at the wheel. In six weeks she covered 1,500 miles, making six locations each morning and eight in the afternoon.

The trailer carried her through the primary with encouraging results for a newcomer: she had only 5,600 fewer votes than her Republican opponent, Common Council member Charles G. Oakman. What she lacked for a November victory, however, were money and the Eisenhower appeal. Oakman also rode high on the anti-Communist crest, telling his audiences that only the Republicans could halt "the repulsive parade of Reds, Parlor Pinks and Communist sympathizers into high office in Washington." Griffiths' campaign, on the other hand, was within the Roosevelt-Truman tradition. Reminding her listeners of her progressive record in the Michigan Legislature, she promised to control inflation without paralyzing the labor market into unemployment. She also pledged herself to thwart the spread of Communism—but in the Truman way of building good allies through economic aid. She made the unusual bid to put Congress on television, which she felt was an antidote for the soap operas to which most homemakers were daily subjected. "Mrs. Citizen," chanted Griffiths' campaign workers, "Seeing is believing, / You know her record in this state. / It stands to reason, she will make us / An upright and honest candidate."[52]

A month before the elections, Eisenhower stopped in

Detroit and announced he would go to Korea if elected. The response to the President was so favorable that Griffiths decided the only way for her to win was to go on television and show people how to split their ticket.[53] Straight-party Democrats cried betrayal and never forgave her. Griffiths lost to Oakman but the slim majority of 10,000 votes, representing a narrow three percent margin, revealed a potential for success. In thanking her constituents for having helped her come so close to winning, Griffiths said she hoped that "as one neighbor to another," she would have the opportunity to interact with them again.[54]

Following her defeat, Griffiths returned fulltime to her law practice which proved to be a short-lived experience. In April 1953, Williams appointed her to an unexpired term as recorder and judge of Detroit's Recorder's Court—the first woman to hold that post in the Court's 127-year history.

The appointment released the venom that had been building for sometime against the Griffiths. The <u>Detroit Times</u> called it "an example of political patronage at its shoddiest" and asked why John J. O'Hara, who had just been elected to the next full term, could not have been chosen for the nine-month interim. "Detroit's court and Detroit's money are being used thus," protested the <u>Times</u>, "to pay a personal and political debt." Some members of the Wayne County CIO were reportedly "doing a slow burn" over the appointment when they recalled how Martha had conducted her Congressional campaign, especially her television appearance. "She was not a team member," they said. "She was more interested in getting Martha Griffiths elected than she was in the welfare of the Democratic Party."[55] Williams, however, felt no hesitation in justifying the appointment on grounds of both friendship and indebtedness. He believed that both Griffiths were "exceedingly capable people" and contended that what might have been construed as "being a little greedy on their part" was outweighed by talent and service. For Williams, the appointment was eminently reasonable and proper and in the best interests of everyone.[56]

Williams did not stand alone in his views. Some saw in the decision the Governor's ability to rise above partisan faction; others shared in the pleasure it gave women generally, and Democratic women in particular. Most concurred that Williams had endowed the Court with a competent and assertive judge and noted that in light of her performance in the Michigan Legislature, Griffiths' court term proposed to be energetic and purposeful. "She pierced many a legislative hide then with sharp-tongued logic," the Detroit News pointed out, "and attorneys agree, her court should be 'interesting.'"[57] Of all persons, Griffiths herself was most delighted. After the economically lean years in the Legislature, the $15,000 salary for the nine-month term was welcome. Above all, she relished the idea of being a judge. "I am happy because you appointed me to this judgeship," she wrote Williams after a month on the job, "I just love the work."[58] As later events were to show, the bench possessed an enduring attraction for her.

Everything about Recorder's Court—the banal and dramatic—tested her ingenuity. As a trial lawyer she was no alien to the courtroom, but saying what the law was and meting out sentences were far different from defending the actions of a client. What was one to do about the woman who throttled the bus driver in a temperamental rage, or how render justice to a father who beat his children in self-hate? What about the five score drunks, petty thieves, prostitutes, and pimps who presented themselves daily for judgment? These unfortunates, labeled by press "the vile silt from the bottom of the bucket," elicited pity from Judge Griffiths. The Detroit Times, which had been as vehement as the News in denouncing her appointment, praised her performance after a month's observation. "It's a dirty job—especially for a woman judge," commented the daily, "yet Mrs. Griffiths has managed to inject a dignity new to the history of 'early sessions' court."[59] Before long, law enforcement personnel behaved more graciously toward the persons they presented to Griffiths each morning.

Besides this daily parade of human weakness, there were the moral criminals who preyed on the weak. Two notable cases occurred during her term. The first involved a movie guild that swindled thirty-five dollars each from 5,000 families. Griffiths fined the guild and jailed the manager. The second concerned several local Teamster unions that grew fat on sums extorted from small entrepreneurs.[60] It was especially in these labor rackets cases that Griffiths showed her mettle. For months she heard how the union chiefs had intimidated, and even bombed, uncooperative jukebox establishments; how they had set up dummy employee lists for autowash operators; and how they had received thousands in payoffs from Detroit-based contractors, many involved in building Michigan's freeway system. Above all, she was appalled by the Teamsters' admission that they cared little about the workers they represented and from whom they collected dues. As a result of these examinations, she turned a number of the Teamster officials over to trial, among them Frank E. Fitzsimmons, who eventually succeeded James Hoffa as international president. "You have pinned a union label on terror and violence," she said in condemnation.[61] Before the ruling, the Teamsters had tried to get Griffiths to back down. She remembered how Hicks had tried to take the edge off the seriousness of the situation by reminding her that they would do her no harm while the trial was in session.[62] From then on, however, she incurred their lasting enmity.

The press praised Griffiths for her courageous stand against the Teamsters. The *Free Press*, which gave her an outstanding woman achievement award, pointed out that in her treatment of organized crime she could be "as tough as a whalebone," and the *News* underscored what perhaps was not so obvious: most judges would have stayed clear of the "touchy" Teamster affair altogether. The *News* further noted that in every instance Griffiths had shown "studious attention to the law and a constant sense of fair play."[63] Having won her laurels in the conspiracy cases, in November 1953 she defeated attorney Maxwell M. Lowe for the six-weeks' term necessary to complete the court year. She had also gained political mileage in ordering a retrial for life convict, Willie Galloway, when two key witnesses confessed to false testimony. A feature of Griffiths' time on the bench was that she convinced her male colleagues that she was worthy of their esteem. On her retirement from the Court they praised her for having brought "a woman's instinctive and oftimes intuitive approach to the many problems that perplex mere men" and they thanked her for having allowed them to draw on her experiences as a legislator and contract negotiator.[64] The lasting significance of having heard 2,400 cases in a nine-month period cannot be underestimated. Months after she had left the Court, she looked to the public acclaim she had won there as the requisite to overturn Oakman's 1952 three percent margin.[65]

As early as June 1953 Griffiths considered running again for Congress, although by the time she completed her term on the bench she hoped another judicial vacancy would open up to her.[66] "I liked being a Judge," she confided to a close friend in January 1954, "it produced a good life for Hicks and me, better than one of commuting between here and Washington. Everybody seemed well pleased with the way I did the work so I would like to return."67 Nevertheless, as a realist, Griffiths kept her options open. Commenting on the state of the nation the day after she wrote of her desire to continue in a judicial position, she told Williams that 1955 was going to be a good year for the Democrats and that when the Eighty-fourth Congress met in January 1955, there would be "darn few Republicans left."68 Her own prospects were yet too unclear to predict how she would figure in that development.

What was clear was that she had a future in politics. As court possibilities dimmed by the spring of 1954, she returned to the idea of running for Congress. Hicks wanted her to try for the Senate and offered to fly her throughout the state as part of her campaign strategy.69 Martha demurred, however, once Williams backed former U.S. Senator Blair Moody.70 When Moody died suddenly after filing for the primary, the Senatorial candidacy went to his sole contender, union leader Patrick V. McNamara. By this time, Griffiths was in the House race in what was to be the most bitterly fought election in Michigan and one of the most closely watched in the nation.

The Seventeenth District—comprising Detroit's 22nd Ward, Livonia, Northville, Plymouth, and Redford Township—was not only Michigan's most populous, but one of two in Wayne County that had voted consistently Republican. Political analysts agreed that the fight there could affect the outcome in a close race for Governor and U.S. Senator. That Williams' majority in 1952 had been less than 10,000 statewide—the Seventeenth having voted by a 5,000 plurality for Williams' opponent—heightened anxiety over that district.

The district leadership, by now made up mostly of UAW delegates, adopted the policy of endorsing a candidate for the primary, the only Democratic organization in Michigan to do so. The district chairperson, Alfred V. Meyer, whom the press accused of "kick[ing] the precedent of impartiality in sundry directions," justified the action on the grounds of "party responsibility" to select the best candidate.71 Thomas L. Poindexter, a political neophyte, was judged worthy of this trust. The Wayne County CIO and the UAW followed the district Democrats and recommended Poindexter to their membership as "a hard working liberal who stands for a program

of aggressive action."[72] Poindexter, who later was to
embarrass both organized labor and the Democrats by
heading a local racist organization, had religiously
sought party and union endorsements. Griffiths had not.

Poindexter's selection by the unions badly strained
the already fragile relationship existing between them
and the Griffiths. In 1953 the UAW had helped defeat
Hicks for probate court because of his tight-fisted
patronage while state chairperson.[73] Frank Morris of
the Detroit Times reported the estrangement in these
terms: "As the UAW-CIO gradually took over the party,
Mr. and Mrs. Griffiths slid out of the inner circles."
In further remarking that the Griffiths were drawing
handsome profits from their labor relations work with
corporate clients, Morris inferred that, by serving as
contract negotiators for business and in representing
business before the NLRB in labor-management disputes,
the Griffiths had jeopardized their standing with the
very organizations they had so carefully courted only a
few years before.[74]

Seventeenth District leadership still bristled
from Martha's breach of party loyalty in the 1952 election when she had instructed voters to split their
tickets. That she was above seeking party endorsement
in 1954 added fuel to the fire. Distaste for this
brand of independence was stated in a memo from the
district chief to central headquarters. "We strongly
condemn," he wrote, "the practice among some self-
seeking Democrats of deliberately ignoring the democratic organizational channels easily available to every
Democrat, in order to attempt personal aggrandizement
through the press."[75] Given Griffiths' independence,
the district believed it had no alternative but "[to]
teach her a lesson." As a result of party action,
Martha perceived herself as "literally on the outside of
the Democratic Party organization." The district, however, saw it as "a case of Mrs. Griffiths deserting the
Democratic Party rather than the Democratic Party deserting Mrs. Griffiths."[76]

When Griffiths advised Governor Williams in June
1953 of her plan to run again for Congress, she spoke at
length of the conflict that would arise within the
party. Party endorsement, she said, "would precipitate
a fight in which innocent bystanders . . . would be compelled to make a choice between me and the official
organization." She proposed that, in place of an official endorsement, she and any other prospective candi-

date be permitted to sit on the Congressional campaign committee. This would preclude any argument that she was "not cooperating" and would clarify the role of the local party which was to conduct campaigns and not usurp the rights of the electorate. She also believed that the state organization, in collaboration with the National Committee, should immediately decide where to concentrate its efforts. Griffiths told Williams that if she lost the primary, she would support the winner. It was obvious to her that the critical Seventeenth District required an "airtight" strategy if the Democrats intended to win in 1954; and in view of the tenuous gubernatorial and senatorial races, she believed them "morally bound" to try. For her part, she had already begun with the help of several devoted women to set up master files so that, when the time came, a direct mailing could be sent to district voters on issues that interested them because of their professional or business affiliations.[77] In late 1953, however, her desire to run for Congress apparently diminished in favor of continuing on the court. But as that hope waned early the next year, she decided to announce her candidacy despite the opposition of both the UAW and the Seventeenth District leadership. And she did so with elan: she and a bevy of women rode to the Detroit City-County Building in her campaign trailer to file the 2,300 signatures that would make her candidacy official.[78]

Armed with this kind of determination, endorsed by the Detroit-Wayne County AFL, and preferred over Poindexter by the non-partisan <u>Civic Searchlight</u>, Griffiths won the primary by nearly a 7,500 majority. "The size of the Democratic vote," conceded Poindexter, "indicates that you should win the final election with votes to spare."[79] More Democrats had turned out in 167 of the 291 precincts than had Republicans, a fact partially explained by the absence of a challenger to incumbent Oakman. The vote, nonetheless, made the GOP nervous, and the press predicted that its decisiveness pointed to a "'humdinger'" of an election. Even though the Republicans had planned to "make it tough for Martha," privately they were saying that their own candidate had "the fight of his life on his hands."[80] While Griffiths might have taken solace from this, she was a political realist. Oakman, publicly endorsed by Mayor Cobo, had defeated her in 1952 and in his first Congressional term had shown himself a faithful disciple of President Eisenhower. He had likewise been attentive to the needs of Michigan, his support for the St. Lawrence

Seaway being a case in point. Two weeks after the primary, Griffiths informed Representative John J. Dingell Sr., that she would have to spend "every moment" campaigning. "The Republicans will put their major effort in Wayne County against me," she said.[81]

Griffiths' August triumph narrowed the opposition. The UAW now offered support, as did the district leadership, although as Griffiths recollected later, the local party never regarded her as "a real white hope."[82] With labor and the Democrats behind her, only Oakman remained to be challenged. Griffiths intended to capitalize on his close identification with Eisenhower, as revealed in his whimsical slogan, "Ike needs Oak." In 1954 the President was in trouble because of a rather severe recession.

Eisenhower referred to this economic downswing as the "skeleton in the Republican closet, locked in by demagogues." A firm believer in the capacity of the free market to adjust itself, he opposed any tampering with the labor market even after unemployment rose to three million in early 1954. The most the Administration was willing to do was to impose a tight money policy. When the economy experienced a turnabout in the spring, the President believed that he had been vindicated and the "cardinal Republican concept" of self-help validated. Recovery had been the work of the American people, he said, not the result of public works.[83] Griffiths analyzed the situation differently.

Well known by now as the roving candidate, Griffiths drove her yellow and green "town-hall on wheels" up and down the district, talking that summer and fall to over 40,000 constituents. Her special magic was her personal contact with Northwest Detroit homemakers, whose future she related to the <u>issues</u>: their husbands' unemployment, the lack of schools for their children, the high cost of living which they experienced day-in-and-day-out at the supermarkets. She spoke of the Administration's do-nothingism and, worse, its apparent malfeasance in the Dixon-Yates scandal and in the Tidelands giveaway[84]—millions that could have been spent for teachers and classrooms. Emphasizing her experience in the legislature, on the court, and in business, she promised that if elected she would work for laborers through creative solutions to unemployment such as public works modeled on the Tennessee Valley Authority. She also promised to work for amendments to the Taft-Hartley Act such as repeal of 14(b) which allowed the states compulsory open-shop laws. Most especially she pledged support of a wage increase for postal workers, a volatile issue among Detroiters because of Oakman's ambiguous stand on the issue.[85] For farmers she advocated a guaranteed annual income in return for their cooperation in controlling surpluses. And as a direct appeal to the very high concentration of homeowners among the constituents (an appeal also made by Oakman), Griffiths said she was "unequivocally opposed" to any further housing projects in the Seventeenth District.[86]

Televising Congress was also an important issue to her, as it had been in 1952, and she additionally pledged to keep her constituents regularly informed of what occurred in Congressional committees, the locus, as she saw it, of the lawmaking process. The Free Press, supporting Eisenhower and Oakman, thought Griffiths' platform "a little vague" and, though "sincere," said it was no panacea for the country's ills. The News looked to Oakman's continuation on the Banking and Currency Committee as being in Detroit's best interests. Both newspapers, however, noted how well suited Griffiths was for federal office, the News adding, "Whoever wins, the 17th will be better represented in Congress than two or three other Detroit districts are bound to be."[87]

To win, Griffiths had to cut into Republican ranks and garner support from independents. To reach this broader audience she bought a series of five-minute television broadcasts.[88] From her living room she reviewed the issues and instructed the electorate in the mechanics of balloting, this time counseling a straight-Democratic vote. In 1954 three out of five new residents in the Seventeenth District were registered Democrats. According to the Free Press, a Griffiths' victory depended on whether these Democratic gains could outweigh the solid Republican strength.[89] Only the ballot box would tell.

November 2, 1954, was a fateful day for Martha Griffiths. Had she not been elected, conceivably she might never have run for Congress again. She did win, however, carrying the district by a larger majority than Williams, though defeating Oakman by only a slim 6,645 votes. As the hours of balloting revealed the will of the electorate, the months of testing vanished into triumph. The UAW, which had initially balked at her candidacy, was first on the congratulatory line praising Griffiths for her "magnificant [sic] victory."[90]

Griffiths returned thanks with the knowledge that, while she had won despite the foot dragging of the UAW and without the endorsement of the Seventeenth District leadership, she stood to gain by their support.[91] One of her earliest communications in Congress was "off the record" advice to Roy Reuther, UAW-CIO Political Action Coordinator. The only way, she said, to improve the political situation was "to reelect our own long enough to put them in positions of power in the committees."[92] Nevertheless, in the 1954 election Griffiths had achieved a certain independence, which, as her performance was to show, she used to effect the goals she sought as a lawmaker.

¹Griffiths, Diary, January 3, 4 and 28, 1928, in Griffiths Library, Romeo, Michigan. (Hereafter cited as Griffiths Library. Unless otherwise indicated, Griffiths Library refers to the Martha W. Griffiths Papers).

²Interview with Martha Griffiths, Romeo, December 2, 1977; Miriam Keast Brown, Pierce City, Missouri: 1870-1970 (Cassville, Mo.; Litho Printers, 1970) p. 15.

³Interview with Martha Griffiths, Romeo, December 2, 1977.

⁴Diary, March 4, 1929, Griffiths Library.

⁵Interview with Martha Griffiths, Romeo, December 2, 1977; Martha Griffiths, "My Mother No Clinger," Detroit Free Press, May 12, 1974, clipping in Martha W. Griffiths (MWG) Scrapbooks, Griffiths Library. On the death of Mrs. Wright the City Leader Journal (Pierce City), June [ ], 1958, (MWG Scrapbooks) wrote; "She was a friendly neighbor who liked to remember the sick, the old, and the sorrowing with visits and gifts of food. She liked nothing better than to prepare a big meal with foods such as only she could cook and invite her friends."

⁶Martha Griffiths, copy of speech to the University of Missouri, May 7, 1968, in Griffiths Library.

⁷Interviews with Martha Griffiths, Romeo, Michigan, July 29, 1977, and Hicks Griffiths, Detroit, Michigan, January 19, 1978. Hicks had an unusual sense of humor. When Martha was in Congress he used to close his letters to her with "Constituentally yours, H.G.G.—T.P.," the "T.P." standing for taxpayer.

⁸Katherine Murray to Lillian [ ], December 20, 1937, in Griffiths Library.

⁹Interview with Martha Griffiths, Romeo, December 2, 1977. In this conversation Griffiths said: "My husband was always so enthusiastic, always so helpful, always so pleased with the smallest thing I did."

¹⁰Dayton Daily News, August 13, 1973, clipping in Martha W. Griffiths Papers, Michigan Historical Collections, Bentley Historical Library, the University of Michigan, Ann Arbor. (Hereafter cited as Bentley Library.) In a taped interview with Wendy Ross ([n.d.], Bentley

Library), Martha Griffiths stressed that only a highly successful man can sustain a wife in politics.

[11] Interview with Martha Griffiths, Romeo, June 3, 1977; Martha Griffiths to Suzanne Vogt, December 7, 1954, in Griffiths Library.

[12] Martha Griffiths, "What Politics and Politicians have Taught Me," speech to Theta Sigma Phi, Press Club, Detroit, October 16, 1962, in Griffiths Library.

[13] This and Griffiths' subsequent votes are taken from the Michigan Manual.

[14] Interview with Adelaide Hart, Bloomfield Hills, Michigan, November 4, 1977.

[15] Richard Thruelsen, "When Michigan Woke Up He Was Governor," Saturday Evening Post, February 12, 1949, clipping in Lawrence L. Farrell Papers, Bentley Library.

[16] Griffiths to Daniel Thorton, January 17, 1949, in MWG Scrapbooks, Griffiths Library.

[17] Former Vice-President Henry A. Wallace believed Truman had not gone far enough into the New Deal. His Progressive Party advocated gradual socialism, total desegregation, and concessions to the Soviets. Governor J. Strom Thurmond of South Carolina organized his supporters, the States' Rights Democratic Party, around opposition to Truman's civil rights policy.

[18] A good source for the genesis of the new Democratic movement is the Hicks G. Griffiths Papers, in the Griffiths Library, Romeo. See, for example, Hicks Griffiths to Officials of Democratic Party, [n.d.]; John P. Boeschenstein to Hicks Griffiths, March 6, 1948.

[19] Lawrence L. Farrell to G. Mennen Williams, April 5, 1948, in G. Mennen Williams Papers, Bentley Library; Detroit News, February 21, 1948, clipping in Hicks Griffiths Papers, Griffiths Library.

[20] "Minutes of the Continuing Committee of the Michigan Democratic Club," February 21, 1948; "Constitution of _____ County Democratic Club"; Hicks Griffiths to G. Mennen Williams, March 24, 1948, in Hicks Griffiths Papers, Griffiths Library.

21 When State Chairperson, Hicks put out a snappy little publication, "How to be a Precinct Worker," in which he demonstrated in particular the necessity of having strong precinct organizations (Hicks Griffiths Papers, Griffiths Library).

22 Interview with G. Mennen Williams, Detroit, October 25, 1977.

23 Frank McNaughton, *Mennen Williams of Michigan: Fighter for Progress* (New York: Oceana, 1960) p. 194; Williams to Farrell, April 5, 1948, in Farrell Papers, Bentley Library.

24 Martha Griffiths to Frances Norman, April 20, 1948, in Griffiths Library.

25 Hicks to Farrell, July 7, 1948, in Farrell Papers, Bentley Library. Williams wrote Farrell, July 3, "Lack of adequate funds is slowing down the machine but otherwise we are going strong." (Farrell Papers, Bentley Library.)

26 The major work of the questionnaire devolved on campaign headquarters. Key Democrats throughout the State were asked to secure 250 interviews, involving 15 to 30 interviewers. For the questionnaire and its strategy, see Martha Griffiths to Joseph E. Arsulowicz, August 16, 1948, in Williams Papers, Bentley Library.

27 Martha Griffiths to [ ] Sloan, August 6, 1948, in Williams Papers, Bentley Library. See also Stephen B. and Vera H. Sarasohn, *Political Party Patterns in Michigan* (Detroit: Wayne State University Press, 1957), pp. 54-55.

28 Williams for Governor Committee to Gerald J. Clery, October 20, 1948; "Prodigy's Progress," *Time*, September 15, 1952, pp. 26-29, clipping in Williams Papers, Bentley Library.

29 Griffiths to Edwards, August 6, 1948, in Margaret Price Papers, Bentley Library.

30 Griffiths to Frances Norman, March 22, 1949, in Griffiths Library.

31 Griffiths to A.B. Quinton, Jr., December 3, 1948, in MWG Scrapbooks, Griffiths Library.

[32] Griffiths to Katherine Kempfer, December 4, 1948; Griffiths to Milton S. Landau, January 20, 1950, in Griffiths Library; Detroit News, January 30, 1949, clipping in MWG Scrapbooks, Griffiths Library; interviews with Martha Griffiths, Romeo, February 24, 1980.

[33] Williams to Griffiths, November 26, 1948, in Williams Papers, Bentley Library.

[34] Mildred M. Jeffrey to Martha Griffiths, February 27, 1974, in Griffiths Papers, Bentley Library.

[35] Martha Griffiths to Marjorie Munson, January 4, 1949, in Griffiths Library.

[36] Interview with Martha Griffiths, Romeo, December 2, 1977.

[37] Martha Griffiths to William Sturdevant, March 11, 1949, in Griffiths Library.

[38] Martha Griffiths to Editor, Detroit Free Press, November 12, 1951, in Griffiths Library.

[39] Michigan, House Journal, 1950, pp. 84-85, 253, and 338; House Journal, 1952, p. 1905; Martha Griffiths to Howard B. Lewis, October 23, 1951, in MWG Scrapbooks, Griffiths Library.

[40] Frank X. Martel to Martha Griffiths, March 4, 1949; Griffiths to Martel, March 9, 1949, in Griffiths Library.

[41] Martha Griffiths to Lafe F. Allen, April 25, 1949, in Griffiths Library.

[42] The story of party tensions during Hicks' tenure as state chairperson is very complicated. The material presented here was drawn from several interviews: Martha Griffiths (Romeo, October 9, 1977) and Hicks Griffiths (Romeo, December 3, 1977), Williams (Detroit, October 25, 1977) and other close associates of that day, including Nancy Williams (Grosse Pointe Farms, Michigan, November 14, 1977) and Adelaide Hart (Bloomfield Hills, Michigan, November 4, 1977). The following collections at the Bentley Library were also helpful: Williams Papers (see Williams to Paul L. Adams, May 8, 1950; and Russel S. Pope to Williams, November 15, 1949); Neil Staebler Papers, and Democratic Party, Michigan State Central Committee Papers,

1950-1966. See also <u>Sarasohn</u> on the Edwards' controversy, p. 58.

[43] Interview with Adelaide Hart, Bloomfield Hills, November 4, 1977.

[44] Martha Griffiths to India Edwards, June 12, November 20, 1950, and April 21, 1951 (MWG Scrapbooks); also an undated six-page letter written to Edwards, in Griffiths Library.

[45] Interview with Martha Griffiths, Romeo, June 4, 1977. In retrospect—and in good measure based on the rupture of the UAW with the Griffiths during 1953-1954—Martha Griffiths ascribed UAW support in 1952 as that Union's attempt to get her out of politics, first by having her retire from the Michigan Legislature, and, second, by having her defeated in the Congressional election. Whether or not the UAW intended to defeat her in 1952 is something persons associated with the organization cannot or are unwilling to verify.

[46] Interview with Hicks Griffiths, Detroit, May 6, 1977.

[47] Neil Staebler to Adlai E. Stevenson, November 17, 1952, in Williams Papers, Bentley Library.

[48] Telegrams Victor H. Harding to Martha Griffiths, October 10, 1952, and Michael J. Kirwan to Martha Griffiths, November 3, 1952, in Griffiths Library; interview with Martha Griffiths, Romeo, May 11, 1977.

[49] Interview with Williams, Detroit, October 25, 1977.

[50] Interview with Martha Griffiths, Romeo, December 2, 1977.

[51] For the trailer campaign, see Interviews with Martha Griffiths, June 3 and December 2, 1977, Romeo; Martha Griffiths, "What Politics and Politicians have Taught Me" . . .; Interview with Stephanie Stobierski, January 11, 1978, Detroit; Virginia Schnell, "It's that Homey Touch that Counts in Any Campaign," <u>Detroit News</u>, July 14, 1952; and Don O'Connor, "She Talks, Counts Votes," <u>Detroit Times</u>, October 10, 1956 (MWG Scrapbooks), clippings in Griffiths Library.

[52] Martha Griffiths, Campaign Scrapbook, in Griffiths Library. Oakman's speech of September 12, 1952, is

also found here.

[53] Interviews with Hicks Griffiths, Romeo, December 3, 1977, and Dorothy Meehan, Detroit, January 11, 1978. Both agreed that Martha Griffiths turned off a large number of "official" Democrats when she showed her constituents how to split their ballots.

[54] Undated "Dear Friend" letter in Griffiths Library.

[55] Detroit Times, April 8 and 10, 1953, clippings in Griffiths Library.

[56] Williams to Martha Griffiths, April 3, 1953, in Griffiths Library; Interview with Williams, Detroit, October 25, 1977. Because of this appointment, Griffiths was also selected to sit on the three-person City Election Commission.

[57] Russel J. Comer to Williams, April 8, 1953; Detroit News, April 4, 1953, clipping in Griffiths Library; Michigan, House Journal, 1953, pp. 776-7.

[58] Griffiths to Williams, May 16, 1953; Detroit News, April 4, 1953, clipping in Griffiths Library.

[59] Detroit Times, May 10, 1953, clipping in Griffiths Library.

[60] All three Detroit dailies carried the Teamster cases in September and October 1953 (clippings in Griffiths Library). For the juke box scandals, see the Detroit Free Press, September 29, 1953; for the auto wash intimidations, the Detroit News, October 6, 1953; and the Detroit Times and Detroit Free Press, October 22, 1953, for contractor payoffs.

[61] Griffiths to E.E. MacCrone, June 8, 1959, in Griffiths Papers, Bentley Library.

[62] Interview with Martha Griffiths, Romeo, December 2, 1977.

[63] Detroit Free Press, November 5, 1953, and Detroit News, December 27, 1953, clippings in Griffiths Library. Griffiths was particularly sensitive to the manner in which she meted out justice. In 1964 she still held as one of her "most treasured memories" the occasion when a Jackson prisoner told her "he could be sure there would be a fair trial if the case

were heard before Judge Martha Griffiths." (Griffiths to Fred H. Delany, August 3, 1964, in Griffiths Papers, Bentley Library).

[64] Detroit News, October 23, 1953, clippings in Griffiths Library; Gerald W. Groat et al. to Martha Griffiths, December 22, 1953, in Griffiths Library.

[65] Interview with Martha Griffiths, Romeo, December 2, 1977; Martha Griffiths to Victor H. Hardin, May 12, 1954, in Griffiths Library.

[66] Martha Griffiths to Williams, June 23, 1953, in Williams Papers, Bentley Library and Griffiths Library.

[67] Griffiths to Katherine Doran, January 18, 1954, in Griffiths Library.

[68] Griffiths to Williams, January 19, 1954, in Griffiths Library.

[69] Interview with Martha Griffiths, Romeo, December 2, 1977.

[70] Moody filled Arthur H. Vandenberg's unexpired term, 1951-52, but failed to win the 1952 Senatorial election on his own.

[71] "17th District Split Jars Democrats," [n.d.], 1954; Carl Muller, "Michigan Politics," Detroit News [n.d.] 1954, clippings in MWG Scrapbooks, Griffiths Library. The press spoke of the origins of the strain between the Griffiths and the Seventeenth District as being "so obscure and the stories so varied that most researchers have given up trying to figure it out."

[72] Roy L. Reuther to all UAW-CIO members in the 17th Congressional District, July 23, 1954, in Griffiths Library; "Minutes of [Greater Detroit and Wayne County CIO] Policy Committee Meeting, June 14th [1954], 1:30 P.M." and ["Minutes] Special Delegate Body Meeting, Greater Detroit and Wayne County CIO Industrial Union Council-PAC, Local #157 UAW-CIO Hall, June 15, 1954," in Greater Detroit and Wayne County CIO Papers, Archives of Labor History and Urban Affairs, Walter P. Reuther Library, Wayne State University, Detroit, Michigan (hereafter cited as Walter P. Reuther Library).

[73] The data for Martha Griffiths' split with the UAW and

the 17th District were drawn primarily from a number of interviews: Adelaide Hart, (Bloomfield Hills, November 4, 1977), Mildred Jeffrey (Detroit, January 3, 1978), Dorothy Meehan (Detroit, January 11, 1978), G. Mennen Williams (Detroit, October 25, 1977), and Nancy Williams (Grosse Point Farms, November 14, 1977). Two other persons interviewed asked that they remain anonymous.

[74] "Martha Griffiths Out to Sink CIO," Detroit Times, June 27, 1954, in Griffiths Library. In a letter to Secretary of the Treasury Henry Fowler, dated September 1, 1966 (Bentley Library), Griffiths spoke in strong terms of her rift with the CIO, pointing out that August Scholle took pains to keep her out of sight whenever President Kennedy visited Michigan, a fact observed by the Detroit News. "They [the CIO] opposed me the first time I was elected," she told Fowler.

[75] Alfred V. Meyers to Neil Staebler, August 10, 1951, in Williams Papers, Bentley Library. Although this letter antedated the Griffiths-17th District split, it captures the sentiment perfectly.

[76] Martha Griffiths to Marge Munson, April 14, 1954; Carl Muller, "Michigan Politics," Detroit News, [ ], 1954, clipping in Griffiths Library.

[77] Griffiths to Williams, June 23 and July 6, 1953, in Williams Papers, Bentley Library and in Griffiths Library.

[78] "100 File as Deadline Draws Near," [ ], 1954, unidentified clipping in MWG Scrapbooks, Griffiths Library.

[79] The primary votes were as follows: Oakman, 21,930; Griffiths, 17,919; and Poindexter, 10,443 (Michigan, Michigan Manual, 1955-56, p. 394); Poindexter to Griffiths, August 4, 1954, in Griffiths Library.

[80] Carl Muller, "Michigan Politics," Detroit News [n.d.], 1954; "Griffiths to Battle Oakman," [ ], August 5, 1954; Don Whitehead, "How Michigan's Hot Political Battle Looks to Outside Observer," [ ], clippings in MWG Scrapbooks, Griffiths Library.

[81] Griffiths to Dingell, August 20, 1954, in Griffiths Library.

[82] Martha Griffiths to Selig S. Harrison, January 14, 1955, in Griffiths Papers, Bentley Library. As a matter of policy, the State Central Committee had no funds for any Congressional candidate. Chairperson Neil Staebler suggested that Griffiths share in money raised by the 17th District (Staebler to Jack Shon, October 11, 1954, in Staebler Papers, Bentley Library).

[83] Dwight D. Eisenhower, Mandate for Change, 1953-56, (Garden City, New York: Doubleday and Co., 1963), pp. 304-307.

[84] In keeping with President Eisenhower's philosophy to limit federal control, the Atomic Energy Commission bypassed the Tennessee Valley Authority in 1954 and awarded a contract for power to a private concern known as Dixon-Yates. When it was revealed that the consultant who advised the arrangement was connected with an investment firm that marketed Dixon-Yates securities, Eisenhower was forced to cancel the contract. The President also maintained that the states, rather than the federal government, should control the offshore oil deposits within their historic boundaries. In 1953 he signed the Submerged Lands Act to the delight of Texas, California, and Louisiana.

[85] The Martha W. Griffiths for Congress Committee sent out a flyer (Griffiths Library) refuting Oakman's statement that he favored pay raises for postal employees. That he "reluctantly" voted for the postal hike, it said, did absolve him from his prior action of refusing to sign the petition discharging the pay bill from committee. Griffiths later attributed her victory to the postal workers' disenchantment with Oakman over this issue.

[86] Martha Griffiths to Franklin McDonald, November 23, 1954; "Congress Aspirants Answer 15 Questions," Redford Record, October 21, 1954; "Congresswoman Tells How She Got Elected in 17th," Redford Record, January 13, 1955; Isabella Shelton, "A New Congresswoman Expresses Her Views," Evening Star (Washington, D.C.) November 11, 1954, clippings in Griffiths Library; also see 1954 campaign literature in Griffiths Library.

[87] Detroit Free Press and Detroit News, October 19, 1954, clippings in Griffiths Library.

[88] Some scripts for her television shows are in Griffiths Library; Martha Griffiths to Joe Walsh, October 6, 1954, in Griffiths Library.

[89] *Free Press*, October 10, 1954.

[90] Roy Reuther to Griffiths, November 5, 1954, in Roy Reuther Papers, Walter P. Reuther Library.

[91] Griffiths to Roy Reuther, November 11, 1954, in Roy Reuther Papers, Walter P. Reuther Library.

[92] Griffiths to Reuther, June 23, 1955, in Roy Reuther Papers, Walter P. Reuther Library.

CHAPTER II

Martha Griffiths was exhilarated by her election. Within a fortnight she was off house-hunting in Washington. She wrote Mennen Williams that she was contemplating an apartment, but, she added alluding to the 1948 gubernatorial election, "history being what it is, perhaps I had better rent a house with a basement." The Governor concurred. "Great structures from little basements grow," he said.[1] In 1954 Griffiths saw "entrancing possibilities" in having been elected to Congress. She would soon learn, however, that a junior legislator in a conservative administration had little chance of making effective change despite the most imaginative ideas and intense ardor.

President Eisenhower was disappointed by the outcome of the 1954 elections. Not only had he striven hard to check the normal off-year reversals expected of the incumbent party, but, believing that he had never led a legislative majority, he had fought hard to make the Eighty-fourth Congress solidly Republican. In 1952, 221 Republican Representatives had been elected to 213 Democrats and the Administration had but a one-vote lead in the Senate, a balance upset in 1953 with the appointment of Thomas A. Burke to Robert A. Taft's seat. As the 1954 election results rolled in, Eisenhower found himself with more Democrats than he had hoped for. Republicans slipped to 203 in the House and the Democrats retained their one-vote margin in the Senate.

Michigan had been among the severely contested states. There pro-labor senatorial candidate, Patrick McNamara, beat incumbent Homer Ferguson whose prospects for re-election had been badly damaged by the inept campaigning of Secretary of Defense Charles Wilson. Referring to the masses of unemployed, Wilson told a Detroit audience a month before the elections that the Administration preferred a bird dog that got out and hunted for his food to a kennel-fed hound accustomed to "sit on his fanny and yell."[2] This unfortunate slur on labor, added to general dissatisfaction with Eisenhower's laissez-faireism, opened Michigan's normally Republican strongholds to the Democrats, especially in urban areas scourged by lingering unemployment. Charles Oakman, whose only major fault was that he was an Eisenhower Republican, lost to Martha Griffiths in the Republican entrenched Seventeenth District.

If the President was disappointed with the elections, he nevertheless felt a resurgence as the 1954 recession began to ease up. In fact, 1955 looked "marvelous" to him despite Democratic gains.[3] Yet, several unprecedented challenges awaited both President and Congress at home and abroad. Asia was fast becoming the world's ideological frontier as a result of the Indochinese partition in 1954. Shortly, the Russians would launch Sputnik and present an affront to America's apparent technological and military superiority. Massive changes were also occurring in the United States. In 1953 live births soared to an unprecedented 4 million. For the first time, too, the population was more female, older, and more mobile. Easterners migrated West and whites fled to the suburbs, leaving behind vast black ghettos in the heart of nearly every American metropolis. Not even the 1954 Supreme Court decision outlawing racial discrimination[4] could halt the deepening depression of America's huge black minority. Solutions to issues of this magnitude called for the best minds, the most dedicated public servants.

Griffiths' initial days on Capitol Hill revealed what it was like to be both a newcomer and one of seventeen women. Jokingly she told Nancy Williams that she felt "like a fragile little goldfish among the barracuda!" On her first day in the House a sincere well-wisher greeted her as Hicks Griffiths' wife. Another expressed his concern that if the influx of women continued—there were four that year—soon half the House would be women. Griffiths soon discovered that the men, expecting the women to function below par, were quick to credit those who made any sense at all as "'great brains.'"[5] Fortunately, she made sense.

If being a woman in Congress was potentially exasperating, being a junior member of that body was equally trying. After a few weeks in Washington she wrote a close friend that, like a child, a newcomer was to be seen but not heard. On her first day in the Banking and Currency Committee, fourth-ranking member Albert Rains of Alabama addressed the Chairperson with a near-apology. "I realize I've only been in Congress fourteen years," he said, "but I'd like to ask a question." Griffiths quickly grasped the point. Still, she felt an urgency to speak. "I don't know how much longer I am going to be able to keep quiet," she confessed. "There are a few things that I think need be said." She hoped her two committee assignments, Government Operations and Banking and Currency, would give her that opportunity.6

She had asked to be on the Government Operations Committee because of her concern for the hundreds of small Detroit businesses hit by the 1954 recession.7 Although a minor body by Congressional standards, its responsibilities were impressive: it made recommendations regarding the Comptroller General's reports, studied the government's operational economy and efficiency, evaluated the effects of Congress' reorganization plans on the legislative and executive branches, and reviewed the government's relationships to the states and to those international organizations in which the United States held membership. At the conclusion of the Korean War the Committee had assumed additional responsibility as House watchdog over peacetime defense spending. Griffiths' experience as a contract negotiator had prepared her well for these matters.

Her assignment to the Committee on Banking and Currency was even more to her liking. Where could a lawyer deeply concerned about the future of the American city put her knowledge of economics to better use? Housing and banking, consumer credit and price controls, urban renewal and mass transportation, the InterAmerican Development Bank, the Commodity Credit Corporation, and the Federal Reserve System—all fell under the aegis of Banking and Currency. What disappointment, then, to discover that the Chairperson was the eighty-year-old Brent Spence of Kentucky who was physically unable to conduct a meeting and seldom called one.8 The clue that the Committee did nothing was that three women— Griffiths, Lenore Sullivan of Missouri, and Vera Buchanan of Pennsylvania—were assigned to it in one year. In 1956 Griffiths wrote to UAW President Walter Reuther that the only reason she was remaining on Banking and Currency was because its jurisdiction was "the most interesting" in the House. Although she found the leadership "pathetic" and know it would continue to be so for some time, "I hope," she said, "that I am able to do sufficient work on my own to be of some service to the public."9

In the first year, the newness of the environment made up for the frustration. She was also very busy. The Military Operations Subcommittee of Government Operations met almost daily, which pleased Griffiths. The volume and variety of her mail was something she had never seen before. By spring, busloads of students descended on Washington and throughout the summer the visitors continued to come. By this time Griffiths was also into regular weekend travel back to Michigan to be with Hicks and her constituents, a routine that increasingly called for great psychic and physical stamina. The Detroit residence continued to claim her attention and she was concerned about Hicks' wellbeing. At first she insisted on cooking enough food each weekend to keep him supplied for the week, until Hicks assured her that he could fend for himself Monday through Friday.

Before long Griffiths was gaining the recognition of her Congressional associates. Within a month Speaker Sam Rayburn pointed her out as an extraordinarily capable woman, and, at the close of the first session, Democratic Whip Carl Albert expressed his delight. "The girl from Pierce City," Albert wrote, "did herself proud." He was pleased that the older Representatives were actually bragging about the comprehension she brought to her committees. Senator Margaret Chase Smith told a group of professional women that Griffiths was the most talked-about new member in the Eighty-fourth Congress.[10]

What kind of legislator was she? She described herself as about as liberal as any Democrat[11] and she voted consistently with her party. Professionally, she was up on the legislative process. Only one other woman in Congress, Ruth Thompson of Michigan's Ninth District, was an attorney. Griffiths' knowledge of law and her penetrating logic won the admiration of her colleagues. That she reasoned "like a man" was said in praise of her.[12]

As a big-city Representative, Griffiths' first concern in 1955 was the status of the economy. The effects of the 1954 recession were seen in long lines of the unemployed. In Michigan alone their numbers would rise to 200,000 by 1958. Loss of income meant higher welfare costs and less revenue for the states just at the time when the need for public services, especially schools, was being felt everywhere. With unemployment came hunger. Disturbing reports of malnourished school children in St. Louis reached Missouri Representative Leonor Sullivan during the 1954 debate on an unmanageable farm surplus. Indignant over the contradiction between hunger and abundance she urged her colleagues to pass food-stamp legislation.[13] Griffiths promptly joined in the effort when she came to Congress in 1955.

The Sullivan bill provided that eligible persons could exchange stamps for designated foods at their local grocery stores. Griffiths argued that these commodities were not welfare but belonged by right to needy taxpayers as each year they and their fellow citizens paid a billion dollars to store surplus foods. Beyond this elemental justice her hope was that the foodstuffs—left to rot in government bins—would be put to orderly distribution and eventually eliminated.[14]

While food-stamp advocates felt they had in the Sullivan plan a solution to what South Dakota Democrat George McGovern called the two surpluses—food and hunger—the bill's foes, particularly the Administration, were able to delay action for four years. Agriculture Secretary Ezra Taft Benson opposed stamps on the grounds that they would cost too much and would turn his Department into a welfare agency. All the while, Sullivan and Griffiths pledged to see the plan through. "Women don't like to let people, particularly children, go hungry," a Washington editor noted.[15]

By spring 1958 when Griffiths testified for the bill before a subcommittee on food consumption, Detroit unemployment had soared to 17 percent. Over half a million Michigan residents were on food doles, a million pounds being distributed monthly in Detroit and Wayne County alone. In her testimony, Griffiths set these conditions against the burgeoning storage bins that cost the American taxpayers a million dollars a day. She also criticized the impracticality and waste in distributing bulk quantities of the surpluses: five pounds of cheese when a family could only use two or three; hundred-pound sacks of rice when the annual per capita consumption was no more than six pounds.[16]

Governor Williams likewise appealed to Washington against Benson's refusal to adopt a more flexible method of feeding the poor. Griffiths, determined to move the issue off dead center by bringing Michigan's story to the Capitol, prevailed on Daniel J. Ryan, Detroit's welfare director, and William E. Fitzgerald, executive director of a Detroit wholesalers association. Ryan testified that centralized bulk-food depots destroyed independent grocers and kept away needy people who did not have the money to travel to out-of-the-way places for their food. Fitzgerald warned that storage space would soon be gone and he urged Griffiths to make food stamps a campaign issue in 1958.[17]

Griffiths was upset by all the delay. She and Leonor Sullivan literally badgered the consumers study subcommittee and talked repeatedly with members of the Agriculture Committee.[18] The debate began to gather momentum. Opponents stressed their views that the Sullivan plan was an "unwarranted invasion" of state and local rights, that it was a "'foot in the door'" to more complex distribution plans, and that it forced the federal government to pick up the total bill for feeding the nation's hungry. Proponents praised the bill for its compassion, practicality, and simplicity. Griffiths once again advanced her plea for justice: hungry taxpayers had a right to the food they had paid for. Iowan Representative Neal Smith reminded his colleagues that no hog farmer would feed his livestock an inadequate diet and Michigan's John Dingell, an acerbic critic of the Administration, wondered how Benson had money for hungry cattle but not for hungry people. In the food-stamp program Minnesota Representative Coya Knutson found a positive answer to the American challenge of how to live with abundance.

The plan's advocates pressed the Agriculture Committee into action. Soon Chairperson Harold Cooley and Committee Democrats were denouncing Benson for having neither the imagination nor the sympathy in dealing with the small farmer and the needy consumer. The Committee saw no better way to feed 7 million hungry Americans than through food stamps. Sullivan had their support.[19] In late August the House passed the bill on strictly partisan lines, 88 percent of the Democrats voting for it and 82 percent Republicans against it. Jubilantly Griffiths wrote Daniel Ryan: "It was a long, hard pull, Dan, but we finally made it."[20]

Even after the Senate supported the measure and it became law, the struggle continued. Apparently unwilling to believe that there was anything unusual in the numbers of the hungry and unemployed, Benson failed to implement the plan. Griffiths wrote Ryan that it was obvious to her that it would take mandatory legislation to get the Secretary to move. In a House speech in March 1960 she charged him with depriving needy persons of food while continuing to stockpile. She had also discovered through her work on Government Operations that the Agriculture Department had leased commercial bins at a time the government's were empty, had permitted vast surpluses sent abroad to spoil, and had lost $2 million in the resale of cheese purchased at high prices from select dairy farmers. She had further suspicion that the Commodity Credit Corporation, which was responsible for storing and distributing the excess food, had little respect for economy and efficiency.21

Griffiths was anxious to have government surpluses used. She was dismayed when her own state failed to make the most of what was at its disposal. "The State of Michigan," she wrote Lansing officials, "is acting like 'clucks' in this matter."22 In June 1960 she sponsored an unsuccessful bill that would have given charitable institutions surplus grain for livestock and poultry. Reward for her persistence in feeding hungry citizens came in July 1961 when the government designated Detroit as a pilot food-stamp project. Testifying two years later to the success of this $13 million program, Welfare Director Ryan praised the stamps for providing purchasing power to the needy and for strengthening the independent food industry. He reported that in contrast to centralized bulk distribution, food stamps brought down administrative costs, enhanced diets, and returned the food business to where it belonged.23 For many years Griffiths supported the program. But once she had studied the total federal welfare system, she became convinced there were better ways to attack the root causes of poverty. This story will be told later.

Closely allied to the problem of hunger was inadequate housing. During the 50s Griffiths pulled back from her campaign pledge and supported low-income housing. (Her enthusiasm later waned in response to the increasing number of homeowners in her district.) "I voted 'no' as loudly as possible but it didn't seem enough," she wrote Roy Reuther, head of the UAW-CIO Political Action Committee, after an unsuccessful attempt in 1955 to stay a cut in public housing. And she was consistent in her affirmation of urban renewal. "Families displaced by slum clearance have to have some place to go," she said.24 In 1958 the Democrats sponsored an omnibus housing bill, providing $2.5 billion in grants and loans for construction and slum clearance, residences for senior citizens, $500 million for urban renewal, and loans for college dormitories. Fearing the cost, Eisenhower vetoed the measure only to support a weaker housing bill the following year. After the veto, Griffiths wrote her father that the President was "absolutely crazy" for turning the bill down. In her frustration she was for making no further effort on housing. "Let the F.H.A. [Federal Housing Administration] die," she said. "It would teach Mr. Eisenhower a real first-class lesson."25

The forces behind comprehensive housing legislation worked for a cabinet position that would deal specifically with the cities. Urban Affairs or Urbiculture, as it was called in 1955, proposed to bring under its aegis the many scattered city-directed agencies like the Housing and Home Finance Administration. "I don't think we can just leave them [the cities] to die," Griffiths told the Banking and Currency Subcommittee on Housing. Everything was to be gained from long-range planning.[26] Big-city mayors agreed with her and organized labor looked for a voice on the Cabinet. The rapid growth of blacks in the metropolitan area also drew the NAACP into the ranks of the proponents.

Once again the Republicans advanced their classic arguments that a department of urban affairs would cost too much and would imperil the constitutional balance. They reasoned that some federal control would ultimately mean full control over such mundane matters as snow removal. On hearing this, Griffiths mocked: "I would expect everyone to have a shovel of his own," she said.[27] Most of the governors joined the Administration in opposing what seemed to them a threat to their hold over the cities—and the measure died. Not until 1965, and after several unsuccessful attempts by the Kennedy Administration, did the Department of Housing and Urban Development see the light of day. By then it was obvious that urban blight was the nation's key issue. By 1960, 70 percent of all Americans had moved into the cities. The impact of this migration was seen in despicable slums, congested streets, inadequate transportation, dislocated industry and commerce, dwindling space, polluted air, and overcrowded schools.

The school problem was particularly appalling. Even as early as 1952, Eisenhower pledged to do something about the shortage of classrooms. In Detroit, for example, 38 percent of the children attended schools that were obsolete and in many instances fire traps. Lack of space necessitated double or triple shifts for as many as 44,000 students. Despite the acuteness of the problem nothing was done until 1960 to provide for general school construction.

Griffiths was consistently a school advocate because she believed in education and because she had no fear that federal funds meant federal control. She often pointed out that the government had been involved in education for a century without having interfered in local school districts. Big government just could not afford an unresponsive, illiterate people. "In the end," she insisted, "education will have been cheaper."[28] As one of her first public acts, Griffiths joined Republican Ruth Thompson in promoting rural libraries. She was considered an "avid" supporter of school construction funds throughout her career.[29] During the 60s and 70s when federal aid to education was an open issue, she advocated low-interest loans for higher-education facilities, special assistance for poverty areas, tax relief for teachers, and tax credits for non-public education. Griffiths also sponsored legislation that would have provided natural playground areas for children of the asphalt cities.[30] Learning and space were essential ingredients in Martha Griffiths' philosophy of humanization.[31]

The 1957-58 recession was the critical issue of Griffiths' second term. By the spring of 1958 there were more out of work that there had been in 1941. Detroit unemployment rose to 18 percent and each week 2,000 exhausted their workers' benefits. Seventy-five percent of all Detroit families receiving public assistance—some 11,000—had never been on welfare before and this vast number forced the state to spend up to one sixth of its general fund on relief. Despite serious efforts of the Small Business Administration to shore up the sagging economy through increased loans and easy credit, small store owners and manufacturers began to crumble under the weight of the recession and Eisenhower's formulae to relieve it. Tight money and high interest rates unleashed a steady stream of bankruptcies, the highest since 1933. Griffiths grew increasingly troubled by these failures which she ascribed to the government's negligence in protecting small merchants from undue competition. She was furious, then, when the Attorney General announced he would close Detroit's antitrust office.[32] By now even large corporations had cause for worry. In 1958 automobile sales dipped 30 percent below the 1957 level. Having successfully launched Sputnik in October 1957, the Russians made capital out of the recession. Griffiths bristled. "I do not go along with the 'wait and see' attitude espoused by the Administration," she complained. "Certainly the real problem in this country is not to enforce unemployment on more than 50 percent of the country, but to have enough jobs for everybody."[33]

As the recession deepened, the Detroit Common Council asked for repeal of the auto excise, a proposal supported by the entire Michigan delegation in Congress.

Although Detroit produced only 23 percent of all American-made automobiles, one out of every seven workers in the United States was connected with the automotive industry and one out of every six businesses depended on it. Griffiths argued that when costs were less, sales were more. "Consider," she said, "your neighborhood shopping center that parks 10,000 cars and tell me who benefits most, or in what degree, from the use of cars."[34] Not everyone agreed with her theory. Critics like Herbert Stein, Director of Research for the Committee for Economic Development, said Griffiths' was a "will-o-the-wisp solution," arguing that reduced costs actually discouraged consumerism.[35] Besides tax-free cars to assuage the impact of the recession, Griffiths also advocated defense contracts to depressed areas. But she was sure from her work on the Military Subcommittee of Government Operations that Michigan would continue to be passed over for some of the government's favorite clients.[36]

During 1958 the Democrats sponsored two primary depressed-areas bills: the Community Facilities Bill and the Area Redevelopment Act. The intensity of Congressional debate around federal-works projects underscored the polar differences between big-city Representatives and those from small, rural communities. Unhappy that McCormack assigned the vote on the Community Facilities measure for the Friday before primary elections, Griffiths knew that defeat was more the result of political philosophy than poor scheduling. "A coalition of Northern Confederates and Southern Yankees" has done this to us, she wired Williams, Reuther, and Detroit Mayor Louis Miriani.[37] She later wrote Reuther of her deep frustration in being a Northern liberal: "You start at the foot of the class and it takes more than twenty years to work yourself into a position of some influence." Northerners also had the added burden of having to tend continually to their districts or to lose them. Griffiths told Reuther she hoped to live long enough to see a few city Democrats head the important committees "while they are still young and alert enough to pass some 20th century legislation for our 'affluent society.'"[38]

Griffiths predicted that the Area Redevelopment Bill would meet the same fate as the public works program, so similar were they in purpose.[39] In 1958 she was right, but a brief history of the bill shows the reward of persistent prodding. Every year beginning in 1955, Paul Douglas, head of the Joint Economic Committee, introduced a redevelopment measure. Eisenhower pocket-vetoed the 1958 bill on the grounds that it provided for too little local responsibility. He likewise vetoed Douglas' 1959 version as too great an extension of federal authority and as too costly: Douglas wanted $389.5 million in grants and loans, the President $53 million. John Kennedy made the bill a primary campaign issue in 1960, and finally in 1961 Congress passed a $394 million ARA with strong Administration support. By then, Southern Democrats had been convinced that there was something in the act for their districts and every legislator had been educated to the political potency of the depressed-areas problem. That Michigan qualified as a leading recipient of ARA funds must have given Griffiths great joy.

As a Democrat from the Motor City, Griffiths was expected to be a labor advocate. Despite her early campaign quarrels with the UAW, from 1955 to 1974 she voted pro-labor 90 percent of the time. She was, to use labor's term, a "staunch liberal."[40] Nonetheless, Griffiths was quite capable of exercising the most independent judgment on labor issues when she wanted to. And she did.

Her first bill in Congress was a pay raise for post-office employees.[41] Not only was Griffiths the daughter of mail carriers, but postal workers had figured significantly in her election over Charles Oakman in 1954. Oakman's failure to sign a petition discharging a pay bill from committee cost him the vote of 7,000 postal workers in the Seventeenth District.[42] But there was more to a pay raise in 1955 than a campaign payoff. With no wage adjustment since 1951, postal employees had only a 1939 purchasing power. Griffiths was quick to point out that the starting wage for a clerk or carrier was less than that for a hot-dog purveyor, a library janitor, or a comfort-station attendant. As a result, postal workers were forced to indebt themselves heavily and to moonlight. That the volume of mail was up 40 percent from what it had been in 1951 compounded the inequity. Progress toward pay adjustments nonetheless was slow. As late as 1970, pay-raise sympathizers like Griffiths were still fighting to bring postal pay in line with the wage scale of private industry, an effort of great importance in an industrialized community such as Detroit.

Griffiths did not stop with the mail carriers. She supported the demands of construction workers on federal projects for the prevailing benefits and pay of the unionized trades and she considered the right-to-work laws sanctioned by 14(b) of the Taft-Hartley Act as an affront to the unionized North. The use of Pinkerton guards by the government to ferret out potential labor agitators was immoral as far as she was concerned. "I see red at the mention of the name," she told a concerned citizen. She was no less agitated by cheap Mexican labor that permitted agribusiness magnates to drive out family farms and to compete with domestic farm workers.[43]

By the end of the 50s Griffiths began to look more critically at the unions, their practices and their demands, their impact on the public. Like everyone else she experienced increased consumer prices because of union benefits which, she observed, also convinced management not to hire new workers into the labor force.[44] Labor-run-rampant was how she viewed the accelerating number of strikes. In Detroit alone the newspapers were shut down nine times in nine years. Griffiths warned that unjustified labor demands would eventually force Congress to pass anti-strike legislation.[45] This kind of thinking did not endear her to the unions, but what really angered them was her stand on the Labor-Management Reporting and Disclosure Act of 1959, popularly known as the Landrum-Griffin Act. So intense was the opposition that she responded by taking her case to her constituents.

The anti-union sentiment resulting from the McClellan Teamster investigations of the early 50s set the stage for labor reform by the end of the decade. In 1958 Senators John F. Kennedy and Irving M. Ives introduced a moderate disclosure act which the House turned down and Eisenhower opposed on the grounds that it did not go far enough. Several other measures fell by the wayside until Georgia Democrat Philip Landrum and Michigan Republican Robert Griffin presented their proposal to the House.

The first six titles of the Landrum-Griffin bill responded directly to the findings of the McClellan probe by providing protective measures against unscrupulous union leaders for both individual union members and the unions as organizations. A member's bill of rights guaranteed freedom of speech and assembly, established procedural rules for dues and assessments, protected a member against retaliation and violence. Also contained in the bill were rules and standards for union elections, a description of the fiduciary relationship existing between union officials and their unions, and the requirement that each union submit a constitution and bylaws to the Secretary of Labor, as well as report annually on internal operations. Included were additional provisions regarding the conditions under which national and international unions might exercise trusteeship over local unions. Besides these specifically anti-racketeering sections, Title VII offered a controversial collection of amendments to the 1947 National Labor Relations Act which leaned in the direction of greater restriction. The prohibition against secondary boycotts was broadened to cover coersive activity against an employer to force him from doing business with another employer. Picketing directed against a company where a union was lawfully recognized was likewise listed among unfair labor practices. Another controversial issue, the so-called "no-man's land" provision, gave jurisdiction to the states, rather than to the National Labor Relations Board, over disputes between unions and small businesses. Northern liberals—among them Griffiths—decried the severity of Title VII, particularly the "no-man's land" provision."[46]

Hope to produce a more moderate bill vanished, however, when Republicans joined Southern Democrats in passing the entire Landrum-Griffin package by 299 to 201, the largest number of Representatives ever recorded as voting on any measure in the House. As a result of this vote, the liberals had two possibilities: either recommit the bill and kill it altogether or entrust it to a conference committee where a less stringent measure might emerge. Although Griffiths had voted against Landrum-Griffin because of Title VII, she balked at the idea that there might be no legislation at all. Too many of her constituents had asked for reform and since her days on Recorder's Court she had believed in the necessity of anti-racketeering laws. Given a choice between no statute and the chance that Landrum-Griffin be purged of its anti-union provisions, she and one other Michigan Democrat, John Lesinski, voted against recommitment.[47] According to one newspaper account, the clerk of the House was so taken aback by her vote that he had her repeat it three times and later checked to make sure he had heard it right.[48] Whether the story is true or not, it underscores the fact that in the view of many, Griffiths had overstepped party lines. It did not seem to matter that other liberals like George McGovern and Stewart Udall advocated some manner of reform and looked to the conference committee to accomplish it.[49]

Why then was it said that she and Lesinski had "stab[bed] the working men and women of our country in the back"?[50] The floor debate gives strong indication of just how offensive Landrum-Griffin was to many Democrats from strongly unionized areas. In a long impassioned speech, Speaker John McCormack excoriated it as an attack on legitimate unionism and William Green of Pennsylvania conjured up the populist phrase of William Jennings Bryan when he likened the bill to "a crown of thorns" on the brow of the working class. Several Northern critics called it the "killer bill." Michigan Representatives were outspoken in their denunciations. James O'Hara said the bill made it more difficult for workers to organize and much easier for employers to "kick out" unions already organized. Thaddeus Machrowicz hoped that by defeating the bill in 1958 a better one would emerge in the future, and John Dingell saw sinister Administration forces at work in having made pro-labor Republicans buckle under.

In an open letter in "Ford Facts," John Quillico, President of UAW Local 600, told Griffiths and Lesinski that they had betrayed their electorate. "We expected you—who ran for Congress and were elected with the strong support of organized labor—to stand up and be counted when the chips were down." August Scholle said the AFL-CIO would remember Griffiths and Lesinski at the next election. Hoffa lashed out indiscriminately. "Pure hatred," he said, enacted the "vicious" bill.[51] Griffiths felt compelled by this criticism to explain her actions to her constituents.

In a letter to them she pointed out that she had faithfully represented their demands to curb unscrupulous union leaders. When she had had the chance during the floor debate to vote for a milder reform, she had done so. But, she said, the passage of Landrum-Griffin left her no alternative but to hope for its revision. She reminded her electorate that the real work of purging the unions rested with people like themselves. From her experience she reminded them that no law, no matter how severe or lenient, could substitute "for a prosecutor with courage, nor a judge with understanding, nor witnesses who are unafraid, and finally, for a jury that is above corruption."[52] Three weeks after the vote to recommit, the House passed by a 352 to 52 vote the Labor-Management Reporting and Disclosure Act, Title VII having been modified more to the liking of Northern liberals.[53]

The independence Griffiths displayed in the Landrum-Griffin fight characterized her persistent, if unfruitful, struggle for a centralized civil defense system. What concerned Griffiths was the possibility of a nuclear war. The debate as to whether the United States or the Soviet Union had greater missile capacity was of less significance to her than the actual power of both to ignite the earth. In this she was reminded of the Shakespearian character who said about his fatal wound: "'Tis not as wide as a river nor as deep as a well, but it will do.'" The issue was "saving a meaningful civilization."54

As Griffiths sat on the Military Operations Subcommittee of Government Operations and listened to big-city mayors discuss their inadequate means to handle a nuclear attack she grew more alarmed at the prospect for survival. With downtown buildings designated as fallout shelters she wondered who could possibly survive a midnight blitz. "Nobody," she reasoned, "but skidrow characters, drunks, a few people in hospitals and maybe the night shift on the local news." If an attack occurred during the day, who would protect women and children? One hydrogen bomb equaled the lethal force of sixteen years' round-the-clock bombing by the combined air forces of World War II, and nuclear fallout threatened to encircle the globe for ninety years.55

Griffiths thought two preventative measures had to be taken immediately. First, the public had to be aroused to the possibility and gravity of a nuclear attack. Second, the government had to prepare for an anti-attack effort through a Department of Civil Defense. What was new about the proposed Department was its independent status as a Cabinet office. After two-years' hearings on national survival, the Military Operations Subcommittee concluded that internal defense was fundamentally a non-military function and that the tenuousness of global affairs made it advisable to have a ranking official near the President at all times. The bill provided for amalgamating civil defense activities of both the Office of Defense Mobilization and the Federal Civil Defense Administration of the Department of Defense. The Secretary of Civil Defense would be responsible for planning how to forestall or minimize the effects of an enemy attack and, once one had occurred, for returning the nation to normalcy.56

Except for a brief flurry of interest following the Berlin Crisis of 1958-59, Congress remained basically unmoved by Griffiths' plea for civilian readiness. She blamed the Republicans. "It is the theory of this Administration," she wrote a concerned constituent, "that Civil Defense is a local problem. In my judgment, this is to say that war is a local problem." As late as 1970 she still lamented the general lack of concern, concluding that there was no effective money lobby calling for action.[57]

The Government Operations Committee not only provided Griffiths with an interest in civil and military preparedness but it involved her in the government's massive business as a defense buyer. Later when she was appointed to the Joint Economic Committee she continued to pursue issues related to military purchases. Her experience as an ordnance negotiator equipped her to handle these matters aptly and her deep concern for government efficiency and economy gave her the energy to invade what seemed to be a man's terrain. With the years she acquired a reputation as one of the Defense Department's most outspoken critics.

Before the establishment of the Defense Supply Agency in 1962, each division of the armed forces had its own purchasing policies. Even as late as 1964, the government had no fixed norms for military clothing. "If one service stands fast," the Comptroller General reported, "that is the end of standardization." The lack of coordination among the services resulted in duplication and waste and invited corruption and mismanagement. Griffiths learned of these matters through her work on both the Government Operations and the Joint Economic Committees. She was appalled by what she discovered. How justify, she asked, the navy's purchase of obsolete aircraft engines, the practice of the air force to award contracts to only a few suppliers, a deficient missile system bought by the army for $300 million?[58] Griffiths wondered how any of these things could be explained to the taxpayers.

That the Defense Department annually overspent $150 million in operating its commissaries did not escape notice by her, nor did the millions that were lost in stockpiling perishables and unusable spare parts. For the cost-conscious Griffiths, practices such as these pointed to "a mixture of about 50 percent 'don't know' and 50 percent 'don't care.'" In a speech before the House in 1957 she said that the cure for the "'don't know'" was to train negotiators for their jobs; for the "'don't care'" she recommended that the government have consultative power over defense contracts.[59] "When Rep. Griffiths says something like that," reported the Detroit Free Press, "we listen."[60] Reporters were likewise happy when she denounced consultative services of scientists as being in conflict of interest and when she called for an end to incentive-type contracts on the grounds that they boosted costs. "Mrs. Griffiths," said the Nation, "seems to have hold of something which the Congress should not allow to sink into oblivion."[61]

Griffiths hammered hard at abuse and mismanagement, the squandering of billions in tax money. She continued to believe that Congress needed to know what the Defense Department paid its contractors and subcontractors. "[It] burns me," she said, when the Secretary of the Air Force told her that such information would be both costly and superfluous to provide.[62] As long as she was in Congress she defended the Renegotiation Board which had the authority to renegotiate contracts between the Defense Department and private industry whenever there was question of excessive or unnecessary costs. While Griffiths probably gained few friends in the Pentagon by her persistent interrogation of procurement officers, she helped raise consciousness about the misuse of public funds.[63] This was important to her.

In addition to complicated issues of public policy, Griffiths was concerned about issues that affected the daily quality of life. Educated during her first year in Congress to the gravity of the nation's dwindling water supply, she was alarmed that such few people could be aroused to the potential magnitude of the problem.[64] As a homemaker she early identified with consumer protection, including fair packaging. Because of this interest, a district office of the Food and Drug Administration was established in Detroit in 1959.[65] She consistently sought high standards in meat and poultry inspection. When the Michigan inspection statute was being threatened because its norms were higher than the federal minimum, she urged all states to raise their requirements. She fought the use of refuse in processed meats. To an Agriculture subcommittee studying the problem she said, "I would much prefer to see the pigskin thrown and carried by professional football players than wrapped in a bun and spread with mustard and relish!"[66] Griffiths also objected to the major outlay of Agriculture research funds in food and home management, the "cherry pie concept" as she called it; in her thinking, modern homemakers could be better served by being educated to the hard economic facts with which they daily had to cope.[67]

In 1957 she asked radio and television networks to give equal time with their tobacco advertisers to the potential hazards of smoking, a cause she hoped the Surgeon General would officially support.[68] But her favorite consumer interest was televising the House so that the public could see their Representatives in action. From 1956 to 1963 she fought to redeem this campaign pledge but each time Speaker Sam Rayburn effectively thwarted it. The Griffiths' bill, though not original—New York Jacob Javits had introduced one in 1951—would have limited coverage to a few networks at a time, with a pool of tapes available to all. According to Griffiths, this orderly method of collecting the news guaranteed the right of the people to see how their interests were being protected.[69]

Before 1960, Griffiths' most noted legislative achievement was a bill concerned with the humane slaughter of meat animals.[70] Introduced to the idea by one of her campaign workers, Griffiths discovered that the House had never had such a bill although Hubert Humphrey had introduced one in the Senate. In 1955 Griffiths presented the substance of the Humphrey measure which called for stunning animals before the kill. This proposal was immediately endorsed by the American Humane Society and the American Welfare Institute of New York headed by Ann Arbor socialite, Christine Stevens.

The bill's supporters argued that sticking, the then most popular method of killing meat animals, was cruel and barbaric and that a more enlightened approach was inexpensive, had been used successfully, and resulted in less bruising and therefore less waste. Labor enthusiastically applauded stunning because it proposed to reduce slaughterhouse accidents and Democratic Candidate Adlai Stevenson endorsed the Humphrey-Griffiths plan as worthy of his support.[71]

The bill's opponents were equally strong in their denunciation. Agriculture Secretary Benson thought the proposal was premature and he feared compliance would increase meat costs, disrupt the market, and jeopardize the meat-surplus program. Meatpackers were against any change whatsoever and livestock producers were certain that added slaughterhouse costs would be passed on to them. Because stunning interfered with their kosher practices, Orthodox Jews objected strenuously. House critics basically viewed the measure as an expensive innovation, some heaping ridicule on it. This opposition held off passage for three years.

In the meantime, Christine Stevens mobilized her lobby for a massive letter-writing campaign. Eisenhower once remarked half in jest that if the size of his mail was any indication of what was of primary importance to the American people it was to spare cattle and hogs a cruel and prolonged death. In 1958 the humane slaughter forces once again got their bill to the House floor and singled Griffiths out to steer it through the legislative labyrinth. This she did with "devoted efforts."[72] In February a compromise passed which made it mandatory for the federal government to buy from meatpackers who complied with stunning regulations; the bill, however, did not make sticking a criminal act. The Senate then took up the debate in what turned out to be a "bedlam of conversation," but in July the Humane Slaughter Act emerged with the caveat that Jewish ritual slaughter be exempt from regulation.

Having gotten their law, the protectionists turned the next year to government control of animal experimentation. An alleged incident involving clandestine research on a family dog was all that was needed to move the action forward. In Griffiths the protectionists found a willing advocate. Her so-called "dognapping bill" required the licensing and inspection of federally funded laboratories. That the bill excluded government regulation of experimentation aroused some protectionists like Stevens' lobby; that it allowed for animal experimentation at all incurred the wrath of the antivivisectionists with whom Griffiths disclaimed any connection. In a stinging letter to a Michigan Democratic chief she wrote: "Please do not refer to my bill as an 'anti-vi[vi]section' bill. This is exactly what it is not. You are falling for Reader's Digest propaganda."[73]

Medical researchers protested the Griffiths' bill. Pharmaceutical companies and medical schools criticised Griffiths as unenlightened and mistrustful, as causing useless red tape and obstructing the advancement of science. "Can it be possible," she replied, "that the scientists in this country really object to certainty of humane treatment of lives, which they themselves may be able to prolong, but are not able to create?"[74] Fearful that the antivivisectionists might pressure for an anti-research statute, President Johnson reluctantly accepted what became the Humane Treatment Act of 1966.

Desirous of advancing humane legislation to its next step, Stevens approached Griffiths for a law regulating actual experimentation. By now Griffiths had grown cold to the idea. Not only had promoting the previous bills been costly in time and resources and distracted her staff from their routine responsibilities, but she had reaped little legislative mileage from her efforts. She also was deeply engrossed in the Ways and Means and Joint Economic Committees. When Paul Rogers of Florida approached her in 1967 to co-sponsor the humane-treatment-in-research bill, her response was unambiguous. "If you think I am ever going to get my name on one of those humane bills again," she told him, "you should be taken to St. Elizabeth's [a mental hospital] right now."[75] Griffiths, nonetheless, remained a devoted animal protectionist, the best evidence being the care she and Hicks lavished on the menagerie that became part of their lives when, after her retirement from Congress, they moved to a farm sixty miles north of Detroit.

In December 1958 Griffiths surprised the public by announcing she would run again for Detroit Recorder's Court. Coming within two months of her third successful Congressional campaign, the announcement "fell like a bombshell."[76] The Detroit newspapers were quick to ascribe motives.[77] The News, which said Griffiths' candidacy was bound to have national reverberations, advanced the notion that she had been ordered home by Hicks, an allegation she promptly denied. The News offered a clue in Griffiths' remark that "'advancement here [in Congress] is too slow.'" The Free Press thought that she had been enticed by the salary, which was $2,000 more than what she was earning in Congress. Exhausting weekend travel was the thesis proposed by the Detroit Times. Conjectures notwithstanding, the reporters were surprised that Griffiths should leave Congress now when she was so close to a seat on Ways and Means. Some were also angry as evidenced in the remark of Detroit Times' Don O'Connor: "Today Mrs. Griffiths is in Bermuda," he wrote, "probably lying on a sunny beach and not thinking of the fact it will cost Detroit taxpayers $60,000 to hold a special election to fill her seat should she win the judgeship." Griffiths' response to criticism of this kind was that it was discriminatory. "I would be interested in knowing," she wrote one critic, "if you felt the same way in 1952 when Charlie Oakman left the Council seat and ran against me for Congress."[78]

The newspapers had also observed how Griffiths' announcement "quickly touched off grumblings in local political quarters." Organized labor, in particular, felt betrayed for not having been consulted. "There were sounds from the CIO bleachers like baseball fans stabbed by an umpire's decision," noted one reporter. August Scholle said he heard nothing but "caustic comment" from the rank and file, a sure indication that there would be no union funds for her campaign.

What really moved Griffiths to run for Recorder's Court in 1958? A look at Congress reveals a good part of the answer. Despite all the hopes and all the work, there were still no food stamps, no housing or community-facilities laws. There was no equitable social security legislation for women, to say nothing about an equal rights amendment. There was no Department for Urban Affairs, no Department of Civil Defense. The exise on automobiles had not been repealed and Eisenhower had vetoed the Area Development bill. The Humane Slaughter Act, Griffiths' one achievement, was good, but laws were needed for human beings suffering from malnutrition and substandard housing, from high taxes and high prices; laws were needed for the cities and Griffiths did not perceive herself in a position to make changes.[79]

Not to be forgotten either were the rigors of frequent campaigning. Though universally recognized as an adroit vote-getter, especially among women,[80] she still had to exert tremendous energy each full summer and fall before an election in hauling her ubiquitous trailer throughout the district. Furthermore, there was always the guarded endorsement and negligible support of organized labor and the local Democratic organization. In 1956 she won by a slim 14,000 votes, the Republicans having put more money behind Lucas S. Miel than all the other Wayne County candidates combined. Although her margin of victory more than doubled in 1958, she saw Lesinski go down in the primaries under open attack of the UAW. And that year her opponent, George E. Smith, was endorsed by the Free Press and equally preferred by the influential Civic Searchlight.[81] She had to ask herself whether or not these biennial exertions were worth it all.

Against this backdrop, Recorder's Court looked exceedingly inviting in 1958, now that two judges had reached retirement age. Griffiths had come to think, moreover, that she would have a greater impact on Detroit as a judge than as a member of Congress. Besides, had she not already proved herself an able magistrate? "I am not asking the voters to buy 'a pig in the poke,'" she told people puzzled by her decision. She further argued that her experience in Congress had increased her understanding of the law. The main thing, however, was that it would be a relief to get back to Michigan. "Detroit is home to me," she said. She was willing to test the support of the electorate.82 Although the Democratic Party and the AFL-CIO refused to endorse her, Griffiths had the endorsement of the Detroit Bar Association and the News, the latter calling her "a court gain for Detroit." By spring she was considered the incumbents' "most feared of aspirants."83

Why then did the voters turn her down in the April 1959 elections? First, although she garnered the highest vote of the non-incumbent candidates, she was running against a slate of known judges. The News highlighted this factor. "She lost apparently because of the potency . . . of the incumbents and the fact that even the less competent of them were not wholly incompetent." Second, as noted above, she did not have AFL-CIO support. At the outset of the campaign the editor of the News alluded to union opposition in observing that "no pressure group looks kindly upon legislators who express the belief, as Mrs. Griffiths has, that they represent all of the people."84 Finally, loss of memory played its part: "People had forgotten that I once sat on that court," Griffiths mused, "that I worked very hard, and I trust had used more than ordinary amount of courage."85

Knowing what it meant to lose, Griffiths bore her defeat philosophically.86 As a member of Congress, she would continue to fight for the cities and to do what she could, especially for women. Above all, she could hope that in the next year and a half her party would gain enough strength to vote in both a Democratic President and Congress. With six years' seniority she might then have a chance to bring about the changes she wanted.

¹Griffiths to Williams, November 22, 1954; Williams to Griffiths, December 7, 1954, in Martha W. Griffiths Papers, Griffiths Library, Romeo, Michigan. (Hereafter Griffiths Library will designate these Papers.)

²Quoted in Dwight D. Eisenhower, Mandate for Change, 1953-56 (Garden City, New York: Doubleday and Co., 1963, p. 437. Eisenhower's defense of Wilson's poor judgment is difficult to reconcile with his stated desire: "I earnestly wanted a Republican Congress." p. 431.

³Ibid., pp. 484-89, 492-94.

⁴Brown v. Board of Education of Topeka, 347 U.S., 483 (1954).

⁵Griffiths to Williams, November 22, 1954, in Griffiths Library; Griffiths to John V. Lindsay, February 25, 1960, in Martha W. Griffiths Papers, (Griffiths Papers), Michigan Historical Collections, Bentley Historical Library, University of Michigan Ann Arbor; Clauda Capos, "That's Martha Griffiths: No Radical Lib Chic . . . Just Folksy Charm," Michigan Alumnus 81 (April 1975): 20-22.

⁶Griffiths to Fern Palmer, February 2, 1955, in Griffiths Papers, Bentley Library.

⁷Interview with Griffiths, Romeo, Michigan, June 4, 1977. John D. Dingell Sr., thought Griffiths was needed on Public Works, but two Democrats on the Ways and Means Committee, which assigned House Democrats to the Committee, were willing to support her for Government Operations, if Dingell approved. Elva W. Bell to Griffiths, December 17, 1954, in Griffiths Library.

⁸Interview with Griffiths, Romeo, June 4, 1977.

⁹Griffiths to Reuther, January 18, 1957, in Griffiths Papers, Bentley Library.

¹⁰Carl Muller, "Michigan Politics," [?], [February 1955]; Carl Albert to Griffiths, August 3, 1955, in MWG Scrapbooks, Griffiths Library; Interview with Griffiths, Romeo, December 3, 1977. At the conclusion of the Eighty-fourth Congress Rayburn wrote: "You have been cooperative, your judgment has been sound, and your voting record is one that has been appreciated by us all." July 30, 1956, in MWG Scrapbooks, Griffiths Library.

[11] Interview with Griffiths, Romeo, June 5, 1977. Griffiths' only departure from the party was on the farm vote and then on only three out of fifteen major issues.

[12] Interview with Robert P. Griffin, Detroit, December 5, 1977.

[13] Debate on the food-stamp plan is found in the Congressional Record. Especially informative is discussion in the House, (85th Cong., 2d sess., August 18, 1958, 104:18333-45); see also Senate debate, (86th Cong., 1st sess., August 20, 1959, 105:16568-87).

[14] Griffiths to Leslie Moore, May 8, 1958; Griffiths to George J. Burger, February 7, 1957, in Griffiths Papers, Bentley Library.

[15] "Food Stamp Bill," Labor, March 3, 1956, in MWG Scrapbooks, Griffiths Library.

[16] U.S. Congress, House, Committee on Agriculture, Food Stamp Program, Hearings before a Subcommittee on Consumers Study. 85th Cong., 2d sess., April 16-17 and May 14, 1958 (1958), pp. 49-52.

[17] Ibid., pp. 52-65, 67-75; Williams to Griffiths, March 7, 1958; Fitzgerald to Griffiths, August 20, 1958, in Griffiths Papers, Bentley Library.

[18] Griffiths to Fitzgerald, June 6, 1958, in Griffiths Papers, Bentley Library.

[19] U.S. Congress, House, Committee on Agriculture, Establishment of a Food-Stamp Plan, H. Rept. 907, 86th Cong., 1st sess., August 15, 1959.

[20] Griffiths to Ryan, October 2, 1959, in Griffiths Papers, Bentley Library.

[21] Griffiths to Ryan, February 29, 1960, in Griffiths Papers, Bentley Library; U.S. Congress, House, 86th Cong., 2d sess., March 16, 1960, Congressional Record 106:5752; Newsletters, 1956-74 (July 30, 1959 and October 17, 1960), Griffiths Library.

[22] Griffiths to Charles S. Brown, [n.d.]; Griffiths to G. Mennen Williams, January 11, 1960, in Griffiths Papers, Bentley Library.

[23] Ryan to Griffiths, June 4, 1963, in Griffiths Papers, Bentley Library. The designation of Detroit as a "guinea pig" was mentioned to Griffiths by William Fitzgerald in 1958. (June 10, 1958, in Griffiths Papers, Bentley Library). She urged President Kennedy to consider seriously the proposal. (Griffiths to Kennedy, February 2, 1961, in Griffiths Papers, Bentley Library.)

[24] Griffiths to Reuther, June 23, 1955, in Roy Reuther Papers, Wayne State University Labor History Archives, Detroit, Michigan; Paul A. Miltich, "Rep. Griffiths Beats Drum for Urban Renewal," Ann Arbor News, May 19, 1959, in MWG Scrapbooks, Griffiths Library; Griffiths to Meeting of Pre-Convention Platform Committee of Mich., February 19, 1959, in Griffiths Papers, Bentley Library.

[25] Griffiths to Charles E. Wright, July 8, 1959, in Griffiths Papers, Bentley Library.

[26] U.S. Congress, House, Committee on Government Operations, Bills to Establish a Commission on Metropolitan Problems and Urban Development and to Create a Department of Urban Affairs, Hearings before a subcommittee of Government Operation. 86th Cong., 1st sess., June 3, 9, 19 and July 21, 1959 (1959), pp. 13-24; U.S., Congress, House, Committee on Banking and Currency, General Housing Legislation, Hearings before the Subcommittee on Housing. 86th Cong., 2d sess., May 16-20, 23-27, 1960 (1960), p. 363.

[27] U.S.., Congress, House, Committee on Government Operations, A Bill to Establish a Department of Urban Affairs and Housing and Other Purposes, Hearings before a subcommittee on Government Operations on H.R. 6344, 87th Cong., 1st sess., (1961), pp. 99-100.

[28] Griffiths, "The Responsibility of Christian Women in Today's World," Speech to Congressional Women, June 28, 1966, in Griffiths Library; "A Hard Look at Results of Starving Our Schools," Detroit Free Press, August 20, 1963, in MWG Scrapbooks, Griffiths Library.

[29] U.S., Congress, House, 85th Cong., 2d sess., June 10, 1958, Congressional Record, clipping in MWG Scrapbooks, Griffiths Library.

[30] U.S., Congress, House, 87th Cong., 1st sess., April 24, 1961, Congressional Record 107:6633-34 and June

21; 1961, 107:10932; "Report from Washington: Housing Bill," [n.d.], tape, in Griffiths Papers, Bentley Library.

[31] Griffiths had a great love for nature. One of her favorite books was Loren Eisely, The Immense Journey (New York: Vingage ed., 1959).

[32] U.S., Congress, House, 85th Cong., 1st sess., April 4, 1957, Congressional Record 103:5184; U.S., Congress, House, 85th Cong., 2d sess., June 19, 1958, clipping in MWG scrapbooks, Griffiths Library; also, U.S., Congress, House, 85th Cong., 1st sess., March 18, 1957, Congressional Record, clipping in MWG Scrapbooks, Griffiths Library.

[33] Griffiths to Jack Haines, March 11, 1958, in Griffiths Papers, Bentley Library; U.S., Congress, House, Committee on Banking and Currency, Legislation to Relieve Unemployment, Hearings before the Committee on Banking and Currency. 85th Cong., 2d sess., April 14-18, 21-23, 25, 28-30, May 1-2, 5-9, 13-16, 19-22, 1958 (1958), p. 343; Undelivered speech, March 1958, in Griffiths Library.

[34] U.S., Congress, House, 89th Cong., 1st sess., February 16, 1965, Congressional Record 111:2712-13.

[35] See Committee on Banking and Currency, Legislation to Relieve Unemployment Hearings, pp. 486-87.

[36] Memorandum of January 8, 1959, Breakfast Meeting with Michigan delegation in Washington from G. Mennen Williams to Griffiths, January 26, 1959, in Griffiths Papers, Bentley Library.

[37] Griffiths to Williams, Reuther and Miriani, August 1, 1958, in Griffiths Papers, Bentley Library.

[38] Griffiths to Reuther, August 11, 1958, in Griffiths Papers, Bentley Library.

[39] Griffiths to Williams, Reuther and Miriani, August 1, 1958, in Griffiths Papers, Bentley Library.

[40] "Kind of Lady to Elect to Congress," Labor (Washington, D.C.), July 21, 1956, in MWG Scrapbooks, Griffiths Library. According to the AFL-CIO News, September 7, 1974, Griffiths' cumulative record was 107 to 12 votes. The records of other Michigan Domocrats were: John D.

Dingell Jr., 117 to 5; Charles C. Diggs, 112 to 4; James G. O'Hara, 107 to 6; and Lucian N. Nedzi, 93 to 4.

[41] Griffiths, "Statement before the House Post Office and Civil Service Committee, February 15, 1955," in Griffiths Library. A typical response to her consistent efforts on behalf of post-office employees is found in Edward Ozak to Griffiths, July 1, 1960, in Griffiths Papers, Bentley Library. "The morale of the postal employee has been sufficiently boosted by actions like yours to raise the efficiency of the employees and make the Post Office a more desirable career."

[42] Interview with Griffiths, Romeo, December 3, 1977.

[43] For her stand on right-to-work laws see Griffiths to Charles Hackett, February 24, 1966; and on the use of Pinkerton guards, Griffiths to James C. McGahey, April 26, 1960, in Griffiths Papers, Bentley Library.

[44] On the minimum wage, Griffiths to H. Glenn Bixby, August 18, 1965—"I assure you," she wrote, "that most Congressmen are extremely nervous over this bill."— and Griffiths to E. Edwin Slater, February 2, 1965, for increased fringe benefits, in Griffiths Papers, Bentley Library.

[45] On May 9, 1962, she delivered a stinging attack against striking Detroit newspapers (U.S., Congress, House, 87th Cong., 2d sess., *Congressional Record* 108: 7403-4; also Griffiths to Robert M. Holland, August 17, 1966, in Griffiths Papers, Bentley Library.)

[46] Griffiths form letter, "Dear Friends," August 18, 1959, in Griffiths Papers, Bentley Library.

[47] *Ibid.*; Griffiths to George N. Carleton, August 3, 1959, in Griffiths Papers, Bentley Library.

[48] Unfortunately this clipping in the MWG Scrapbooks, Griffiths Library, gives no indication of source.

[49] For House debate on the bill see especially U.S., Congress, House, 86th Cong., 1st sess., August 13-14, 1959, *Congressional Record* 105:15824-68 and 15870-72.

[50] John Quillico, open letter to Griffiths and Lesinski, "Lesinski and Griffiths Stab U.S. Workers," *Ford Facts*,

August 29, 1959, in MWG Scrapbooks, Griffiths Library.

[51]Ibid.; Steward Didzun, "Politicians Desire No Rides on Teamsters' Bandwagon," Detroit News, November 8, 1959; "A Black Day for Labor," International Teamster 56 (September 1959): 4-8, in MWG Scrapbooks, Griffiths Library.

[52]Griffiths form letter, "Dear Friends," August 18, 1959, in Griffiths Papers, Bentley Library.

[53]See Benjamin Aaron, "The Labor-Management Reporting and Disclosure Act of 1959," 73 Harvard Law Review (1960), 851 ff and 1086 ff. Aaron contends that the conference adjustments helped create additional problems such as the interpretation of federal-state jurisdiction in the "no-man's land" provision.

[54]U.S., Congress, House, Committee on Government Operations, Civil Defense for National Survival, Hearings and Reports. (84th Cong., 1955-56), 84th Cong., 2d sess., March 8, 1956, 1:574; 84th Cong., 2d sess., May 7, 1956, 2:1627-31; "Report from Washington: Civil Defense," video tape for August 6, 1961, and Griffiths to Patrick Pernick, February 5, 1959, in Griffiths Papers, Bentley Library.

[55]"Report from Washington: Threat of Nuclear War," [n.d.] video tape in Griffiths Papers, Bentley Library; William Kulsea, "Congresswoman Tells Horror Tale of Results if Bombs Hit State," Ann Arbor News, December 10, 1957, in MWG Scrapbooks, Griffiths Library; Interview with Griffiths, Romeo, July 21, 1977. See also, Civil Defense for National Survival, 1:107; "Woman Solon Raps A-Shelter Program," Florida Times-Union (Jacksonville), August 3, 1961; Griffiths to Secretary of Defense Robert S. McNamara, September 28, 1961, in Griffiths Papers, Bentley Library; Newsletter 1956-74 (November 1962), in Griffiths Library. Griffiths wrote a correspondent: "In my judgment the present Civil Defense system is ridiculous. It would hardly defend from a tornado, less a bomb. Unless we are willing to establish a reasonable system, it might as well be wiped out." Griffiths to Sidney E. Taylor, December 2, 1960, in Griffiths Papers, Bentley Library.

[56]Griffiths argued for civilian status for the Secretary of Civil Defense in "Status of National Civil Defense Legislation," Journal of American Medical Association (February 15, 1958) 166:793-94, in Griffiths Library.

[57] Griffiths to Donald Levinson, April 4, 1960, in Griffiths Papers, Bentley Library; U.S., Congress, House, 91st Cong., 1st sess., March 20, 1970, Congressional Record 116:E2282.

[58] Memorandum of January 8, 1959 Breakfast Meeting with Michigan delegation in Washington from G. Mennen Williams to Griffiths, January 26, 1959; "'Reckless Capitalism' Does Wonders for Aircraft Industry—and You Pay!" Labor's Daily, June 13, 1957, in Griffiths Papers, Bentley Library; "GOP Fighting Griffiths Bill to Stop Defense Profiteering," Michigan AFL-CIO News, July 2, 1959, in MWG Scrapbooks, Griffiths Library. Also, U.S., Congress, House, Committee on Government Operations, Navy Jet Aircraft Procurement Program, Hearings and Reports before the Subcommittee on Military Operations. 84th Cong., 1st sess., October 24-27, 1955 (1956), pp. 45-47; clipping of Congressional Record, 86th Cong., 2nd sess., March 9, 1960, in MWG Scrapbooks, Griffiths Library.

[59] U.S., Congress, House, 85th Cong., 1st sess., May 28, 1957, Congressional Record 103:6961.

[60] "One Long-Term Cure for Military Waste," Detroit Free Press, May 29, 1957, MWG Scrapbooks, Griffiths Library.

[61] U.S., Congress, House, 86th Cong., 1st sess., May 26, 1959, Congressional Record 105:8227; U.S., Congress, House, 86th Cong., 2nd sess., June 9, 1960, Congressional Record 106:12312-14; Pearson, "The High Cost of an Incentive," Washington Post and Times Herald, May 31, 1959; "Double Agents in Procurement," Nation, June 25, 1960, in MWG Scrapbooks, Griffiths Library.

[62] Griffiths note on letter of Carl Vinson to her, May 12, 1961, in Griffiths Papers, Bentley Library.

[63] U.S., Congress, House, 88th Cong., 2d sess., April 29, 1964, Congressional Record 110:9145; U.S., Congress, House, 89th Cong., 2d sess., May 18, 1966, Congressional Record 112:10418, and June 15, 1966, 112:13295; also U.S., Congress, House, Joint Economic Committee, Impact of Military and Related Supply and Service Activities on the Economy, Hearings before the Subcommittee on Federal Procurement on the Economy. 88th Cong., 2d sess., April 16 and 21, 1964, pp. 130 ff. and Economic Impact of Federal Procurement. 89th Cong., 2d sess., January 24, March 23-24, 1966 (1966), p. 110. In the latter document, Lawson B. Knott Jr.,

the Administrator of the General Services Administration, told the JEC that its hearings "more than any other single factor" helped change procurement procedures.

[64] Griffiths to Patricia Walker, June 2, 1965, in Griffiths Papers, Bentley Library; Dan O'Connor, "Plan Water Probe Here," *Detroit News*, October 18, 1955, MWG Scrapbooks, Griffiths Library; Interview with Griffiths, Romeo, February 12, 1977.

[65] On her responsibility for establishment of Detroit district office see Griffiths to Norval L. Slobin, February 9, 1961; for her concern of FDA practices, "Memo to Mrs. Griffiths," November 19, 1963, in Griffiths Papers, Bentley Library.

[66] "Testimony of the Honorable Martha W. Griffiths, before the Livestock and Grains Subcommittee of the House Committee on Agriculture," July 18, 1973, in Griffiths Papers, Bentley Library.

[67] "Back to the Kitchen" (editorial), *Washington Post*, May 16, 1955, in MWG Scrapbooks, Griffiths Library.

[68] "Filter Tips Leave PHS in a Haze," *Washington Post and Times Herald*, July 24, 1957; Jack Anderson, "Crackdown on Cigarette Ads by House Probers Due," *Detroit Free Press*, September 24, 1957, in MWG Scrapbooks, Griffiths Library. In 1953, the *New England Journal of Medicine* linked cigarettes to cancer. Not until 1968, however, did anti-smoking messages appear on television. In 1971 both cigarette and anti-cigarette ads were barred.

[69] Griffiths interview with Florence Hoff [n.d.], tape, in Griffiths Papers, Bentley Library; "Smith to Put TV up to Committee," *Washington Post*, February 21, 1961, in Griffiths Papers, Bentley Library; J.F. Ter Horst, "Rayburn-Smith Feud Prevents TV in House," *Detroit News*, February 23, 1961, in MWG Scrapbooks, Griffiths Library.

[70] For the 1958 House and Senate debate see U.S., Congress, House, 85th Cong., 2d sess., February 4, 1968, *Congressional Record* 104:1653-74 and Senate, July 29, 1958, 194:15368-85; also argument offered by Humphrey in introducing the bill in the Senate, U.S., Congress, Senate, 84th Cong., 1st sess., April 1, 1955, *Congressional Record* 101:4188; U.S., Congress, House, Com-

mittee on Agriculture, <u>Humane Slaughter of Livestock</u>, H. Rept. 706, 85th Cong., 1st sess., July 9, 1957.

[71] Griffiths' arguments found in her "Statement before the Senate Agriculture Subcommittee 'On Humane Slaughter,'" May 10, 1956, in Griffiths Library. In addition to the gains mentioned she pointed out that new equipment would be subject to depreciation rates; Stevenson to Griffiths, November 1, 1956, in Griffiths Papers, Bentley Library.

[72] Stevens to Griffiths, February 14, 1958, in Griffiths Papers, Bentley Library; U.S., Congress, House, 85th Cong., 2d sess., February 4, 1968, <u>Congressional Record</u> 104:1654.

[73] Griffiths to Neil Staebler, April 28, 1961, in Griffiths Papers, Bentley Library.

[74] There are several strong letters against her bill in the Griffiths Papers, Bentley Library, including her response, Griffiths to R.S. Schreiber, April [n.d.], 1961.

[75] Interview with Griffiths, Romeo, September 10, 1977; Griffiths to Rogers, September 13, 1967, in Griffiths Papers, Bentley Library.

[76] "Martha Griffiths Loses: Stays in Capitol," <u>Detroit Times</u>, April 7, 1959, in MWG Scrapbooks, Griffiths Library.

[77] <u>Detroit News</u>, December 23 and 28, 1958; January 25 and [n.d.], 1959; <u>Detroit Free Press</u>, December 24, 1958; <u>Detroit Times</u>, December 23 and 25, 1958, and January 6, 1959, in MWG Scrapbooks, Griffiths Library.

[78] Griffiths to Milton B. Shaber, January 6, 1959, in Griffiths Papers, Bentley Library.

[79] U.S., Congress, House, 90th Cong., 1st sess., October 3, 1967, <u>Congressional Record</u> 113:27656; Interview with Griffiths, Romeo, February 24, 1980.

[80] Neil Staebler, Michigan Democratic State Chairperson, told Christine Stevens, August 10, 1956, that Griffiths was "her own best insurance for re-election." Staebler Papers, Bentley Library. Frank Morris of <u>Detroit Times</u> called her the "most successful woman campaigner in Michigan Democratic history." ("No

'Landslide' for Dems, GOP," July 30, 1956, MWG Scrapbooks, Griffiths Library.)

[81] The reason the Free Press supported Lucas S. Miel over Griffiths was that it thought he was an extraordinarily good candidate. "Our Recommendations on the 16 Candidates," October 31, 1958, MWG Scrapbooks, Griffiths Library; Interviews with Griffiths, Romeo, July 24, 1977 and December 2, 1977; "Wayne AFL OKs Governor," Detroit Times, June 21, 1956, in MWG Scrapbooks, Griffiths Library.

[82] Griffiths to Helen V. Smith, February 3, 1959; Griffiths to Ella G. Roller, January 6, 1959, in Griffiths Papers, Bentley Library; Interview with Griffiths, Romeo, December 2, 1977.

[83] Detroit News, March 15 and 17, 1959; Detroit Free Press, April 1, 1959, in MWG Scrapbooks, Griffiths Library.

[84] Detroit News, January 26 and April 8, 1959, in MWG Scrapbooks, Griffiths Library.

[85] Griffiths to L.B. Parrish, June 16, 1959, in Griffiths Papers, Bentley Library.

[86] Interview with Griffiths, Romeo, December 2, 1977.

CHAPTER III

In the final hours of 1969, Life looked back over the 60s as the "Divided Decade." The editors observed that the first five years had been characterized by "a brisk feeling of hope, a generally optimistic and energetic shift from the calm of the late '50s." Then came Watts in 1965 and, as in a chain reaction, violence erupted all over the nation.[1] In July 1967, angry blacks burned and bombed Detroit. Viewing the ruins from an armed squad car, Martha Griffiths noted with shock: "We have some hard thinking to do about our urban areas and considerable work."[2]

Even before 1965, Griffiths had been awakened to violence as a global reality. In addressing the National Association of Women Lawyers in August 1960, she had pointed out Japan's recent failure to guarantee a safe visit for an American President, the unspeakable brutality loosed by the Congolese on resident Belgians, and Soviet exploitation of anti-American hatred in the Western Hemisphere by stepped up aid to Fidel Castro's pro-Communist government. "The world is no longer a stage," she said, "but an audience prepared to throw rotten tomatoes, some of which might be loaded with hydrogen bombs."[3] In September that same year she had reported to her constituents that the end of detente with Khrushchev had drastically reduced America's influence across the world.[4] And she expressed the same sober realism on the eve of the Eighty-seventh Congress when she told friends, "I feel that if Kennedy can delay the bombs being dropped upon us, he will have done a great deal."[5]

Yet, buoyant and venturesome, Griffiths approached the New Frontier with dreams for traveling the road of peace at home and abroad. "In problem solving," she told the NAWL, "this nation must lead the way" and she meant to do her share.[6] For Griffiths, the 60s actually held great promise for an invigorating journey. Overcoming whatever antagonism her 1959 bid for Recorder's Court might have engendered, she had carried her district in 1960—including AFL-CIO support[7]—by nearly 58 percent of the vote, a figure that rose steadily toward 80 percent over the decade.[8] By the mid-60s Griffiths was assured of re-election, even though it took a lot of hard work such as back-breaking pancake suppers in the early decade and shopping mall safaris in the late 60s and early 70s to keep pace with her changing constituents.[9]

The Kennedy-Johnson era fired Griffiths' enthusiasm. She loved Kennedy for his elan, but she identified with the pragmatism of Johnson. "He was an alchemist of dreams," she said at the time of Johnson's death. What he did may not have been perfect but one could "see it, touch it, use it, test it, live with it, or improve it." Johnson was a person after her own heart. "His name really should be 'Action,'" she once remarked.[10] She was particularly energized by Johnson's belief that the future of the city was the national priority. Thus, she supported the President's War on Poverty, describing it as "an attempt to mobilize the human and financial resources of the nation in a conscious and focused attack on want and deprivation."[11]

Griffiths fought hard during the 60s against soaring unemployment rates, especially in Detroit where the unemployment rose way beyond the national average. As a palliative, Griffiths advocated a significant dose of federal contracts.[12] She also believed that money spent for urban renewal was money well spent: it provided housing and jobs. "Urban renewal made many errors. . . . But urban renewal did some beautiful things," she argued in its defense.[13] Active concern for the cities provoked in her a vivid anger over the metastasis of black ghettos. Panic selling engineered by home realtors was, in her opinion, "one of the most important—and most vicious—causes of spreading segregation of our cities." If she had had her way, there would have been a constitutional amendment requiring that in every sector of a city the number of blacks be in proportion to the national census.[14]

To address the problem of urban sprawl, Griffiths introduced a bill to research mass transportation systems. Furthermore, she advocated returning to the cities the income taxes of the federal employees hired there.[15] An active regard for urban dwellers moved her to defend rent subsidies, made her "madder than a hornet" over cost discrimination in depressed areas, and prompted her to propose a three-day meal plan for hungry children.[16] She analyzed the merits of the farm subsidy from its impact on the cities: how it would affect employment, production, and the price of bread.[17]

Concern for the cities likewise shaped her into a a protector of the environment,[88] into a foe of firearms,[19] smut[20] and rats. One of her most publicized speeches in the House was in response to ridicule heaped on Johnson's 1967 $40 million rodent extermination plan. On that occasion, she spoke in the manner that had become her hallmark: a short burst of spontaneous oratory resulting from a sense of outrage.[21] "You could hear a pin drop in that chamber," reported Dan Rostenkowski of Ways and Means. "It was a most embarrassing episode for the Republicans."[22] With a mass of facts at her disposal, Griffiths discussed the origin, characteristics, and habits of rats, which she called the "living cargo of death." "They have made Genghis Khan, Hitler, and all the other men look like pikers," she said. "Their tails swish through sewers and over the food we eat. Their stomachs are filled with tularemia and amoebic dysentary. They carry the most deadly diseases, and some think it is funny." She was amazed that Congress could pour billions into defense and do nothing to kill "the most devastating enemy man has ever had."[23] Her short exposition galvanized the press and the public behind Johnson's program and before the end of the session, the money cleared Congress.[24]

During the Nixon years Griffiths did not let up on her concern for urban America; if anything, her activity increased as evidenced in her exhaustive JEC welfare study. She continually fought cuts in HEW appropriations as grave losses to the service needs of the central cities.[25] She served on a select panel dealing with the harsh problem of drug traffic so endemic to depressed areas and, as a result of this effort, sponsored several bills relating to drug control.[26] Her primary activity on behalf of the cities, however, was more profound than suggested by these individual undertakings. By serving on JEC and on Ways and Means she was brought into daily contact with urban affairs. The involvement of JEC with the overall effects of the nation's economic measures provided her breadth of vision and contact with the experts. "I know that all the members of Ways and Means would have been delighted to have sat on Joint Economic," Griffiths said in reflecting on her dual membership.[27] The prestigious and hardworking Ways and Means gave her opportunity to deal with the particulars of taxes and trade, of welfare reform and social security, "the things," as John McCormack put it, "that go to the hearts and the hopes of countless of millions of Americans."[28] The interplay between JEC and Ways and Means gave Griffiths a legislative perspective not afforded many members of Congress—and to that date, no other woman.

Fortunate though she was in having these assignments—
"very lucky," she described it—fate did not have the
upper hand. Griffiths planned her future. "I saw what
was coming up," she recounted in reflecting on her
appointment to JEC, "and I asked for it. You see, I had
gotten all the women to go in and see Sam Rayburn to get
me on Joint Economic. And he had already promised the
seat, but he said, 'The next one that occurs I will give
it to her.' . . . And, by gum, one opened up the next
year and I got it." Griffiths was the first woman to
serve on this prestigious Committee and the second Representative from Michigan, Jessie P. Wolcott having been
the first. From the outset, Griffiths loved JEC. "You
were sitting there listening to the real brains tell you
how it [the economy] worked," she noted appreciatively.[29]

The Joint Economic Committee to which Griffiths was
appointed in February 1961 had grown with the national
income during its fifteen years. Designed in 1946 to
deal specifically with postwar unemployment and social
unrest, the Committee's analyses of major economic issues had become as important as both its annual recommendations on the President's budget and its reports to
Congress' budget committees. Bernard D. Nossiter of the
Washington Post underscored JEC's influence when he
wrote: "Its documents are often a useful clue to the
congressional temper, a guide to campaign arguments, and
an omen of future legislation."[30] That the studies
broached some of the knottiest problems of the big purse
—30 percent of the national income flowed into Washington in taxes and revenue—gave JEC a primacy on Capitol
Hill. Its scope instinctively appealed to Griffiths as
did the colleagues with whom she worked. The names of
Paul Douglas and Hubert Humphrey, the two Senators she
admired most,[31] suggest the quality of JEC.

Griffiths served on a number of JEC subcommittees
from 1961 through 1974, but especially intriguing to
her were those dealing with military purchases, foreign
economics, urban affairs, and fiscal policy. Two subcommittees—Defense Procurement and Economy in Government—concerned with military duplication, overlap and
waste, allowed Griffiths to take up the probe initiated
years before on Government Operations. The resultant
publicity she directed to shoddy and costly procurement
practices continued to make her persona non grata to the
Pentagon.[32] Her interest in foreign economic policy,
stimulated by a desire to foster Michigan sales abroad,
found an outlet in the Subcommittee on Inter-American
Economic Relationships, which introduced her to the

southern continent particularly through a Central American field study she conducted in 1962.[33] Concluding from this on-the-spot inquiry that prevailing land patterns were more decisive to the future of this hemisphere than the ideological struggle between communism and democracy, she argued for increased foreign aid in the form of low-interest loans and technical assistance. She reasoned that the United States would fail in its own best interests were it to ignore the geographic and demographic significance of Central America to both global peace and hemispheric solidarity.[34] Her special concern over the safety of the Canal Zone led her further in 1964 to advocate statehood for the intercontinental artery. "Let us fly one flag, use one army, and [let] that [be] the flag and Army of the United States," she told Congress.[35]

In addition to these three subcommittees, another concerned with urban affairs harmonized with her own Subcommittee, Fiscal Policy. Named as chair in May 1964, she was acknowledged by the media to be a "middle-roader [who had] confidence of business and labor alike." The anticipation was that she would fashion Fiscal Policy "in the great tradition" established by Wilbur Mills in the 50s.[36] In reactivating the Subcommittee, JEC Chairperson Douglas earmarked its agenda: continued national debate on tax structures, federal expenditure policies, and the manner of presenting the budget to Congress.[37] While the direction set for the Subcommittee was distinctly futuristic—to move the dialogue beyond the 1964 tax law—Griffiths was no less optimistic that her Subcommittee would educate the public on existing economic facts; that it would explain, for example, how the 1964 tax cut was meant to raise revenue and how a GNP edging toward a trillion dollars affected the current federal budget. In her role as chairperson, her personal ambition was not to be only as good as Mills, "I simply have to be better," she confided to a close friend.[38] Public and personal confidence, as well as an outstanding membership, executive director and staff, were all grounds for believing that Fiscal Policy would be first-rate.

Almost every year while Griffiths was chairperson, the Subcommittee dealt with a major issue: during 1964-65, fiscal concerns for 1965-75; in 1966-67, private pension plans; revenue sharing and its options, 1967; income maintenance options, 1968; the relationship of the budget to inflation and full employment, 1969; and the federal welfare system, 1971-74. The week after its re-establishment, the Subcommittee agreed to the recommendation of Executive Director James K. Knowles that its first task was to get a cross-sectional view of what leading economists thought were the crucial issues for the coming decade.39 From this symposium the Subcommittee hoped to shape its long-range agenda.

Forty-eight experts from labor, business, the universities, and the foundations identified five central issues for future analysis: "fiscal drag" resulting from the excess of federal revenues over expenditures, fiscal policy as a flexible anti-cyclic tool, the national debt, tax reform, and revenue sharing.40 The last item, also referred to as "fiscal federalism" by its chief proponents, Joseph A. Pechman of the Brookings Institution and Walter W. Heller, former chairperson of Kennedy's economic advisers, was one debate in which Griffiths took a position from the outset: she opposed giving the states unencumbered federal money.

Revenue sharing received public attention during the 1964 campaign when both candidates, Lyndon Johnson and Barry Goldwater, endorsed the idea. Following the Vietnam War it drew serious attention as postwar adjustments collided with the heavy demands made on state and local governments for costly public services like schools, hospitals, and roads. The federal government added to the complexity by its unwillingness to spend surplus revenue on the states. As the various JEC subcommittees went about their respective studies, they invariably ran into this multi-level problem. The Fiscal Policy Subcommittee took this as its cue to face the issue of revenue sharing directly—the first Congressional body to do so. When Griffiths announced that hearings would be held, she asked that revenue sharing be considered but one option in redressing the fiscal imbalance.41 Her caution suggested that revenue sharing had already become a popular concept.

Heller indicated why. Revenue sharing was a simple way of automatically guaranteeing to the states a large source of unrestricted revenue, a strategy which avoided the hardening categories of conditional grant programs and equalized financial burdens among all units of governments. Revenue-sharing advocates further argued that large doses of monetary self-determination proposed to realize a real partnership between Washington and the states. "States and localities," Heller contended, "are still the most essential part of a mechanism for feeding ideas up the line and having them come back down with money attached."[42]

This reasoning riled Griffiths for three reasons. First, she believed in the "puritan ethic" that whoever had authority over the funds was also responsible for controlling them. For the federal government to have nothing to say about how its money was spent and to exact no accountability from the states was, in her view, illogical and immoral. Secondly, she had yet to see the states work toward solving their financial problems. Outmoded governmental structures and archaic taxing strategies, lack of sympathy for the cities and indecisiveness in dealing with local governments called for self-reform before federal largess. Furthermore, her experience in Lansing had taught her to resist leaving federal funds to "the untender mercies" of state legislatures, more subject to political chicanery than Congress and more attached to the rural areas than to the big cities where services were needed most. "It will be the Ways and Means Committee versus the Governors," Griffiths argued, "and each one of them will have his own ax to grind. . . . You are going to have a greedy group of people seeking the money with every conceivable device to try to get it."[43] In 1967 her preferred solution to state-sponsored services required: first, the discontinuance of grants-in-aid, which she had observed to be too complex and inflexible to be of value; and, second, the revision of the IRS code to allow taxpayers credit for supporting their state and local governments, a boon to progressive taxation. Moreover, for Griffiths, tax credits proposed to be a more authentic expression of self-determination than the "pie-in-the-sky" remedy of the revenue-sharing advocates.[44]

In 1969 President Nixon sent a "no strings" plan to the Hill, requesting $500 million for FY 1971 with increments up to $5 billion by 1976. Neither Ways and Means nor the Senate Finance Committee, however, acted on the bill, nor on the more restrictive distribution formula offered by Senators Edmund S. Muskie and Charles E. Goodell. In 1971 the Administration stepped up its demands by a massive $15 billion package which met opposition commensurate with its size. Two of Griffiths' JEC colleagues, Hubert Humphrey and Henry S. Reuss, also co-sponsored a bill providing the states with incentives for retaining or augmenting their federal revenues. The Advisory Commission on Intergovernmental Relations likewise adopted the Muskie plan. Despite these efforts, revenue sharing showed little sign of going anywhere throughout 1971 as long as Ways and Means and the Senate Finance Committee held out.[45]

In the extensive Ways and Means hearing, Griffiths and Treasury Secretary John B. Connolly exchanged strong views regarding the merits and demerits of unconditional federal grants. Griffiths continued to argue that they would open the floodgates to indiscriminate spending, would be used as political leverage in the boondocks, and would be a burden to the most populous states. "You send some money back to Cleveland, New York, and Detroit," she told Connolly, "but the truth is that they are paying the bill that you are sending also to Podunk." Connolly reminded Griffiths that Podunk, also a part of America, would receive funds according to the needs-equity proviso of the administration bill. Griffiths nevertheless called Nixon's proposal "pie" and "manna" for governors and mayors. "Manna saved Israel," the Secretary replied tongue-in-cheek, "and pie has calories for everyone, so that it has value as food." Griffiths then dropped the loaded question: "Does Texas have an income tax?" To Connolly's negative response Griffiths declared that Michigan and Detroit taxpayers were not interested in financing the Lone Star State. Moreover, she was concerned that a sizable portion of the federal money would be used to cover the cost of escalating public pensions and never reach its proposed destination. As Griffiths saw it, revenue sharing was nothing but a "fast solution to a long-term problem."[46]

In her conversation with Muskie, Griffiths reiterated her contention that "no strings" allowed the unscrupulous to pull strings. She did, however, like Muskie's poverty ratio which apportioned greater revenues to poor areas. She had hoped, she told him, to have built something like his ratio into the most recent welfare bill.[47] What particularly bothered Griffiths was that revenue sharing, like welfare, carried no price tag of its cost to the government over a twenty year period—bad business, in her opinion. As one Detroit newspaper put it, revenue sharing "set up Uncle Sam as the sugar daddy who picks up the bills without asking questions." By the summer of 1971, the fate of Nixon's proposal seemed fairly settled: "The irresistible force," noted the <u>Wall Street Journal</u>, "is no match for the immovable object."[48]

Yet the concept proved beguiling—even to "the immovable object." In November, Mills and some of the other members of Ways and Means proposed a version of revenue sharing that ultimately drew the support of the majority, including Griffiths. The bill provided that over a five-year period one-third of $30 billion would be plowed back into the states and two-thirds into local jurisdictions. By this formula, the bill's proponents acknowledged that urban problems surpassed those of the states, that city residents paid more for what they got, and that city administrators had less than they needed. The measure placed restrictions on the recipients by requiring the states to maintain the level of assistance they had given the cities prior to the act and by obliging local governments to use the money solely for public safety, environmental protection, and public transportation.

Despite the ratios and "strings," within a year Michigan Democrats were regretting the day they had voted for the State and Local Fiscal Assistance Act of 1972. They considered the banking of the funds and the use of the money to cut taxes and pay deficits—all in the name of revenue sharing—as "political hijinks." Had it not been for the importuning of Detroit Mayor Roman Gribbs, Griffiths admitted later that she would never have capitulated to revenue sharing. She thought it a "tremendous mistake" then, and seeing how the money was subsequently being used made her angry and ashamed that she had let herself be swayed. For fear of what revenue sharing was fast becoming, in 1973 Griffiths tried to prevail on JEC for a comparative study of state and local budgets a year before and a year after revenue sharing went into effect. She hoped by this means to show how the money was really being spent. JEC, however, did not think the recommendation important enough to implement. "What you really did," she said by way of final assessment, "was to require that Ways and Means levy the taxes, and you passed it back all over the country and relieved all those politicans from their own folly."[49] Having lost this battle, she could at least find solace in the progress made in another area of primary concern to her and the Fiscal Policy Subcommittee: pension reform.

Among the legislative achievements of the 70s, the Employee Retirement Income Security Act of 1974—ERISA— must be mentioned. For giving impetus to this long overdue statute, Griffiths' Fiscal Policy Subcommittee has to be credited on at least three counts: first, for the original comprehensive hearing on private pension plans; second, for a compendium of select views on the relationship of private pensions to social security insurance and other retirement programs; and third, for injecting new data into the pension debate through other Fiscal Policy Subcommittee analyses such as the pension studies of the 1971-74 welfare probe.[50]

By 1970 the pension question was in a state of financial and moral chaos. Statistics reveal why. Between 1950 and 1970, employee-employer contributions to private pension funds rose from $2.1 billion to a worth of $16.6 billion. In 1970, 5.2 million retirees drew $8.4 billion in benefits. These recipients represented a tenfold increase of those who received $370 million in pension benefits in 1950. In 1980, 42 million pensioners were expected to be covered as compared to the 4 million beneficiaries of 1940. Pension assets were also projected to mount to some $250 billion. This rapid, uneven growth transformed the latent deficiencies of a relative "non-system" into gross problems. When Griffiths' Subcommittee began its inquiry, six troublesome areas were evident: inequitable coverage, inadequate vesting, insufficient funding, fund mismanagement, loss of benefits with plan terminations, and tax discrimination against the self-employed and against employees not covered by retirement plans.[51] The Fiscal Policy hearings initiated an early disclosure of these egregious conditions.

Inspiration for the 1966 hearings came from a curiosity in Griffiths to find out what was happening to "the incredible hoard of tax-free money" lodged in some 34,000 registered pension plans. Two moral considerations also moved her to act: one, tax privileges on employer contributions not directly benefitting retired workers; and, two, the use of taxpayer money in paying for non-taxable pension benefits. From Griffiths' perspective, retirement money that never reached its beneficiaries was theft on two counts. For those JEC members who served on either Ways and Means or the Senate Finance Committee the study of pension economics was natural and welcome. Especially anxious to get the probe under way were James Knowles, JEC executive director, and Nelson D. McClung, a Griffiths' staff appointee who was to engineer the volume on select pension views.[52]

While the most vigorous body in the 60s to deal with private pensions, the Fiscal Policy Subcommittee was not the first to do so. In 1962 President Kennedy mandated an interagency review headed by Secretary of Labor W. Willard Wirtz. In reporting to President John-

76

son in 1965, the task force asked for fuller corporate funding and the establishment of minimum vesting standards. Yet the Administration submitted no legislation to Congress, nor did Ways and Means act on Wirtz' recommendations. In the spring of 1965, a Senate subcommittee on retirement income also held hearings on the inadequacy of pension coverage and, as a result, advised expanded retirement benefits for the self-employed. Chairperson Jennings Randolph urged Griffiths to keep his subcommittee's recommendation in mind as she and her colleagues worked for pension reform.[53] Griffiths needed no prodding in this regard, well aware that independent professionals, like her husband, were at a disadvantage in accumulating retirement income.

The long-range goal of the Fiscal Policy study was to design a guaranteed pension system. As original input, Griffiths hoped those persons who had been adversely affected by the "non-system" would testify, but, when this did not materialize, she relied on their correspondence to make her case. One reporter noted how effective she was in using this strategy during committee hearings: "Her questions answered, Congresswoman Griffiths folded her letters into her purse and prepared to adjourn the meeting. But not without a final word. She wanted the record to show again that she felt citizens were not being treated fairly. . . . 'If you are not indignant about this, I am,' she told Secretary Wirtz. 'I'm furious that these people are paying into these pension plans and getting nothing for it.'"[54]

Who, she asked, would not be upset to learn that a worker, forced by illness to retire at 62 after 30 years on the job—10 paying into the union—had neither social security because of his age, nor pension benefits because he had only 13 of 15 years' required vesting? Who would not be angry that a laborer lost 28 years' benefits because he had not reached vesting age when he left his firm? Who, moreover, would not experience something of a union administrator's "long, lonely and mostly useless effort" to design a reciprocal multi-employer plan for two locals of the same trade and same international?[55] The experiences of ordinary people were important to Griffiths both in shaping her views and in providing leverage in pressing for legislative change.

No less significant and no more comforting was testimony from corporate executives and pension trustees. The Subcommittee learned that five-sixths of the

Teamster membership supported pensions for the other one-sixth; that at its closing, Studebaker paid an average cash settlement of $600 to workers of 23 years' employment; that organized garment workers received no benefits from their union's non-contributory plan unless they remained with it until retirement. The Subcommittee was also told that engineers working on federal aerospace projects could not transfer benefits, although their employment necessitated their move from one plant to another. Federal bureaucrats added their own bad news to these revelations. They blamed the pension push on the pitifully low social security base, admitted to the absence of an official definition of funding, and acknowledged that the law provided only mild IRS enforcement of plan disclosures. "The social architecture, social planning, social invention," confessed Secretary Wirtz, "is so far short of the scientific invention here."[56]

Each new set of testimony reinforced for the panel the hard fact that between one-third and one-half of all prospective pensioners received nothing in their retirement. Writing to Walter Reuther at the conclusion of the hearing, Griffiths outlined the sine qua non of pension reform. "It is absolutely essential that pensions vest," she declared. "I feel that 10 years is too long a period of time and that pensions should be insured, and that there should be some stringent government controls over them. It is bad enough that people are bilked and defrauded of pensions, but I strongly surmise there have been some real shenanigans with the funds." What lay ahead? Congress could delay no longer in facing up to its responsibilities. But, she predicted, "there is going to be some very strong and powerful lobbying against any action whatever. The pension funds have been a happy bonanza for altogether too many people."[57]

Griffiths' hearings did a great deal to arouse workers to the financial precariousness of their retirement years.[58] Knowing she was responsible for the next step, Griffiths urged Mills to take up the matter with Ways and Means. It remained for others, however, to initiate pension reform. In 1971 Nixon proposed the Employee Benefit Protection Act while the Senate Labor Subcommittee initiated a study on retirement guarantees. The next year Senators Jacob K. Javits and Harrison A. Williams prodded Congress for action on a measure providing vesting rights, authorizing federal insurance, and allowing benefit portability. A jurisdictional dispute with the Senate Finance Committee together with the distractions of the approaching national elections brought this latter effort to a temporary halt. In the meantime, the House Labor Subcommittee, busy with its own reform version, had tangled with Ways and Means. Griffiths was still with those who preferred a Ways and Means bill since she had come to the conclusion that it would take "ironclad [tax] protections" to prevent companies from "looting the funds."[59]

In the midst of these intercommittee fights, Griffiths opened a Pandora's box on public pensions. Upset about the little her husband could accumulate toward his retirement as a self-employed professional, she investigated the kind of pension she would receive as a member of Congress. She estimated that if she paid $3,400 for 20 years, at 60 she would draw a $20,000 pension in addition to a $12,000 survivor right. Similar benefits for Hicks would cost $500,000 in investments or $25,000 a year after taxes, a disparity Griffiths considered grossly unfair.

The magnitude of the injustice could be seen by looking at what was happening to the taxpayer dollars which supported public pension funds. Threatening to tax state and local budgets out of sight were the 15 million public employees participating in some 2,200 pension systems that cost $15 to $20 billion each year. Added to this was the rate of acceleration in pension receipts and withdrawal payments—15 and 13.6 percent respectively for 1969-70. During the Ways and Means hearings on revenue sharing, the Committee had learned that Cleveland paid 60 percent of its total budget in salaries and pensions for its police and fire fighters. Given facts like these, it was conceivable that public pensions might triple by 1980. Furthermore, the liberal retirement benefits that were being built into union contracts actually doubled or tripled future salaries. What was Griffiths asking? Simply, that everyone wake up and object to what was going on.[60]

Throughout 1973 Congress continued to struggle over private pension reform. The Senate broke the impasse in early fall by adopting a compromise measure combining the views of its contending committees. The House Labor Subcommittee then offered a revision but looked to Ways and Means for the tax provisions. In February 1974, Ways and Means introduced its own comprehensive plan that paved the way for a joint substitute. What followed bordered on the ironic for Griffiths. A complicated

House rule excluded the Ways and Means section of the bill from debate, except for her proposal that tripled the retirement tax deduction for the self-employed. Griffiths had consistently fought on Ways and Means against the tax deductible limitation of $2,500 set by the 1962 Keogh plan.61 At her urging—and the heavy lobbying of the American Medical Association and the American Bankers Association—the Committee recommended that the Keogh ceiling be raised to $7,500. During the House debate, Griffiths' JEC colleague, Henry Reuss, led the opposition against her proposal on the grounds that it favored the independently wealthy, the equivalent, he contended, of "pil[ing] loophole upon loophole." Griffiths' rejoinder, drawn from her own experience as a legislator and as her husband's law partner, was that the restriction discriminated against the very person who took the greatest economic risks: "the grocer, the candlestick maker, the baker, the farmer. . . ." She was annoyed that Reuss did not see that the law already protected the very rich—to say nothing of the members of Congress—and that, through an innovative feature of the pending bill, those not covered could deduct as much as $1,500 annually toward an individual retirement account. Key in her defense were Herman T. Schneebili, ranking minority member of Ways and Means; Barber B. Conable Jr., leading Republican on both Ways and Means and JEC; and Ways and Means Acting Chairperson Al Ullman. In offering his support, Ullman indicated that Griffiths' role in the pension reform had been "vital" to the bill's broad contours as well as to its specific dimensions.62 She had wanted everyone who had a right to a retirement benefit to get it, and she was concerned that pension rights be extended to as many as possible—to small entrepreneurs as well as to corporate executives and employees, to women as well as to men. Although she had not succeeded in procuring equal voice for both spouses in choosing or rejecting their survivors annuity, she was pleased that up to three years' recognition was given toward vesting for those persons employed before they were 25 years old—a boon to women who worked in their twenties, raised a family, and then returned to the labor force.63

On Labor Day 1974, President Ford signed ERISA into law. Some criticized the reform for failing to require a pension fund of every business. Griffiths, however, took the position that ERISA was a start and could be amended with time.64 It had to be seen for what it was: the federal government's first attempt to deal with the largest sum of unregulated money in the nation. ERISA required compliance with minimum funding standards, fixed sound fiduciary norms, granted portability of benefits, guaranteed vesting rights, and established a federal insurance corporation against plan terminations. In December 1974, Griffiths unsuccessfully introduced an amendment which could have obliged corporations to inform their employees annually of their potential benefits and to furnish new and survivor beneficiaries with information about the taxes paid toward their benefits.[65] Despite her disappointment, she must have taken heart in the substantial gains made in pension reform since her Fiscal Policy Subcommittee first began its analysis in 1966.

For Griffiths, JEC continued to be an exciting committee on which to serve. As one prominent staff member observed, she seized on its unique forum to do some of the things she thought important for her time.[66] Undeniably, she gave the Fiscal Policy Subcommittee its style and directed its activities to consequential issues as revenue sharing and private pensions. In 1968 the Subcommittee held hearings on income maintenance which later developed into an extensive welfare probe. This will be fully considered in Chapter V.

Because of its importance as a committee, membership on Joint Ecomonic seemed to preclude service on one of the three exclusive House committees: Appropriations, Ways and Means, and Rules. When the prospect of Griffiths' election to Ways and Means began to emerge, Chairperson Mills voiced his concern that she remain on JEC. Griffiths argued that her JEC colleagues, Hale Boggs and Thomas B. Curtis, were on both and newly elected Speaker John McCormack supported her view that what was permissible for the two men was permissible for her. Accordingly, when she took her place on the co-called "salt mine of Congress" in January 1962, she did not abandon JEC. "It is cause of much happiness to me that I did not have to leave the Joint Economic Committee," she informed one of her associates.[67]

The Ways and Means vacancy had occurred in mid-1961 when President Kennedy appointed Michigan's Thaddeus M. Machrowicz district court judge. Two challenges subsequently faced the Michigan Representatives: first, whether or not they could keep the political plum within the family; and, second, whether or not they could agree on a single candidate. Although most of the potential contenders were satisfied with their own committees and were therefore unavailable for Ways and Means, two candidates besides Griffiths would have welcomed endorsement: John D. Dingell, whose father had eminently served the Committee as an early force behind Medicare, and James G. O'Hara, reportedly the favorite of both the White House and Lansing. The <u>Detroit News</u> strongly urged Michigan Democrats to get behind one aspirant or lose the seat to Ohio. "There is quite a lot of backstairs maneuvering going on," reported James Reston of the <u>New York Times</u> and Griffiths admitted in 1967 that bringing her colleagues around to her appointment had taken "a bit of doing."[68]

Her personal worry was that the Democratic caucus would not elect her because she was a woman. Mills perceived the matter differently and told Griffiths he would prevail on the House leadership to foster her candidacy. Both the then Speaker Say Rayburn (Rayburn died before Griffiths' appointment was made) and Majority Leader McCormack agreed to the proposition if the Michigan Representatives would go along. When Dingell and O'Hara pledged themselves to support the delegation's choice, Griffiths had the votes she needed. McCormack also remained true to his word and, as Speaker of the Eighty-seventh Congress, campaigned for her. A former member of Ways and Means himself, he looked to Griffiths as an asset to the Committee because he saw her as someone who would further Kennedy's program, although he thought of her as having a mind of her own.[69] In December 1961 another vacancy occurred on Ways and Means with the resignation of Texas Democrat Frank Ikard. Southerners, anticipating that the post would be filled by a Texan, awaited the selection of Clark W. Thompson. On January 18, 1962, Thompson was elected fourteenth ranking member of Ways and Means and Griffiths, fifteenth.

The media assessed Griffiths' election more as a tribute to ability than to femininity. "Very fitting," mused Fletcher Knebel of the <u>Atlanta Constitution</u>. "Women already own most of the means—and know the ways to get the rest." Hale Boggs predicted that not only would his JEC colleague be an outstanding member but that there would be a sharp decline in absenteeism.[70] Griffiths herself felt "[like] a raw recruit from Iowa at the Battle of the Argonne Forest. . . . The shooting had already begun."[71]

To understand Griffiths' influence in her thirteen years on Ways and Means is to understand in some measure the impact of Mills on his Committee; it is likewise to discover how twenty-four men reacted to having a woman collaborate with them on taxes, debt ceiling, and balance-of-trade payments. Most of the members already knew Griffiths from her committee work on JEC, Government Operations, and Banking and Currency, but they had yet to deal with a woman as one of their own. In a fundamental sense, in 1962 Ways and Means was a male preserve for those who, in the indelicate opinion of the Detroit News, "[were] holdovers from the brass spittoon era, . . . still loftily imbued with the theory [that] woman's place is in the kitchen."[72]

Under Wilbur Mills, Ways and Means reached an historical peak, although it always had a pre-eminence among Congressional committees. Established by the First Congress, Ways and Means handled most of the financial matters in the House, which accounted for almost 20 percent of all bills. What the 25 members—15 from the majority and 10 from the minority—said about taxes, tariffs, social security, and welfare—generally was law. "As the Committee goes so goes the House," noted a critic.[73] In addition to its manifest legislative power, Ways and Means also controlled the lifeline of House Democrats as the Committee on Committees. Some of the Ways and Means members looked on this political function as more than ample reward for what could be an unmerciful workload.

As chairperson of Ways and Means, Mills clothed the Committee with his own character and Mills was recognized as the best tax lawyer on Capitol Hill. According to Griffiths, he had the House "sewed up" on taxes because the membership-at-large knew little about the intricacies of the subject, did not understand the loopholes, and did not have to learn. On the floor, Ways and Means bills were non-debatable. Mills' power was further enhanced by his relationship to his Committee: he ruled. He decided the agenda, allowed no subcommittees, and rarely permitted anyone but himself to present a bill on the House floor. Above all, he was a master of consensus. Skillfully shaping a statute from the disparate views of the members, he seldom risked less than 80 percent agreement on a major bill. "Mills knew what everyone of us thought, and knew how to get our vote, and always tried to stretch the tent to get everybody in it," recalled Committee member Barber Conable. The result of this "stretching" was legislation that was often unchallenging. The Mills' style, moreover, created what Conable described as a committee with a life of its own, dominated by Mills and the few he allowed to emerge like ranking Republican John W. Byrnes. It was to surmount this anonymity that Griffiths often went public with her views.[74]

The character of Ways and Means, particularly Mills' consensual mode, seemingly required members willing to compromise, willing to abide by what John F. Manley, in his study of the Committee, called the "norm of restrained partisanship."[75] Business Week underscored this fact when it informed its readers: "There are no crusaders on Ways & Means. . . ."[76] Did Griffiths fit this description? That Mills asked her to be on his Committee argues rather convincingly that she did. Those who thought her "too subservient" to Mills would also have said yes, as would those who refused to consider her a reformer of any kind.[77] A further case could be made that she possessed strong attributes of accommodation: a sense of the political, a logical mind, legal training and experience. Moreover, she was never known to have engaged in inflammatory causes; in fact, she had studiously avoided them.

Yet, there was a way in which she defied political negotiation. When the Committee got into Social Security and tax legislation and Griffiths identified areas of discrimination, particularly against women, she held fast. "Martha, as strongminded as she was," Conable pointed out, "was frequently one that was not in the tent." A long-term House counsel on Social Security matters observed the same. "She compromised a lot less than most," he remarked. "She took unpopular positions, but that didn't stop her or wipe the smile off her face." But, he added knowingly, she might have gotten further had she given in a little.[78]

Strange, then, that to some of the media, Griffiths was Mills' "pet."[79] Her influence on the Chairperson was noticeable. "The most influential member on the Committee with Wilbur," noted one of her former colleagues. Another: "When Griffiths challenged Mills, Mills backed down. . . . Mills was able to count. . . ." The reasons? Mills admired brains and hard work. Never a dilettante on a legislative interest, Griffiths delved into her subject and spoke with force and authority. That was Mills' way. He also appreciated attendance at meetings. Mills thought of Griffiths as "always dedicated, always present."[80] "If you really did the work, you were working all day," Griffiths explained to an inquirer interested in Ways and Means. "Sometimes it would meet until 7 o'clock at night; and, of course, if it were in conference, it could go to 12 o'clock. . . .

It worked just all the time." Griffiths attributed her influence on both Mills and her colleagues to this daily perseverance through committee meetings. She became so practiced in observing Mills that she sensed the moment he had the consensus he was striving for.[81]

Except in the case of those members for whom she was not "the sweet, self-effacing, accommodating person that many expect[ed] their women to be," Griffiths scored high with her Ways and Means associates. "Quite politic," yet "dominant," was how most perceived her. One former colleague admitted that if he wanted something in the Committee, the first person he would go to after Mills would be Griffiths. "I would feel that would be the thing that would be most apt to lead to my success. . . . I always wanted to have [her support]." Griffiths was their equal. That she worked harder than most was immediately recognized. But, most importantly, she contributed a woman's point of view, a dimension missing from Ways and Means for nearly two hundred years.[82]

Griffiths' colleagues also quickly recognized her "formidable" side which she displayed most often in committee hearings. To tangle with her was, in the estimate of one, to have "walked into a buzz saw." Her technique was to pose the unsettling question. For example, she asked one of the Rockefellers: "Why don't you pay taxes?" And of Treasury Under Secretary Robert V. Roosa she inquired: "Why do we care about gold [in Fort Knox]?" "What do you have against women?" was the question asked of HEW Secretary Robert H. Finch.[83] Former HEW chief Wilbur J. Cohen declared that she came at his people like a "prosecuting attorney." Starting with Mills, her colleagues thought she was "tough" on her adversaries, could be devastatingly sarcastic, but usually concluded a tense colloquy on an upbeat. "You could almost see the beads of sweat rolling off the brows of the membership of the departments," observed Griffiths' junior, Dan Rostenkowski.[84] Robert M. Ball, Social Security Commissioner, who came in for some of her most severe interrogation on Ways and Means, retrospectively ascribed Griffiths' anger as directed more toward Mills and the Committee than toward bureaucrats like himself. In upbraiding Ball she was really pleading with the twenty-four men, with whom she often clashed, to put aside their male prejudices and stop discriminating. She was particularly irritated by their favorite argument that equality would cost money. When she heard talk like that she became "mad at the whole world."85 Did she have a right to her fury? "If she didn't get somewhat exercised . . . , nobody would pay any attention," was how a high ranking Ways and Means staffer explained what he observed. Another thought of her as something of "a John the Baptist," especially in matters of sexual equality.86 Because of the importance of women's rights today and Griffiths' role in promoting them an entire chapter—Chapter IV—is devoted to this issue.

When Griffiths mentioned that "the shooting had already begun" before she arrived on Ways and Means, she was specifically referring to the work that had taken place on the Trade Expansion Act of 1962 (TEA). The irony about this, as far as Griffiths was concerned, was that she had sought appointment to Ways and Means principally to shape trade legislation. Nearly four years after her retirement from Congress, she still expressed an overriding interest in international commerce. "The thing that was the most fascinating thing to me in the world," she said, "is the movement of goods between nations."87

Not only had Griffiths missed out on the TEA hearings, but Ways and Means did not produce another major trade bill until 1974. Blame, if one looks at it from Griffiths' perspective, was due to Mills whose chief interest was tax legislation. Griffiths was particularly disappointed when Mills refused to appoint a Ways and Means subcommittee to monitor the developments set in motion by the 1962 trade act. She believed that maintaining world economic and political balances did not afford Congress the luxury of deciding whether or not it wished to handle international trade policy. She thought, moreover, that Congress was morally responsible for gathering its own trade data in developing a legislative position and should not be caught uninformed and have to rely on the Executive branch to tell it what to do.88

A staunch freetrader, Griffiths was naturally drawn to the liberal contours of the TEA.89 The international trade status of the United States in the early 60s was cause for basic optimism. There was a favorable balance-of-trade; also the prospect of increased employment and the absence of competition with two-thirds of what was imported. But there were also pressures, such as U.S. dependence on key raw materials like zinc, competition for the business of developing nations, and the intensification of the challenges of both the Soviet bloc and

the Common Market. Griffiths warned that unless the
United States adapted to the economic realities of Western Europe, it would soon be in serious trouble.[90] As
a Michigan Representative, Griffiths had a special interest in seeing the tariff walls come down. Sixth in
the nation in the volume of manufactured exports, Michigan promised to be a prime beneficiary of trade expansion.

In Ways and Means, Griffiths fought for the retention of trade adjustment assistance for industries
adversely affected by tariff concessions. Without this
proviso, the labor unions would not have gone along,
even though they considered TEA one of the most important
bills of the Eighty-seventh Congress.[91] Griffiths clearly recognized that the trade act walked the middle
ground on some very controversial issues. The heart of
the bill, tariff reduction on the authority of the President, was at best ambiguous to her. She would have
preferred that Congress retain its power over rate-setting rather than permit the Executive to use tariff
reduction or elimination as a negotiating tool. Nevertheless, she was willing to permit testing of what President Kennedy called the most important piece of international legislation since the Marshall Plan.[92] Her
hope was that American manufacturers would awaken to the
bill's potential and aggressively compete with the new
trade opportunities at their disposal. She had discovered that the Western Europeans had mastered their trade
much better than her own compatriots.[93]

In 1965 Griffiths praised the U.S.-Canadian free-trade agreement on automobiles and automotive parts as
one of the very few new trade ideas of the last half of
the century. Increased prosperity for one sector of the
Northern Hemisphere, she argued, redounded to the economic well-being of the United States. She told Congress
that only "the timid" would engage Canada in a trade
war. On the basis of an $8 billion exchange of goods,
both countries had too much at stake "to now start playing beggar-your-neighbor." Although the bill faced
strenuous opposition from American auto part manufacturers and from some members of Congress who decried Canada's special treatment as a violation of the TEA tariff
negotiations, the proposal ultimately received heavy
endorsement from both Houses. Griffiths referred to the
accord as the beginning of a North American Market, and
she hoped Mexico would soon follow Canada's lead.[94]

The expiration of TEA in 1967 brought heavy pressure

from the White House for further liberalization of tariff restrictions. In 1968, however, Ways and Means killed Johnson's trade bill; two years later Nixon's proposal died in the Senate. What had happened? Congress, including Ways and Means, had clearly backed away from its previous antiprotectionism. Griffiths, too, was speaking differently. "I was practically born a free trader," she told witnesses during a JEC hearing on investment credits for overseas industry. "I was for free trading—boy, when I look at what they [multinational corporations] are doing, I wonder if I really am for free trade." Later she explained her about-face as the result of "too many things hav[ing] evolved in complex industrial nations."[95]

Dramatic changes had indeed occurred on the trade scene since 1962. The value of imports, for example, had risen 143 percent by 1969, while exports had only increased by 85 percent. The use of cheap labor by overseas manufacturers had adversely affected American workers on two counts: in the reduction of jobs and in the influx of inexpensive foreign-made goods. By the early 70s, Griffiths was particularly concerned about Michigan and Detroit unemployment rates, which in turn influenced the profit-margin of domestic manufacturers.[96] The situation was worsened by other factors: runaway inflation, resulting in more expensive goods to foreign buyers; a high standard-of-living which placed heavy demands on foreign products; the continued threat of the Common Market; and the astronomical growth of foreign productivity, especially in Asia. "Made in Japan. . . Hong Kong. . . Taiwan" turned free-trade advocates like Griffiths into mild protectionists.

In its unsuccessful attempt to revive the tariff in 1970, Ways and Means nonetheless made a bid to establish import quotas on textiles and footwear. Between 1960 and 1969 the value of imported textiles had risen 146 percent, resulting in high unemployment among low-paid, semi-skilled workers, especially older women and minorities. The volume of imports likewise caused a rash of bankruptcies among small firms—69,000 in the first half of 1970. Footwear producers fared no better. Foreign boot and shoe imports had doubled between 1964 and 1969; by 1975 it was expected that 70 percent of all American purchases would be manufactured abroad.[97] Reluctantly acceding to the textile quota, Nixon nevertheless threatened to veto the entire trade bill if Ways and Means went any further.

The hearings on footwear gave Griffiths the opportunity to complain about American shoes. She little wondered that Americans bought foreign shoes when those made at home fit so badly. But, more to the point, she worried about America's lack of assertiveness in the world market. "We don't have anybody out breaking their backs to sell," she pointed out to Secretary of Commerce Maurice H. Stans. The country needed expert incentives and manufacturers needed to agree among themselves to get out and share the market. And, she warned, where trade relations were meant to be reciprocal, the United States should not be expected to bear the burden of the arrangement.[98] Responding to a correspondent who chided her for abandoning free trade, she wrote that there was "great misunderstanding" on why Ways and Means had found it necessary to set limits: it was "a tap on the wrist to warn other nations that international trade agreements are not a one-way street." When a cynic asked whether or not she would be as enthusiastic about eliminating free trade in automobiles as she had been in textiles and footwear, she said she would if it jeopardized employment. "I don't think," she asserted, "anyone is going to let Japan destroy the American automobile market."[99]

Although Congress failed to revise the tariff in 1970, it could not delay doing so indefinitely. The expiration of the Trade Expansion Act in 1967 and the round of international negotiations scheduled for early 1975 prompted Nixon to seek Congressional guidelines without which no major nation would be willing to parley. Accordingly, in 1973 Mills forced a comprehensive package through the House, only to have it languish for ten months in the Senate Finance Committee over a rider dealing with Soviet restrictions on Jewish emigration. The trade law finally signed by Ford in January 1975 empowered the President to harmonize, reduce, or eliminate tariff and nontariff trade barriers. The five-year grant further sanctioned Nixon's requests for authority to meet balance-of-payment deficits, to brake inflation, and to retaliate against nations endangering U.S. commerce. The trade measure, however, markedly restricted the use of Executive power in these broadened areas, formulated a Congressional veto procedure over nontariff agreements, and established an advisory committee to the President. The law additionally relaxed the criteria by which industries and workers adversely affected by the tariff revisions could seek relief, authorized trade preferences for developing countries, and extended the most-favored-nation clause to Communist states which permitted the free emigration of their citizens.

In approaching this major trade effort, the first since 1962, the Mills Committee considered the harm that had been done to non-participants in the TEA accords, the complicating role played by multi-national corporations, and the effects of the 1971 international monetary reform on world commerce. Ways and Means also took note of the increasing inability of the General Agreement on Tariffs and Trade to deal with trade complexity. In the context of these developments, the committee adopted a middle course between a free and a protected market.[100] In concurring, Griffiths put herself at odds with organized labor which by the mid-70s had gone protectionist for fear of what expanded trade relations might do to employment.

In other trade matters Griffiths showed herself sympathetic to the unions' point of view. She inveighed against tax incentives for the multi-nationals precisely because they undercut U.S. goods and jobs by their foreign privileges and cheap labor. She likewise argued against furthering profits for America's competitors. "Today's technology," she said, "will be Japan's export tomorrow." She was not for opening the sluice indiscriminately. Nor did she look serenely on the continued depletion of America's natural reserves for sale abroad. In her opinion, the protection of America's human and material resources was of primary importance in any liberal trade agreement.[101]

In the formulation of the 1974 tariff bill, Griffiths had also been concerned about the Soviet Union's restriction of Jewish emigration to Israel. In 1972 she had protested this policy before Congress; in 1973 she had co-sponsored the freedom of emigration amendment forbidding government-backed credits to the Soviet Union as long as it did not lift its ban. The pivotal issue of the 1974 reform, however, was not Soviet policy but Congressional willingness to support Nixon's request for discretionary control over world trade. Griffiths took her Committee's position that presidential authority on the world market was primarily a matter of fair trade rather than power politics. The President, therefore, had best be limited both to preserve the constitutional balance between the executive and legislative branches in trade matters and to temper the propensity of the White House to use tariff negotiation as a political tool. Nevertheless, Griffiths and other Committee trade liberals believed that the President needed some authority to secure an open and nondiscriminatory market since Congress' power to legislate tariffs did not make that body a negotiating agent.[102] Following the 1973 hearings, Griffiths was quoted by the <u>Wall Street Journal</u> as having said that the Administration's bill would be "very sharply rewritten"—and it was.[103] The law that ultimately emerged was basically the Ways and Means version with its multiple and specific limitations on Executive action. While the Trade Reform Act of 1974 probably pleased no one—organized labor least of all— it did give the President the power he needed at the trade table. Moreover, having survived a Mideastern crisis and both the Watergate and Mills' scandals, the bill attested to the determination of Congress to function as an international stabilizing influence even in the worst of circumstances.

During her thirteen years on Ways and Means, Griffiths spent more time on the tax code than on anything else. Nearly every year Mills initiated a revision so that during her tenure Griffiths went through the entire code four or five times. "Over and over and over again" was how she experienced it. In Griffiths' thinking, concentrating on tax legislation resulted in the neglect of other vast jurisdictions like trade, social security, and welfare.[104] She also believed that Mills failed in not bringing Ways and Means to an indepth assessment of its tax legislation, which may explain in some measure why he found it advisable to revise the code repeatedly.[105]

Did Griffiths have a tax philosophy? Only that the law be simple and equitable. She would have abolished all tax exemptions in favor of a small levy on gross income. But, she mused, "everybody loves his own loophole." Her greatest concern about the code was that it discriminated against women. "All you have to do is read the tax law," she observed, "and you realize that the work of women has never meant anything. A wife is the least protected person in the law in this country." She was among the first to raise objection to what she termed the "marriage tax," the difference paid in taxes by a married couple and by two single persons with the same cumulative income. She also fought for a tax-free inheritance for spouses, arguing that the contribution of a woman to the family income, whether as a homemaker or a wage earner, gave her an unconditional title to the full inheritance, especially when that estate could be donated tax-free to some charity. Is a wife worth less than charity, she asked?[106]

When Griffiths joined Ways and Means in January 1962, the Committee was six months into its deliberations on the first of the Kennedy-Johnson round of tax reductions. At the time, she and Walter Heller, head of Kennedy's Economic Advisers, were tangled in JEC over the President's request for discretionary authority to lower taxes. For Griffiths it was "dubious pleasure" to leave increases to Congress and decreases to the Executive. She assured Heller, however, that if the Administration had a case for a tax cut, it would move through Congress "faster than a declaration of war," a prediction as "impressive" to the economist as he had found his encounter with Griffiths "grueling."[107] The talk of a tax cut in 1962, nonetheless, planted the seed for Johnson's major cut of 1964.

Central to the 1962 revision was a 7 percent investment credit by which Kennedy and his councilors hoped to stimulate national growth through increased capital improvements. To offset the revenue loss, as well as prevent tax-dodging, they asked that the federal government be permitted to withhold levies on interest and dividends. Griffiths supported both aspects of the plan, defending the investment credit before Congress on the grounds that unless American entrepreneurs modernized, they could not be effective competitors for the developing nations of Asia and Africa. Later, as she reflected on the investment-credit feature, she would have liked to have seen it used as an economic regulator. As for withholding taxes on interest and dividends, she was anxious to close the loopholes, especially when she learned that interest was the biggest of all—even bigger than the oil depletion allowance. Her theory on all loopholes, as she came to understand them in her several reviews of the codes, was that what had originated as remedies for deserving individuals and causes had become escape hatches for designing enterprisers.[108]

The next two years, linked by Kennedy's assassination, were spent in complicated debate over the 1964 tax cut. In the fall of 1962, Griffiths anticipated the controversy by sending a questionnaire to her constituents asking what they would do with an $100 additional income. Her purpose was two-fold: one, to educate the public on the miniscule personal effect of the proposed massive $11.5 billion tax reduction; and, two, to show Congress what people would actually do with the money, since the theory behind the bill was that consumers would pour most of it back into the economy. The Administration had estimated that a dollar in the hand was worth 2.5 to 4 in the till.

The widely publicized poll revealed that the public did not intend to spend a fourth of the anticipated nest egg. Moreover, 62 percent were against the reduction altogether, expressing a why-bother attitude for so few dollars. Griffiths believed two lessons could be learned from the response: first, people had to be educated on why even a small tax cut could be directed toward balancing the budget; and, second, the government needed to note from consumer comment that at the local level tax reduction that came as a cut in property taxes was more meaningful than a decrease in federal income taxes.[109] In commending her on her inquiry, one correspondent reported that Griffiths had kept the complex issues simple and had given the lawmakers some idea why the public was lukewarm toward a tax cut without a corresponding cut in the budget. She had, in sum, accomplished her two-pronged objective.[110]

The poll served to generate another JEC Griffiths-Heller debate.[111] The presidential adviser would not be dissuaded from the prospects of tax reduction despite Griffiths' poll which demonstrated that the proposed cut was meaningless to most Americans. "I think the problem you have is that the individual taxpayer has an economic theory of his own, and it doesn't really fit in with yours," she told Heller. "They are looking at taxes as a pretty personal affair. The moment you state to them. . . [that] an $8.6 billion tax reduction. . . turns out to be that $8.33 that her husband got additionally in his paycheck last week, [you have] the far step between the dream and the reality." Heller reminded Griffiths that "good things often come in small packages" and, in a further attempt to build his case, pointed out that in the cut lay the homemaker's long-awaited mink. The press took up the challenge, suggesting that Mrs. Heller purchase "an adequate little Democratic stole" to give her husband "a lesson in basic economics, the kind they apparently didn't teach at Harvard." Heller provided the newspapers further criticism when he said he was amazed that the "puritan ethic" was so deep that Americans would deny themselves a tax cut if it meant deficit spending.[112] Griffiths had made her point out of Heller's mouth. Paul Douglas praised Griffiths for the "brilliant and penetrating questioning" that had forced the Administration to face its tenuous position.[113]

Griffiths was nonetheless willing to give the cut a try. She had been assured by the Treasury Department that by the additional property taxes resulting from increased residential and business construction, the bill would generate $1.5 billion for the states and $1.4 billion for local jurisdictions—Michigan being fourth in the nation in anticipated gains. Finally, she pleaded with her Congressional colleagues to collect their own tax data so that come future tax reform, they could exercise an independent judgment and not have to rely on what the President told them.[114]

Before passing on to the 1965 revision, mention should be made of Griffiths' little "intrigue," as she called it, concerning the tax dividends credit proviso of the 1964 code. A supporter of tax relief for small investors, Griffiths also decided to use the issue in forcing, though unsuccessfully, a reduction of the 27.5 percent oil depletion allowance.[115] When the Administration requested that the 4 percent credit be dropped from the proposed code, Griffiths joined the anti-Administration members of Ways and Means in voting for its retention. Fearing that the entire revision would be lost without the amendment, President Kennedy asked Ways and Means for a reconsideration. Absent the day the Committee voted 12 to 12 on the President's request, Griffiths was sought out by both Kennedy and Speaker McCormack to break the tie—which she did. The Chicago Tribune charged that the "about face" would merit a sizable area development contract for Detroit, an imputation Griffiths firmly denied. Having been told by House leadership that the code hung on her vote, she had had to weigh the consequences. "My only anxiety," she wrote an enquirer, "was that taxes should be reduced."[116]

In 1965 the emphasis shifted to excise reduction, the third major cut since the Democrats had taken office in 1961. A long-standing foe of wartime levies, Griffiths had written a constituent in 1960 that she was for the repeal or reduction of every excise on the books.[117] Her target in 1965 was the auto tax, a campaign begun the previous June when Congress passed a one-year extension on existing excises. The talk then, which impressed her as being more political than economic, was for the eventual repeal of all taxes on stipulated luxury items and a partial repeal of the 10 percent excise on the manufacturers' price of cars and car parts. Women, she insisted, could use only so much facial paint and powder; what they really wanted was the money that would come from the increased auto production resulting from repeal of the excise.[118]

In February 1965, Griffiths introduced a bill calling for immediate repeal. She estimated that $225 could be saved on each car purchase, a real boon to two-or-three-car families. She likewise calculated that increased auto sales would boost the economy by some $5 billion. Detroit's Big Three—Chrysler, Ford, and General Motors—heartily endorsed her point of view, although Ways and Means thought the proposal too costly. In May, President Johnson asked that the excise be immediately reduced from 10 to 7 percent and then stabilized at 5 percent in 1967. Griffiths warred. Ways and Means compromised by proposing incremental reduction toward a total repeal by 1969. "The next time the male motorist begins to complain about women drivers," the Detroit News editorialized, "perhaps he ought to reconsider in view of what Mrs. Griffiths is trying to do for him."[119]

Despite all that Griffiths was trying to do in the mid-60s to cut taxes, which included forcing the Big Three automakers to back down on a proposed price hike,[120] the automobile excise was too substantial to be readily surrendered by the federal government. In his 1966 budget message calling for Vietnam funds, Johnson requested a temporary rescission on reducing either the auto or telephone tax. Griffiths was furious and pledged to fight postponement. In 1969 and again in 1970, however, the reductions were discontinued and the frontier of total repeal pushed to 1982. All this tampering greatly annoyed Griffiths and apparently proved her right: phased reduction invited interminable delay.[121] In August 1971, a month after she had co-sponsored another repeal bill, Nixon called for immediate elimination of the excise to help create new jobs through increased car sales. By the year end Congress passed the Revenue Act of 1971 providing for total repeal. Griffiths rejoiced that six years of struggle had passed into victory.[122]

By the spring of 1966, the press of the Vietnam War on the War on Poverty triggered an inflationary spiral, the reverse of what had been anticipated from the tax cut. The Democrats on the Joint Economic Committee called for an immediate halt on the investment credit and for the enactment of a tax increase. In October, Congress suspended the benefit on capital improvements—ten months too late as far as Griffiths was concerned. She was equally upset over her colleagues' lethargy in forcing a cut in spending. "At one point they were reluctant to vote tax reduction," she reminded a friend, "now they neither want to vote for expenditure reduction nor tax increases—just talk." Yet, a tax increase was inevitable. In an attempt to explain the reason to her constituents, she pointed out that many states had violated the intent of the 1964 cut by passing income tax laws. Moreover, Social Security taxes had risen so high that wage earners had less buying power every year.[123]

In an effort to combat this fiscal derangement, in 1967 Johnson proposed a surcharge on individual and corporate income taxes, beginning with 6 percent and accelerating to 10 percent over a seven-month period. While many economists, business executives, and labor leaders supported the President's solution, Ways and Means held firm against the President throughout 1967 for failing to give an assurance that he would cut spending. "The new economics," Griffiths told Secretary of the Treasury Henry H. Fowler, "is running into old politics." She was not certain that inflation would be curtailed were customers deprived of purchasing power. Besides, how explain to the public that a tax increase would balance the budget when they still did not understand how a cut was supposed to have done the same in 1964? The more deeply she became involved in the controversy, the more she was convinced that the surcharge was "lazy economics" which threatened to destroy any possibility for a meaningful tax reform.[124] Therefore, in 1966 when Congress tacked the 10 percent surtax on the bill extending auto and telephone excises, Griffiths sized up the legislative conglomerate as having "built a road to yesterday."[125]

Between 1961 and 1969, Presidents Kennedy and Johnson, using the power of the Executive office, masterfully engineered three major reductions and one surcharge through Congress. The changeover to the Republicans in January 1969 brought about a reversal: within a month of Nixon's inauguration, Ways and Means initiated a very complex revision. The law that emerged ten months later was almost totally the work of Congress, despite efforts of President Nixon to intervene with his own proposals and with the threat of a veto.

Pressured by the overtaxed middle-class, Congress realized it had to move quickly to forestall a "citizens' revolt." The revelation that 154 individuals with adjusted gross incomes of $200,000 or more paid no income taxes made Ways and Means look "stupid." Reform, therefore, demanded a system that taxed the wealthy and relieved the over-burdened.[126] In February 1969, Griffiths told Congress that it was responsible for "the absolute certainty that every American pays taxes and that he is not given a choice." To allow the rich to determine the taxes they would pay—if any—was in her opinion inexplicable and unconscionable.[127]

Griffiths' contribution to the extremely complex act can be assessed in some measure by looking at those critical areas in which she attracted public notice either in support of Congressional action or as "one that was not in the tent." Chief among these areas were the extension of the surcharge, the postponement of the excise reductions on automobiles and telephone service, the repeal of the 7 percent investment credit, and the reduction of the oil and gas depletion allowance. In 1969 she was also deeply involved in the tax status of both private foundations and state and municipal bonds, as well as the tax burdens of singles.

Griffiths voted against the majority of her Committee on the auto excise as has already been noted above. She also opposed a six-month extension of the surtax without a reform of the oil allowance.[128] Her support for repeal of the investment-tax credit logically followed her stand of 1966 in voting to suspend that benefit. Between 1966 and 1968 she had observed how the investment-tax credit had wooed industry out of high-tax, profoundly depressed areas. Griffiths nonetheless sympathized with small entrepreneurs who suffered disproportionately from the repeal, suggesting that their loss be offset by closing the loopholes on big business.[129] A foe of the oil depletion allowance, Griffiths was delighted when Congress began to chip away at the exemption by reducing domestic benefits from 27.5 to 22 percent. When Ways and Means first challenged the allowance by recommending a reduction to 20 percent, Griffiths' elation made the news.[130]

Griffiths was particularly agitated by tax-exempt state and municipal bonds. She could not understand, for example, why Anna Dodge, the widow of Detroit auto pioneer, Horace Dodge, would pay nothing on the $2 million in dividends she received annually. "There is something to me that is really inherently wrong [in this]," she told Ways and Means. Despite criticism that she made Anna Dodge look like "the Lucretia Borgia of income tax abuse" Griffiths was unrelenting. "The truth is," she said, "the American taxpayer is taking a beating because those holders of those bonds are not paying their fair share." Griffiths believed that cities which depended on bonds for their income also had a right to whatever taxes those bonds could generate. By way of compromise, Ways and Means proposed that state and local bonds be subsidized. The Senate, however, dropped the amendment for a tax on arbitrage bonds, which convinced Griffiths that the importuning of governors and mayors was more compelling than the question of whether or not the government could affort to exempt rich bondholders from paying taxes—or morally should.131

Griffiths' role in curbing private foundations was more successful. By 1968 some 25,000 foundations controlled assets totalling $20.5 billion—half of which were in the hands of 33 organizations. This advanced stage of philanthropy suggested to the editors of *Fortune* that the big foundations vied with government and business as the three most powerful American institutions.132 Critics, like Griffiths, therefore were anxious to open foundation trusts to public scrutiny, a task begun earlier in 1965 by the Treasury Department.133 That body had identified six areas of foundation abuse: donor involvement in foundation transactions, delays in distributing benefits to charity, foundation engagement in unrelated business, the use of funds to control family property, financial transactions at variance with charitable giving, and the preponderance of donors and family members on boards of trustees. By 1969 a seventh abuse had come to light: the use of foundation funds for political purposes. Despite these dubious practices, the Treasury examiners had been careful to point out that the foundations were making a substantial social contribution by supporting select research activities and, for this reason, hoped Congress would be benign in legislating controls. Griffiths, however, told the Michigan Foundation Conference in 1974, that when the issue came up for review in 1969, Congress had intended the eventual demise of the foundations.134

Foundation heads were understandably upset by the preliminary Ways and Means proposals which limited stock ownership, prohibited grants to individuals, and forbade activities affecting government decisions. They argued as well that an audit tax on investment income would seriously jeopardize their charitable activities.135 Griffiths disagreed. Philanthropy seemed to her the least of the foundations' worries. Rather, she said, they awarded trips to their friends under pretext of research and were not above involvement in international politics. They were also free from government control. How, for example, could anyone think that New York would police the Rockefeller Foundation when the Governor was a Rockefeller?" Most of all, Griffiths was convinced that private foundations were really tax shelters. She insisted that everyone would be better off once foundation heads admitted this.[136]

Griffiths' sharp criticism sparked a lively exchange between her and Ford Foundation President McGeorge Bundy—enlivened by Bundy's disclosures that Ford funds had been used for Senator Robert F. Kennedy's staff.[137] Griffiths unmercifully reacted to what she termed Bundy's "palaver" about all the good Henry Ford had planned to do in establishing his Foundation. "I couldn't stand it any longer," she remembered herself replying, "and I said, 'I represent the district in which Henry Ford was born and in which he lies buried, and Henry Ford didn't intend to do any of that stuff with that Foundation. What he intended to do was keep that stock from being bought by the general public. . . .' And I said, 'All the things you are saying are absolutely nonsense.' And Mr. Bundy, who had never been questioned in his life on anything, was simply furious." Griffiths wanted Bundy and the other foundation executives to know what was at stake: "Should we have some of us paying taxes and other large amounts of wealth not paying taxes?"[138] She was pleased, therefore, when Congress passed several restrictions on the foundations, including a 4 percent levy on investment income. As a result of this legislation, the foundations began to experience significant curtailment of their activities.

Another area of the 1969 tax revision that concerned Griffiths was relief for singles. She had already succeeded in procuring guidelines for divorced or separated parents who had custody of their children so that they could normally claim the dependency exemption;[139] she was less fortunate in securing benefits for single persons who maintained a home.[140] After 1969 she worked to extend child-care deductions to single male foster parents and to adjust income inequities between low-paid single women and ADC mothers receiving multiple welfare benefits.[141] When the issue of singles was raised for the 1969 code, Griffiths told Ways and Means it had to do something. Congress eventually legislated a break for singles, limiting their taxes to no more than 20 percent of the tax rates paid by married persons with the same income. The adjustment, however, had an unfortunate side-effect. In correcting the inequity for singles, the law created the situation whereby a working couple filing a joint return paid more than two singles with the same combined earnings. In Griffiths' view, this discriminated against both marriage and women. The issue gained national prominence when couples publicly chose to live "in sin" rather than pay the differential. Griffiths had a solution: tax everyone with an income, but make allowances for heads-of-households or those responsible for dependents.[142] It would take years, however, before something would be done about the "marriage penalty."

Although the 1969 tax law was the last major code effort in which Griffiths was involved (there were some lesser changes in 1972 like the reinstatement of the 7 percent investment credit), during the 70s Griffiths continued to support tax relief for low- and moderate-income families. In 1971 she co-sponsored a measure to reduce social security taxes for 63 million wage earners,[143] and in 1974 joined Senator Walter F. Mondale on a tax-credit bill providing a $200 option for parents and their dependents in lieu of the existing $750 personal exemption.[144] The previous year she opposed an increase in federal gasoline taxes. She argued that at their local gas pumps motorists already subsidized the oil companies. And, she asked, how could Congress morally require a widowed homemaker in her district to pay more on consumable goods while the surplus income of the Rockefellers and the Dodges went untaxed?[145]

In conjunction with tax reform, Griffiths introduced the first recycling bill in Congress in 1972, which she proposed be financed from taxes that would come with repeal of the oil depletion allowance. It seemed "practically obscene" to her for oil magnates to hold on to their privileges while annually the federal government was responsible for disposing of 4.3 billion tons of solid waste; and the states, 250 million tons additional refuse. Griffiths hoped Congress would be generous in rewarding recyclers and proposed that they be assisted: first, for producing raw materials and saleable commodities from the waste; and, second, for constructing anti-pollution reprocessing facilities. When told by a Treasury Department staffer that her solution to environmental clutter would do nothing substantial to clean up the nation's junk yards, she bristled. "Don't just sit there and say it won't do it," she said. "I think it will do it. Let's try."[146] Pollution control unfortunately was not on Congress' agenda for the early 70s.

As Griffiths reflected on the hours she had spent on tax matters as a member of Ways and Means, she concluded sadly that genuine tax reform was not possible. As she saw it, two factors stood in the way. First, the government had no spending priorities. "There is nothing that calls any of us to act," Griffiths noted. "You don't know whether you are making a profit or loss." It was not as though she had shirked personal responsibility in seeking a solution: she had studied the matter both as a member of a joint committee and on JEC.[147] The second factor militating against reform, as she saw it, was the devil loophole. "As I prepare to leave this Congress," she wrote a library head in October 1974, "I have come finally and conclusively to feel that it is virtually impossible to reform the tax code because among other things, charities, art institutions, universities and others who have no understanding of the tax code whatsoever are permitting themselves to be used by the rich to plead their cause of further tax avoidance."[148] A truly just tax code required the end to all privileges.

The Mills' Committee will not only be remembered for the time spent on the tax code but for its debates on national health insurance. Griffiths was right in the middle in the tradition of her Michigan predecessors. In 1943 Representative John D. Dingell Sr. co-sponsored the first of the health-insurance bills financed out of payroll taxes and sixteen years later Senator Patrick McNamara recommended health benefits to all persons covered by the Old Age Survivors Insurance of the Social Security Act. Griffiths couched her philosophy on national health insurance in a question: "If health care is going to be given to select groups [i.e., to aged and the poor], then under the Constitution shouldn't health care be equally available to all?"[149]

When Griffiths arrived on Ways and Means in 1962, the Committee was six months into hearings on the King-Anderson Medicare bill which provided, through the Social Security Act, hospitalization and nursing-home care for the elderly. As Griffiths watched the Committee deliberate, she soon concluded that Mills would act only when he reached consensus among the members. "Mills is afraid to take chances," she had noted during the 1961 Medicare debates.[150] Her own position on the 1962 proposal was positive but nuanced. She believed it was the best bill that could be anticipated since the state-administered Kerr-Mills enactment either did not function on behalf of the indigent-sick or, where it did, was "a replica of the ancient poorhouse operation." In her home state, the first to adopt Kerr-Mills, only 1.85 percent of persons over 65 benefited in the first year of operation, an indication to Governor John Swainson that the act was a "significant failure." Nonetheless, Griffiths had wished that non-governmental agencies—the hospitals, insurance companies, the American Medical Association (AMA)—would have come up with their own "sensible plan" of health care for the aged and, thereby, have rendered a Congressional solution unnecessary. She also maintained a lingering doubt about the general direction health-care planning was going in regard to prepaid insurance. "I personally have never been very sure that hospitalization plans are desirable for healthy people," she informed her father when Medicare first attracted public notice at the end of the 50s.[151]

By 1963 the prospects of a Social Security health bill began to brighten as the margin of resistance in Ways and Means shrank 13 to 12. Pressure correspondingly heightened as evidenced in Griffiths' spirited criticism of the AMA during the Committee hearings. Addressing AMA President Dr. Edward A. Annis, she accused the organization of serving only patients who guaranteed payment and of creating a professional elite by limiting students in the nation's medical schools. (She was particularly dismayed by the growing number of foreign practitioners in American hospitals, resulting from the enforced admission rates.) She further charged the doctors of being the only professionals who escaped the consequences of their mistakes. Most of all, she indicted AMA for violating its sacred trust in its multimillion dollar political drive to defeat Medicare.[152] Johnson's accession to the presidency in November 1963 gave her some hope that this medical oligarchy would come to an end.

Throughout 1964 Johnson battled Medicare adversaries. Although the President seemingly got nowhere, principally because of the opposition of Thomas B. Curtis, the second ranking Republican on Ways and Means, Johnson announced he would take health care for the aged to the voters. His election in November 1964, along with a Democratic Congress—the legendary Eighty-ninth—meant that Medicare foes were in for a fight.

The new Congress far surpassed the President's expectations. From January through May 1965, Ways and Means spent five hours in daily executive session hammering out a law that was a tribute to Mills' legislative genius.153 Under package of one plan, Medicare provided three interdependent but distinct health-care strategies: first, the Kennedy-Johnson Social Security bill; second, the voluntary insurance program of ranking Ways and Means Republican John W. Byrnes, partially paid for by both the user and the Treasury; and third, the extension of Kerr-Mills for the medically indigent (Medicaid). Disappointed that this Social Security revision did not also amend the insurance benefit inequities for remarried widows and couples, Griffiths was generally pleased with the direction of the bill, although she was quick to point out what she considered were Medicare's philosophic flaws. Doctors were sure to find the law a sesame "to Ft. Knox." In the same vein she wrote a confidant: "The statistics of the Bill are irrevocably welded to the theory that all men are mortal, and that before too long. Therefore, a few more wonder drugs; a little more artistry in the surgical profession and the payment part will be a shambles. Of course," she concluded, "the mark-up on aspirin and appendectomies will be so good, that it may be a saving safeguard."154 Aside from the inference of what doctors might be tempted to do with prepaid insurance, Medicare appeared to effect greater justice in health care. It pointed to universal health coverage; and, as the second social security program to give benefits without reference to sex, it represented, to Griffiths' great delight, "a start of equal rights."155

When Griffiths retired from Congress in December 1974, the debate on national health insurance was well under way. The five-year interval spanning the passage of Medicare and the first of her insurance bills had been a time of continuing crisis in the nation's third largest industry. A 1971 Ways and Means study revealed that while hospital spending in 1970 was five times what it had been in 1950 and medical cost increases during the 60s twice those of consumer goods, the United States had slumped internationally to eighteenth place in male life expectancy and fourteenth in infant mortality. Four-fifths of the population under 65 had hospital and surgical insurance, but for many it was inadequate and for the poor practically non-existent. Three-fourths of all poor children were not covered by any health plan. As a group, the poor were less healthy as evidenced by their absenteeism from work and their minimal use of doctors and dentists for preventive care. The number of physicians had not kept pace with the growing population, nor had health services been improved in the ghettos or impoverished counties. That so little was being done, although the federal government's portion of every medical dollar was thirty-seven cents, was cause for heightened concern.156

Griffiths had always been in the forefront to secure a healthy nation. In the Michigan legislature, she had opposed medical student quotas and, in her second year in Congress had vigorously advocated nationwide distribution of the Salk vaccine. During the population boom, she had consistently supported hospital construction under the Hill-Burton Act and, once immersed in her JEC welfare study, had sponsored a meal plan for malnourished children.157 Medicare took her further into the health dilemma. In a short time she came to lament the health-delivery system as "sick." On the day she introduced her national health bill, she told Congress that fragmentation, encrustation, and non-competitiveness had resulted in some form of medical indigency for most Americans.158

The Kennedy-Griffiths Health Security bill, as it was called after 1971 when the Senate and House versions merged, was the work of the AFL-CIO and the UAW Committee of 100 for National Health Insurance. These groups prevailed on Griffiths in 1970 to sponsor their bill because they considered her good publicity both within and outside of Congress.159 Kennedy-Griffiths, the most extensive health strategy ever to come before Congress, covered every person in the United States with at least a year's residency. Financed by both the Social Security Act and the Treasury Department, the bill provided a broad range of services from hospitalization to preventative medicine, including prescription drugs. Furthermore, unlike any other health-care bill, it required no deductibles or other cost-sharing. In its original form it called for a one percent payroll tax up to $15,000 annual income and a three percent tax on employers, the latter to be matched out of general federal revenues. Central to the plan's operation was contract for services with hospitals, doctors, and dentists, the government allowing these groups to retain whatever savings they accrued beyond their budgets. The act offered additional financial rewards to doctors who would work in medically deprived communities.

As expected, the bill unleashed a barrage of diverse public comment. The reaction of Detroit's two leading newspapers highlighted the polarities. Warning the doctors that a lack of self-discipline invited public control, the News decried the prospects of astronomical administrative costs and increased federalization. Free Press correspondent Saul Freedman, on the other hand, not only labeled the plan "exciting" but because of it lauded Griffiths as "one of the smartest members of the House."[160] Despite the initial reaction, during most of 1970 Congress did not stir on national health insurance except for a few days of Senate hearings. Former HEW Head Wilbur J. Cohen pressed Griffiths for House action. "It is only by having hearings on the subject by the Ways and Means Committee," he wrote "[that] we will make people sit up and take notice of problems and issues involved."[161] In July Griffiths pledged, with the support of over twenty colleagues, to return to the Ninety-second Congress with her bill which she planned to improve by an additional one percent payroll tax shared equally by the federal government and employers.[162]

If the Ninety-second Congress thought it had enough in considering the comprehensiveness of the Kennedy-Griffiths bill, it soon discovered it had to deal with a spate of health-care proposals. The Administration forwarded the National Health Insurance Partnership Act and AMA sponsored Medicredit, promising Ameriplan at a later date. The insurance companies endorsed the National Health Care Act and Senator Jacob Javits proposed to extend Medicare to the general population. Carried over from the previous Congress was Senator Russell B. Long's catastrophic insurance bill based on the principle that the high costs of severe illness or accident was America's number one health-coverage need. Within a month, the issues had become so complex that the Detroit News doubted Congress could ever cut through the insurance thicket by the end of the year. The 1972 elections promised further delay on any definitive action for some time.[163]

During the last quarter of 1971, Ways and Means held twenty-one days of hearings on the health-care bills, Griffiths stressing that comprehensive national insurance was the only way to go. Convinced that her bill or one similar to it would eventually become law, she told HEW Secretary Elliot L. Richardson that she opposed the beguiling rhetoric of some of the other proposals, including Nixon's Partnership plan.[164]

She believed the merits of her proposal far surpassed all others for the following reasons. First, the Health Security Act covered all persons in a comprehensive manner. The Javits' bill extended Medicare benefits in stages; the rest offered lesser benefits; Medicredit, the least of all. Second, the Health Security Act attacked one of the root causes of exorbitant health costs by eliminating private insurance carriers. Griffiths especially hoped to get rid of Blue Cross.[165] Third, the Health Security Act built in cost containment by the contract-for-service mechanism. Fourth, the Health Security Act offered incentives to health providers for cutting expenses and for distributing medical resources more equitably. Fifth, the Health Security Act faced the true cost of health care by absorbing all health expenditures. Whether the system was financed through taxes or by private insurance, whether it was centralized or decentralized, universal coverage was expensive. "It's a question of from which pocket are you going to pay this thing," Griffiths insisted.[166] Sixth, the Health Security Act federalized the system and thereby provided greater coordination, cost efficiency, and access. Dr. Russell B. Roth, speaker of the AMA house of delegates, reminded Griffiths that federalization was at the heart of AMA's disagreement with Kennedy-Griffiths. Richardson also criticized the bill for assuming that only a "radical intervention by the Federal Government. . . in an inflexible, predetermined, and monolithic manner" could redeem the system. Griffiths responded that the only monolithic aspect of her program was the comprehensive benefits available to all on an equal basis and that a federal structure was inherent to a national guarantee of health care. For her it was a matter either of allowing the government to run the system or of permitting others to do so by "socializing . . . finance." There simply was no escaping federalization.[167]

The 1971 Ways and Means hearings concluded all formal legislative action on national health insurance until April 1974 when Mills announced that his Committee would again consider the issue. In the meantime, informal debate focused on two of the health-care bills: Kennedy-Griffiths and Nixon's Partnership Act. The latter allowed employers the option of instituting approved health-care plans for their employees. It also provided government-sponsored insurance for poor families not covered by employer plans and called for the establishment of health-maintenance organizations. Critics of the White House plan charged that it offered too little for too few.

Meanwhile, within Congress Mills tangled with Senator Kennedy over the elimination of private insurance carriers stipulated in the Health Security Act. Griffiths told a UAW audience that the exclusion of these intermediaries would be matter for "the biggest fight. It's just going to be us against them," she warned, "and in that I hope that we win." AFL-CIO President George Meany repeatedly hammered away at the private carriers as "costly middlemen. . . with their gluttonous profits, and their policies that only an attorney can read. . . ."[168]

In 1973 Griffiths reintroduced her bill with several liberalized features. Among these were the phase-in of dental care for adults, increases in the tax base to reflect increases in the social security-tax base, establishment of a quality care commission, allocation of funds for both manpower training, and provision for pilot projects to test the feasibility of home-maintenance care for the chronically ill and disabled. With Ways and Means absorbed by the trade bill and caught in the crunch of Mills' alcoholism, the only additional activity on national health insurance in 1973 was some inconsequential hearings held in December by the House Interstate and Foreign Commerce Subcommittee. Given these circumstances, Griffiths' criticism of Nixon for stalling on any insurance plan as too costly was unwarranted.[169] Incidental to her major health push during this period of relative inaction, Griffiths co-sponsored a bill for a separate Department of Health with the primary responsibility of concentrating on the nation's diminishing well-being.[170]

In the spring of 1974, the issue of national health insurance once again came before the public. In April, Senator Kennedy announced to the dismay of organized labor, that he was abandoning the Health Security Act in favor of a compromise with Mills. Asked later how she felt about her former co-sponsor's defection, Griffiths said jokingly that the reason she was a feminist was that so many fathers deserted their children.[171] Kennedy's accommodation, nonetheless, prompted Mills to reopen the Ways and Means hearings at the end of the month.

During the debates, three health strategies predominated—Griffiths' not being one of them. "You gentlemen can't stand comparison with the thing which would really be health insurance coverage," she told her co-workers half in jest. She predicted that as the costs of the other plans reduced small employers to bankruptcy, a future Ways and Means would be "competent enough to institute my bill."[172] The gradualism pervading Congress in 1974 simply precluded consideration of the Health Security Act, now co-sponsored with Griffiths by Representative James C. Corman of California.

The three contending programs with which Mills was then willing to deal were: first, an Administration revision mandating compulsory employer plans but allowing optional employee participation; second, the Long-Ribicoff catastrophic illness insurance bill containing a health plan for the poor; and third, the Kennedy-Mills enactment of compulsory insurance that was to be financed by a 4 percent payroll tax and run by an independent Social Security administration. Kennedy-Mills also incorporated private insurance carriers as fiscal intermediaries. Of the three bills, the Kennedy-Mills formula was closest to the Health Security Act, although Griffiths and Corman objected to its limited coverage, its use of private insurance companies, and its provision for deductibles and co-insurance.[173] Griffiths was unalterably opposed to the catastrophic plan as "a cruel hoax." In her way of thinking, the bill promised to increase all health expenses by tempting doctors and hospitals to classify most medical incidents as catastrophic. She further disagreed with the measure's incremental approach and its health provisions for the poor, arguing that the latter forced recipients to choose between work or benefits. With a good portion of her JEC welfare study in print she wondered why former HEW Secretary Abraham Ribicoff repeated the error of not considering all welfare benefits that a family received in determining health-care eligibility. "It just highlights what I am trying to say," the Senator told Griffiths. "How difficult it is to have a huge social or economic program to handle basic problems. It is tough."[174]

Given Congress' apparent desire for some payroll financing, it appeared as though the Nixon bill would be excluded in a final compromise. Griffiths wanted it understood, nevertheless, that even revised it was too minimal to effect change in the health delivery system. In a heated conversation with HEW Secretary Casper Weinberger, she attacked what she considered to be the bill's weaknesses besides its voluntarism, limited coverage, dependence on insurance companies, and use of deductibles. She charged that the plan buried costs, subsidized the rich, and discriminated against older citizens, especially the aged-sick. Using data from the welfare study she was conducting through JEC, she also criticized the proposal's welfare provisions for offering benefits unrelated to other welfare programs, for using a sliding income scale in determining eligibility, for creating work disincentives by high benefit-loss rates, and for allowing the states to administer the plan after they had proved themselves incompetent to handle welfare.[175]

By the time Ways and Means had concluded its hearings in early July, the nation had become so completely distracted by Nixon's impending impeachment that further work on health insurance seemed useless. Ford, however, picked up on the previous momentum when he became President in August and asked Congress to continue its activity "with the greatest spirit of cooperation." Griffiths was pleased. The paralytic effect of Watergate and Mills' alcoholic condition, as well as his failure to get anything but razor-thin votes from his Committee, nonetheless brought the deliberations to a halt by fall.[176]

The Ninety-fourth Congress gave little evidence in January 1975 that health reform would be an agenda item and President Ford, alarmed over the deteriorating state of the economy, dropped national health insurance from his budget priorities. Mills' successor, Al Ullman, likewise opposed any plan financed through increased payroll taxes. Griffiths retired from Congress that winter concerned about the fate of a comprehensive insurance plan but arguing that every American could be covered by the money spent annually on health services—if services were distributed equitably. She had formed certain conclusions as to why the latter was not the case. The prevailing health-care delivery system allowed insurance companies to reap up to 10 to 15 percent of the total health expenditure in profits. It opposed centralized fiscal management and persisted in treating the myth of free choice as fact. "Try calling a doctor in the middle of the night in a strange town," she advised. It was Griffiths' contention that when it became self-evident to voters that their health care was a "matter of right, rather than a matter of privilege or pity," the nation's legislators would act.[177]

Griffiths' concern for universal health insurance was matched, if not surpassed by her promotion of equity in the distribution of the broad range of benefits under title of the Social Security Act. Martha Griffiths consistently fought against legal distinctions based solely on sex differences. The discriminatory distinctions affecting men will be treated below; those affecting women will be considered in Chapter IV.

Although Griffiths devoted greater energy toward the elimination of legal sex bias against women, she was not unmindful of legislation which worked to the disadvantage of men—because these laws more often than not discriminated against women. As a result she was perceived as a champion of benefit equity for both sexes. A long-term counsel for Social Security matters noted that Griffiths "did more for men as opposed to women than anyone else I know because when she said equality, she meant equality." Ways and Means member, Barber Conable, was intrigued by Griffiths' involvement in men's benefits. "'Well,' she'd say, 'I want to look out for my husband on this. . . . He has just as much rights as I do.'" In this matter, Social Security Commissioner Robert Ball thought Griffiths scored two points: first, in the considerable attention she gave equal entitlement; and, second, in her independent quest for the information on which to base her judgments.[178]

In the Ways and Means deliberations on Social Security amendments, Griffiths was quick to point out how men suffered because the law was written differently for women. A husband was hurt by the fact that a working wife could not pass her retirement or survivor benefits on to her spouse unless he proved his dependence on her. A deceased woman's husband and children were hurt by the legal proviso that disqualified minors from receiving their mother's benefits if she was out of the work force a year and a half before her death. Quite simply, Griffiths' attention to women's rights drew her into more universal social security concerns.[179] Accordingly, she worked to establish the same age computation point for men as for women, as well as the same age determination for a reduced annuity and for total dependency benefits. Her abortive fight to secure Social Security benefits for veterans without diminution of their pensions might also be interpreted as being on the side of men since they were the primary beneficiaries of her efforts.[180]

Fundamentally, Griffiths quarreled with Social Security as the "most unfair law that was ever drafted." Speaking of the statute's origin she said:

> Didn't those men realize that in 1936 [1935] there had to be widows of World War I men who were supporting children, but they didn't help them. What about the woman who was working

whose husband never had worked under Social
Security. . . . She works, she's covered,
she's rearing their children, she dies. Her
children can't draw. How can you do things
like that? How can you see life through
those eyes? I can't understand that. . . .
The drafters of the law really believed, in
my opinion, that a woman's work was worth
nothing, that a woman's work in the home was
worth nothing. . . .[181]

Having researched the men who drew up the Social Security Act, Griffiths concluded that some could not have comprehended the sociological changes that were taking place in the American family after 1930.[182] Griffiths also believed that whatever was paid in retirement income during the working years had to be equitably returned as an earned right to all retirees—women as well as men. Furthermore, she recommended that Social Security be liberalized by paying benefits according to the number of years worked rather than to the income earned. In the current system, it was possible for a person who had worked longer and paid more in taxes to receive less in retirement benefits than someone who had earned a great deal in a short time.[183]

Griffiths was particularly upset by the direction the Social Security Act had taken since 1935. Intended as old-age insurance, it had become an umbrella for welfare benefits. She told an economist during her 1968 JEC income-maintenance hearings that Social Security should be "at least . . . a pension system. But I get voted down all the time," she lamented. "Everybody else is trying to make it into a welfare system." She therefore opposed taking on more "'do-gooder' programs" or using payroll-tax surpluses for other purposes like defense. "To have old people competing with ABM's . . . [means] old people are going to get short shrift." Constantly faced with the dilemma of the declining power of Social Security as income replacement vis-a-vis the growing burden on industrial states to support Social Security as a quasi-welfare system, Griffiths felt torn between increased Social Security taxes for welfare programs and pension security for elderly citizens.[184]

That a husband did not automatically qualify for his spouse's Social Security also greatly distressed Griffiths from the point of view that he was denied his wife's earned benefits solely because she was female and he was male. The presumption in maintaining a sex distinction was that the man was always the provider. Griffiths once told a credit bureau association that the men on Ways and Means simply could not comprehend how a woman could be either the full or partial support of her family. She further attempted to demonstrate that it often took two checks for a contemporary couple to maintain themselves and their offspring and that, even if the husband were the sole breadwinner, a difference based on sex was illogical and unconstitutional. She was not opposed to a means test in awarding benefits if there had to be one, but she could not see how the law could justify giving a wealthy woman her spouse's retirement and survivor rights while denying them to a less well-to-do male who could not prove dependency. In 1969 the facts showed that the typical man who would immediately profit from a change in the law was in need of the meager payment from his wife's low-paying job.[185]

In supporting her position on benefit equity, Griffiths was fond of quoting case histories. Her favorite involved a man in a state mental institution who had no Social Security of his own and could not claim his wife's because, since she did not pay half his care, he was not considered her dependent. Each month, however, she had to send money for his medicine and spending account. She also had to provide for his clothes, dentures, and other necessities—at the same time trying to live on her paltry check. "Please look into this," she pleaded with Griffiths, "and if there is anything to change it please find it. Then tell the WORLD." There were innumerable stories like this, each raising the same question: "If a woman can get benefits through her husband, why can't the husband get it the same way? Why this discrimination against women?"[186] That was Griffiths' question: Why this discrimination against women?

The men in Washington often argued that equality would cost too much. Griffiths bristled. "You are wanting to pick up orphans, you want to pick up disabled widows; you want to pick up civil service people," she chided Social Security Commissioner Ball, "but not these men for whom women made a real contribution." As far as she was concerned, justice, like charity, began at home. She would show Congress and the White House where to cut Social Security: a billion in college tuition for children of deceased or disabled fathers, $49 million for aged parents living with their retired children, $200,000 paid to the grandchildren of retirees.[187]

Although Griffiths did not succeed in having the

dependency requirement eliminated for entitlement to widower's insurance, in 1967 she persuaded her colleagues to amend Social Security so that minor children could receive benefits from their working mothers who retired, died, or became disabled. Before 1967, a woman had to work eighteen months in the three-year period preceding retirement to be fully insured. This current-employment test left 175,000 minors uncovered, thereby denying families, particularly widowers, $82 million in insurance. As always, the argument was that the family did not depend on the mother's income. Griffiths emphasized the illogic of this presumption by comparing case histories. In one instance there was the young, sizable family who could not claim their mother's survivor benefits because she was out of work a year and a half before she died. In another instance, there was a sole survivor who had never worked outside the home, but on the death of her husband was eligible for both his police pension and his Social Security benefits, although when he died he had been off Social Security for five years.[188] Griffiths' mail over and over again demonstrated injustices such as these.[189]

One of the immediate beneficiaries of Griffiths' amendment awarding survivor rights to minors was Lawrence Filson, a long-term House deputy counsel. "When I told Mrs. Griffiths that her little project had conferred this benefit on me," he recalled with evident satisfaction, "she literally jumped up and down with glee, which I thought at the time was rather incongruous. But it was a delight to see her so pleased and also it indicated how really deep down serious she felt about the things she was trying to do." Filson further noted that while he often disagreed with Griffiths' ideas about what was constitutionally required of Social Security, the Supreme Court subsequently vindicated her "wild attitudes."[190] In Weinberger v. Wiesenfeld (1975),[191] it ruled that a widower, like his children, was automatically entitled to his deceased wife's Social Securith under the equal protection clause of the Fifth Amendment. This decision gave Griffiths "real glee."[192]

Griffiths prevailed on the Ninety-second Congress to permit widowers, as well as widows, to draw a reduced annuity at 60. Even more importantly, at her urging Congress lowered the computation point for men from 65 to 62, thereby increasing benefits for most men. In 1968 the Second Circuit Court had upheld the computation distinction as a legitimate means for reducing the disparity between the economic and physical capabilities of men and women;[193] however, two years before, Social Security Commissioner Ball had already admitted to JEC his difficulty in defending higher benefits for a woman solely "by reason of [her] being a woman."[194] Ball's position strengthened Griffiths in her conviction that standing for equality was not being a "woman's libber" but a "human being for justice."[195] And to be a "human being for justice" had much to do with the great energy and time Griffiths devoted to equal rights for women and a reformed welfare system, the topics of the next two chapters.

[1] Life, December 26, 1969, p.8.

[2] Griffiths to Archie Stabler, July 31, 1967, in Griffiths Papers, Bentley Library.

[3] Griffiths, "The Rising Tide of Violence," Vital Speeches 26 (October 1, 1960): 745-47. Griffiths was particularly proud of this speech probably because it came at a critical juncture of her Congressional career.

[4] U.S., Congress, House, 86th Cong., 2d sess., September 1, 1960, Congressional Record 106:19304-6.

[5] Griffiths to Mr. and Mrs. Robert D. Sweeney, January 10, 1961, in Griffiths Papers, Bentley Library. She likewise wrote David Seigle, February 19, 1960 (in Griffiths Papers, Bentley Library): "I too view our future with great pessimism, not only as it relates to our ability to match the communists, but actually as to whether or not man has sufficient sense to overcome his aggressive instincts and remain alive."

[6] Griffiths, "The Rising Tide of Violence."

[7] "Griffiths Backed for Congress," Michigan AFL-CIO News, July 14, 1960; "Griffiths: Friend of Consumer," Detroit Labor News, July 21, 1960, in MWG Scrapbooks, Griffiths Library.

[8] Election

Election	Griffiths	Republican Contender		Total Vote
1960	134,660	Richard E. Morell	98,721	233,824(57.5%)
1962	122,021	James F. O'Neill	83,870	205,891(59.9%)
1964	136,230	Wm. P. Harrington	50,580	187,041(72.8%)
1966	90,541	Wm. P. Harrington	40,334	130,875(69.1%)
1968	123,376	John M. Siviter	40,906	164,880(74.8%)
1970	108,176	Thomas Klunzinger	27,608	135,784(79.6%)
1972	123,331	Ralph E. Judd	60,337	185,634(66.4%)

Michigan Manual/Page: 1961-62:467; 1963-64:443; 1965-66:482; 1967-68:478; 1969-70:502; 1971-72:525; 1973-74:565.

[9] Will Muller of the Detroit News called her suppers, "the like of which no Republican should be asked to live through. . . . A guest. . . can fall prey to a lifetime of addiction." "Eat with Hubert [Humphrey] at $100—Martha at $1.50," October 5, 1966, clipping in MWG Scrapbooks, Griffiths Library, Romeo). That she was "a gifted congresswoman" was the steady election

appraisal of the press. (See, for example, the <u>Detroit Free Press</u>, August 1, 1962, and the <u>Detroit News</u>, October 21, 1962, clippings in MWG Scrapbooks, Griffiths Library.) During the 1966 and 1968 elections, the Vietnam War significantly figured in as an issue. "I never have approved this war. . .," she wrote an enquirer. (Griffiths to Howard Handleman, August 19, 1968, in Griffiths Papers, Bentley Library.) Busing was an issue in 1972 in the redistricted 17th District.

[10]Interview with Griffiths, Romeo, June 4, 1977; U.S., Congress, House, 93rd Cong., 1st sess., February 6, 1973, <u>Congressional Record</u> 119:3572; Griffiths to William Allgeyer, January 8, 1964, in Griffiths Papers, Bentley Library. She told her constituents that it was easier to vote for Johnson's legislation, whether it won or lost, "than to try to explain the delays to a man who, as Leader of the Senate, passed 87 bills in 87 minutes." (Newsletters 1956-74 [January 1964], in Griffiths Library). Her strong support of the President can be gathered from a note written to him, May 4, 1965 (in Griffiths Papers, Bentley Library):
"Dear Mr. President:
    It is my understanding that you receive some letters that oppose your policies. Therefore, if it is any comfort to you,
    Intreat me not. . . to return from following after thee; for whither thou goest, I will go; . . . thy people shall be my people, and thy God my God.
    (Book of Ruth, Chapter 1 Verse 16)"

[11]Griffiths, "The Responsibility of Christian Women in Today's World," speech to Congregational Women, June 28, 1966, in Griffiths Library. She wrote a constituent: ". . . I have long argued that the nation's most desperate human and social needs are in urban areas." Griffiths to Rev. Alan T. Heggen, February 16, 1968, in Griffiths Papers, Bentley Library.

[12]The constancy of Griffiths' fight for Detroit contracts was impressive. In 1963 John C. Manning of the <u>Detroit Free Press</u> (August 5, 1963) wrote that if the City kept its Defense Center, credit would have to be given to Griffiths and Mayor Jerome Cavanaugh. Griffiths was the only Detroit representative "not alibiing." The <u>Free Press</u> editorial, March 24, 1965, agreed "when Mrs. Griffiths says: 'I think Detroit ought to put up a fight on this one [Federal Customs

Office]." Clippings in MWG Scrapbooks, Griffiths Library.

[13] Griffiths to John H. VanWart, September 6, 1966, in Griffiths Papers, Bentley Library.

[14] Griffiths, "The Responsibility of Christian Women . . ."; Interview with Griffiths, Romeo, July 29, 1977. "The question on open housing," she wrote James Lagana, March 25, 1968 (in Griffiths Papers, Bentley Library), "is whether you have open housing statewide or black-controlled cities."

[15] See her bill, U.S., Congress, House, 89th Cong., 1st sess., H.R. 9996, a <u>Bill to Amend the Mass Transportation Act of 1964 to provide for additional technological research</u>, July 22, 1965. Larry Carino, Vice President and General Manager of WJBK-TV2 (Detroit), mentioned his disappointment over the Michigan delegation's lethargy on the withholding tax (December 20, 1971, in Griffiths Library): "After a successful effort by Representative Martha Griffiths to move the bill out of the Ways and Means Committee," he said, "six of our state's Congressmen favored it and only four were opposed—but <u>nine</u> did not vote."

[16] U.S., Congress, House, 90th Cong., 1st sess., October 25, 1967, <u>Congressional Record</u>: 113:29852. In 1974 Griffiths co-sponsored with a number of the Detroit delegation the Abandonment Disaster Demonstration Relief Act to deal with the crime of abandoned HUD-related homes, of which Detroit had 12,000. Griffiths to Robert Tindal, October 4, 1967, in Griffiths Papers, Bentley Library; U.S., Congress, House, 91st Cong., 1st sess., March 20, 1969, <u>Congressional Record</u> 115:7046-7.

[17] Griffiths, Newsletters 1956-74 (June 1963), in Griffiths Library.

[18] In 1969 she co-sponsored the National Environmental Policy Act to provide long-range environmental planning. In 1971 she also co-sponsored legislation for a thorough review of the nation's energy resources and in 1973, she joined four other members of the Michigan delegation in a proposal for the restoration of land denuded by strip-mining. In 1973 the League of Conservation Voters noted that Griffiths had supported 12 out of 19 of their interests, voted against 3, and was absent for 4. (Material in MWG Scrapbooks,

Griffiths Library.)

[19] She co-sponsored legislation for riot control and for banning interstate commerce of guns and switchblades. She likewise supported anti-bombing legislation and the reimbursement of law enforcement officers for costs incurred in apprehending criminals.

[20] In 1969 she co-sponsored legislation banning obscene mail to minors. During this same period she sought citizen awareness about physical child abuse. U.S., Congress, House, 91st Cong., 1st sess., May 22 and 27, 1969, Congressional Record 115:13532 and 14136.

[21] Interviews with Margaret Heckler, Washington, D.C., January 24, 1978; Barber B. Conable Jr., Washington, D.C., January 27, 1978; and Edna F. Kelly, Briarcliff, New York, March 5, 1978. As reported by former Representative Kelly, when Griffiths was aroused by a floor debate, "She'd say, 'Edna, I've got to speak.'"

[22] Interview with Dan Rostenkowski, Washington, D.C., January 24, 1978.

[23] U.S., Congress, House, 90th Cong., 1st sess., July 20, 1967, Congressional Record 113:19551. Griffiths recalled that whenever she rose thereafter to address Congress, the murmur was heard: "Here comes another rat speech!" Interview with Griffiths, Romeo, July 29, 1977.

[24] The Boston Globe, July 22, 1967, in MWG Scrapbooks, Griffiths Library. Writing in the Houston (Texas) Post, July 27, 1967 (in MWG Scrapbooks, Griffiths Library), Robert G. Spivack chided Congress for having "played the role of Marie Antoinette" on the rat bill. While Griffiths received some criticism for squandering the taxpayer's money "in order to follow your own ideas. . . for a people [Puerto Ricans] whose latest contribution to society is anarchy," (Margaret Jefferson to Griffiths, July 23, 1967, and Evelyn H. Davison to Griffiths, July 25, 1967, in Griffiths Papers, Bentley Library), most of her mail joined in the crusade. (See, for example, Daniel S. Bedell to Griffiths, July 27, 1967, in Griffiths Papers, Bentley Library: "Your points were so well put, and many of your colleagues in the House have expressed to me admiration for your forthrightness on this issue.")

[25] Griffiths to George W. Garman, February 2, 1970, in

Griffiths Papers, Bentley Library; U.S. Congress, House, 93rd Cong., 1st sess., February 8, 1973, Congressional Record 119:4144.

[26] U.S., Congress, House, 91st Cong., 2d sess., March 23, 1970, Congressional Record 116:8646-7. For a complete review of panel proceedings, see U.S., Congress, House, Select Committee on Crime, Hearings and Reports. 3 vols., 91st Cong., 2d sess., 1969-70.

[27] Interview with Griffiths, Romeo, February 22, 1978.

[28] Interview with John McCormack, Boston, Massachusetts, January 5, 1978.

[29] Interviews with Griffiths, Romeo, June 3, 1977, and February 22, 1978; also, Rayburn to Griffiths, December 7, 1960, in MWG Scrapbooks, Griffiths Library.

[30] "Economic Policy Draws Hill Democrats' Fire," Washington Post, March 8, 1962, clipping in Griffiths Papers, Bentley Library.

[31] Interview with Griffiths, Romeo, July 29, 1977.

[32] See, for example, Frank C. Porter, "Proxmire Assails Defense Firms," Washington Post, January 6, 1968, and Sanford Watzman, "Ex-Arms Buyer Hits Profiteers," (Cleveland)Plain Dealer, January 28, 1968, clippings in MWG Scrapbooks, Griffiths Library; Griffiths, "Statement for Rules Committee: Two-Year Extension of the Renegotiation Act of 1951 (H.R.7445)," in Griffiths Papers, Bentley Library.

[33] Ann Penning, Griffiths' administrative assistant, wrote John Lehman, February 17, 1961 (in Griffiths Papers, Bentley Library) that Griffiths wanted to be on the Subcommittee of Foreign Economic Policy because "Michigan as a producer of automobiles is the bellweather of the American Economy."

[34] U.S., Congress, Joint Economic Committee, Economic Policies and Programs in Middle America: A Report to the Subcommittee on Inter-American Economic Relationships of the Joint Economic Committee, by Martha W. Griffiths, Joint Committee Print (Washington, D.C., Government Printing Office, 1963); Griffiths, "Report from Washington," videotape to constituents on aid to the Latin Americas, in Griffiths Papers, Bentley Library; Griffiths, Newsletters 1956-74 (November 1961),

in Griffiths Library; Griffiths, "In Support of the Alliance for Progress," Washington World 6 (August 1966):23-25. In 1962, she reported to her district that "the primary obligation of foreign aid is to the United States." U.S., Congress, House, 87th Cong., 2d sess., October 13, 1962, Congressional Record 108: 23634-5.

[35] U.S., Congress, House, 88th Cong., 2d sess., January 15, 1964, Congressional Record 110:443.

[36] U.S., Congress, House, 88th Cong., 2d sess., Leonor K. Sullivan, "Extension of Remarks," June 8, 1964, Congressional Record, clipping in MWG Scrapbooks, Griffiths Library; Joseph R. Slevin, "Taxes and Spending—New Probe," New York Herald Tribune, May 21, 1964, clipping in Griffiths Papers, Bentley Library.

[37] Paul H. Douglas to Members of JEC, May 1, 1964, in Griffiths Papers, Bentley Library.

[38] Griffiths to Henry T. Bodman, May 6, 1964, and Griffiths to Robert A. Cislo, June 9, 1964, in Griffiths Papers, Bentley Library; Griffiths, "NAM and Its Members Asked for Economic Views," NAM Reports 9 (June 15 1964), 5.

[39] Knowles to Griffiths, May 18, 1964, in Griffiths Papers, Bentley Library. Knowles has been credited as shaping the fiscal thought of the Kennedy-Johnson Administrations.

[40] U.S., Congress, Joint Economic Committee Subcommittee on Fiscal Policy, Fiscal Policy Issues of the Coming Decade: Statement by Individual Economists and Representatives of Interested Organizations, comp. Alan P. Murray, Joint Committee Print (Washington, D.C., Government Printing Office, 1965); U.S., Congress, Joint Economic Committee, Fiscal Policy Issues of the Coming Decade, Hearings before the Subcommittee on Fiscal Policy, 89th Cong. 1st sess., July 20-22, 1965 (1965); "The Big Issues: Debt and Taxes," Business Week, March 6, 1965, pp. 66-68. In its editorial, Business Week (p. 69) stated: "If the Joint Economic Committee, the parent group of Mrs. Griffiths' subcommittee, takes on the crucial task of organizing these studies and pressing ahead on them, it will contribute enormously toward establishing a sound basis for coming Congressional decisions."

[41] U.S., Congress, Senate, 90th Cong., 1st sess., July 27, 1967, Congressional Record 113:20412. For the hearings and reports on the study, see U.S., Congress, Joint Economic Committee, Subcommittee on Fiscal Policy, Revenue Sharing and Its Alternatives: What Future for Fiscal Federalism, 3 vols., ed. Harley H. Hinrichs, Joint Committee Print (Washington, D.C., Government Printing Office, 1967) and U.S., Congress, Joint Economic Committee, Revenue Sharing and Its Alternatives: What Future for Fiscal Federalism, Hearings before the Subcommittee on Fiscal Policy. 90th Cong., 1st sess., July 31, August 1-3, Nov. 7-9, and 14-15, 1967 (1968).

[42] Hinrichs, pp. 739 and 751.

[43] Hearings, Revenue Sharing. . ., 1:140-41, 145-47, and 173; 2:188-89, 218, 223, 343, and 398; also Griffiths to Zolton Ferency, February 6, 1967, in Griffiths Papers, Bentley Library.

[44] Hearings, Revenue Sharing. . ., 1:145-47; Griffiths, "Revenue Sharing and Its Alternatives: What Future for Fiscal Federalism?" Tax Review 28 (December 1967): 47-50; Griffiths, "Federal Revenue Sharing," speech before the Michigan Municipal League, Lansing Michigan, September 19, 1968, in Griffiths Library.

[45] Griffiths wrote her constituents in June 1971, "For every dollar that Michigan received [from revenue sharing], Michigan taxpayers would pay $1.64. I am opposed to it. There has not been a successful 'no-strings attached' revenue sharing plan operate in any country in the world." Newsletters 1956-74.

[46] U.S., Congress, House, Committee on Ways and Means, General Revenue Sharing, Hearings before the Committee on Ways and Means. 92nd Cong., 1st sess., June 2-3, 7-11, 14-17, 21, 23-24, and 28, 1971 (1971), 1:63-67, 192-94; 2:289, and 5:817.

[47] Hearings General Revenue Sharing. . ., 1:194; 3:472-75; "Revenue Sharing Fails to Meet Cities' Real Need," Detroit Free Press, June 4, 1971, clipping in MWG Scrapbooks, Griffiths Library.

[48] Wall Street Journal, June 7, 1971, clipping in MWG Scrapbooks, Griffiths Library.

[49] Interview with Griffiths, Romeo, April 15, 1978; Allen

Phillips, "Revenue Sharing Doubts Arise in Capitol," *Detroit News*, April 22, 1973, clipping in MWG Scrapbooks, Griffiths Library.

[50] U.S., Congress, Joint Economic Committee, *Private Pension Plans, Hearings before the Subcommittee on Fiscal Policy*. 89th Cong., 2d sess., April 26-27, May 2-3, 9-11, and 16, 1966; U.S., Congress, Joint Economic Committee, Subcommittee on Fiscal Policy, *A Compendium of Papers on Problems and Policy Issues in the Public and Private Pension System*, comp. Nelson McClung, Joint Committee Print (Washington, D.C.: Government Printing Office, 1968); U.S., Congress, Joint Economic Committee, *The Labor Market of the Private Retirement System*, by Robert Taggart, Joint Committee Print, Study Paper II (Washington, D.C.: Government Printing Office, 1973) and U.S., Congress, Joint Economic Committee, *Issues in Financing Retirement Income*, by Alexander Korns, Joint Committee Print, Study Paper 18 (Washington, D.C.: Government Printing Office, 1974).

[51] U.S., Congress, House, Committee on Ways and Means, *Tax Treatment of Pension Plans*, by Staff of Joint Committee on Internal Revenue Taxation, Committee Print (Washington, D.C.: Government Printing Office, 1973), 1:1 and 3-8.

[52] Knowles to Griffiths, June 2, 1965, in Griffiths Papers, Bentley Library; Interviews with Griffiths, Romeo, June 4, 1977, and February 22, 1978; Griffiths, "What is Wrong with Pension Plans?" *NAM Reports* 12 (April 17, 1967), 20ff. In the *Hearings, Private Pension Plans. . .*, 2:358-59, Secretary of Labor Wirtz "point-[ed] out that it is unquestionably true that to whatever extent there are tax benefits to a program of this kind, what that means is that the taxpayers as a whole pick up that much of the cost of these plans. This is not said in criticism of that approach," Wirtz concluded. "In support of it rather." Griffiths replied: "It is very kind of you to state it this way. I have stated it considerably less neutrally."

[53] Randolph to Griffiths, October 12, 1965, in Griffiths Papers, Bentley Library.

[54] Griffiths to Subcommittee, September 2, 1965, in Griffiths Papers, Bentley Library; *Hearings, Private Pension Plans. . .*, 1:1-2; Robert Cahn, "Probing Pension Plans," *Christian Science Monitor*, May 13, 1966, clip-

ping in MWG Scrapbooks, Griffiths Library. In praise of Griffiths, Douglas quoted from this article. Unfortunately, the Vietnam hearings which ran concurrent with the pension probe robbed the latter of some of its publicity. U.S., Congress, Senate, 89th Cong., 2d sess., May 26, 1966, Congressional Record 112:11571.

55E.V. Dupree to Griffiths, May 19, 1966; Louis Anderson to Griffiths, April 28, 1966; and Ernest Murphy to Griffiths, May 4, 1966, in Griffiths Papers.

56Hearings, Private Pension Plans. . ., 1:27-102, 146-7, 178-262; 2:348, 366-68, 370-71, 376, 427, 429, 430, and 435.

57Griffiths to R. Messersmith, February 5, 1974; and Griffiths to Walter P. Reuther, August 25, 1966, in Griffiths Papers, Bentley Library.

58Interview with Griffiths, Romeo, April 15, 1978.

59U.S. Congress, House, Committee on Ways and Means, Tax Proposals Affecting Private Pension Plans, Hearings before the Committee on Ways and Means. 92d Cong., 1st sess., May 8-12 and 15-16, 1972, 3:641-44.

60Griffiths, "Public Pensions: Growth and Impact," Tax Review 33 (January 1972), 1-4. Several newspapers joined in the protest. For example, "Rep. Griffiths Makes a Case," Grand Rapids Press, February 20, 1972. "Public Pensions Need an Airing," Wilkes-Barre Times Leader, February 24, 1972; Robert Dietsch, "The Public Horn of Pensions," Washington Daily News, February 22, 1972; and Theodore Schuchat, "Taxpayers Bear Pension Load," Kansas City Star, March 16, 1972, clippings in MWG Scrapbooks, Griffiths Library.

61Griffiths to Neil B. Hartwig, February 29, 1974, in Griffiths Papers, Bentley Library.

62Interview with Henry S. Reuss, Washington, D.C., January 24, 1978; U.S., Congress, House, 93rd Cong., 2d sess., February 28, 1974, Congressional Record 120: 4766-71.

63Griffiths to Wanda Rajowski, June 12, 1974, and Griffiths to Kathleen McDonnell-Clary, October 1, 1974, in Griffiths Papers, Bentley Library; "Martha Griffiths Calls New Pension Bill Unfair to Women," Detroit Free Press, January 16, 1974, clipping in MWG Scrapbooks, Griffiths Library. In 1973 Griffiths emphasized to the staff of the General Accounting Office how prejudicial late vesting was to women: "It means," she said, "that the wife of your youth, who works to put you through college or whatever reason she may work for, and that you discard when you're forty, her effort has contributed to the support of your second wife." (Speech to the GAO, November 7, 1973, in Griffiths Papers, Bentley Library.)

[64] U.S., Congress, House 93rd Cong., 2d sess., August 20, 1974, Congressional Record 120:29198. Griffiths pointed out that what was important was that money withdrawn from tax-free funds would go to those for whom it was intended.

[65] See H.R. 17621, December 12, 1974.

[66] Interview with John Stark Jr., Washington D.C., January 30, 1978. Stark was executive director of JEC during Griffiths' tenure.

[67] Interview with Griffiths, Romeo, June 3, 1977; Griffiths to Wright Patman, January 27, 1962, in Griffiths Papers, Bentley Library. Griffiths resigned from Banking and Currency and Government Operations on the day of her election to Ways and Means.

[68] Interviews with Charles Diggs Jr., Washington D.C., January 25, 1978; Dingell to Emily George, R.S.M., March 6, 1978; Tom Joyce, "Mrs. Griffiths Eyes Vacant Machrowicz Job," Detroit News, November 26, 1961, and "Can't Ignore Martha," Detroit News, January 5, 1962; Reston, "Changing of the Guard on Capitol Hill," New York Times, January 3, 1962; and Edwin A. Lahey, "Rep. Martha Griffiths: Charming, Competent," Detroit Free Press, September [ ], 1967, clippings in MWG Scrapbooks, Griffiths Library.

[69] Interviews with Wilbur Mills, Arlington, Virginia, January 23, 1978; McCormack, Boston, Massachusetts, January 5, 1978; and Griffiths, Romeo, January 6, 1978; Louis C. Rabaut et al. to Sam Rayburn, August 24, 1961; James G. O'Hara to Sam Rayburn, September 22, 1961; and John Lesinski to Sam Rayburn, September 22, 1961, in Griffiths Papers, Bentley Library. Rayburn died November 16, 1961, and McCormack was elected Speaker by the Eighty-seventh Congress.

[70] Knebel, Atlanta (Ga.) Constitution, February 13, 1962 and several other clippings in MWG Scrapbooks, Grif-

fiths Library; Boggs to Griffiths, January 17, 1962, in Griffiths Papers, Bentley Library.

[71] Griffiths, "My First Two Years on Ways and Means," Women Lawyers Journal 50 (Summer 1964), 100.

[72] "Can't Ignore Martha," Detroit News, January 5, 1962, clipping in MWG Scrapbooks, Griffiths Library; Interview with Conable, Washington D.C., January 27, 1978.

[73] John F. Manley, The Politics of Finance: The House Committee on Ways and Means (Boston: Little, Brown and Co., 1970), pp.20-21. The sense of power was emphasized by William M. Brodhead, Griffiths successor on Ways and Means, as reported by the Detroit News, January 10, 1978: "Ways and Means is where the power is. If you want to make a difference, you want to get your hands on the money, and that's where the money is," the Representative allegedly said. "It's exciting, exhilarating. It's tense. It's fun. It's exhausting."

[74] Interviews with Barber B. Conable, Washington, D.C., January 27, 1968; and Griffiths, Romeo, June 3-4, 1977, January 6-7, 1978, and April 15, 1978. Griffiths was the only member of Ways and Means who Mills allowed to present a bill—a renegotiation act—on the floor. On the issue of consensus, Griffiths agreed with an HEW official reported by Manley (p. 108) as saying "'Mills is an eminently successful opportunist. He does not announce his position and force it through. He sits and listens to the members and knows what will go. I'd say 80 percent of it is consensus, 20 percent Mills, but certainly not 50 percent Mills.'" (Griffiths, January 7, 1978).

[75] Manley, p.64.

[76] Business Week, May 8, 1971, pp. 72-75.

[77] "Our Choices for Congress," Free Press, [summer 1972] and "How Nader Sees 3 Congressmen," Observer Newspapers, October 25, 1972, clippings in MWG Scrapbooks, Griffiths Library.

[78] Interviews with Conable, Washington, D.C., January 26, 1978; and Lawrence Filson, Washington, D.C., January 26, 1978.

[79] Saul Friedman, "Red-Haired Rebel Battles Tax Czar in

House Revolt," <u>Detroit Free Press</u>, June 26, 1969, in MWG Scrapbooks, <u>Griffiths Library</u>.

[80] Interviews with Gerald R. Ford Jr., Vail, Colorado, July 19, 1978; James C. Corman, Washington, D.C., January 26, 1978; Rostenkowski, Washington, D.C., January 24, 1978; Conable, Washington, D.C., January 26, 1978; Mills, Arlington, Virginia, January 23, 1978; and John M. Martin Jr., Washington, D.C., January 24, 1978. Martin said that a member's influence on Mills depended "on how hard an individual wanted to work and how industriously and assiduously they followed—pursued—the legislation they were sponsoring. . . ."

[81] Interviews with Griffiths, Romeo, January 7, 1978, and April 15, 1978. Griffiths knew the moment Mills had reached consensus on Medicare.

[82] Interviews with Conable, Washington, D.C., January 26, 1978; Corman, Washington, D.C., January 26, 1978; Rostenkowski, Washington, D.C., January 24, 1978; and J.P. Baker, Washington, D.C., January 25, 1978.

[83] Helen Fogel, "Martha—'A Powerful Chick' in Congress, a Cook at Home," <u>Detroit Free Press</u>, September 13, 1970, clipping in MWG Scrapbooks, Griffiths Library; U.S., Congress, House, Ways and Means, <u>Social Security and Welfare Proposals, Hearings before the Committee on Ways and Means</u>, 91st Cong., 1st sess., October 15-16, 21-24, 27-28, 30-31, November 3-7, 10, and 12-13, 1969 (1970), 2:367; U.S., Congress, Joint Economic Committee, <u>The United States Balance of Payments</u>, <u>Hearings before the Joint Economic Committee</u>, 88th Cong., 1st sess., July 8-9, 1963 (1963), 1:119-22.

[84] Interviews with Wilbur J. Cohen, Ann Arbor, December 14, 1977; Conable, Washington, D.C., January 27, 1978; Corman, Washington, D.C., January 26, 1978; Rostenkowski, Washington D.C., January 24, 1978; Mills, Arlington, Virginia, January 23, 1978. Mills said she had a "very cutting tongue when she wanted to bite." Ways and Means Counsel J.P. Baker (Interview, Washington, D.C., January 25, 1978) pointed out how her sense of humor usually took the bite off her sarcasm and Edna F. Kelly (Interview, Briarcliff, New York, March 5, 1978) noted how she could devastate by the little twist of humor. Judd Arnett ("emember—Ray is—Thay?" <u>Detroit Free Press</u>, October 1, 1965, clipping in MWG Scrapbooks, Griffiths Library) quipped, "To have Griffiths with you would be a joy; but to have her against

you would be hell with hair curlers."

[85] Interviews with Robert M. Ball, Washington, D.C., January 30, 1978, and Griffiths, Romeo, February 22, 1978. Griffiths told the Economic Club of Detroit the same thing on April 18, 1978.

[86] Interviews with Baker, Washington, D.C., January 25, 1978; Martin, Washington, D.C., January 24, 1978; and Filson, Washington, D.C., January 26, 1978. The term, "John the Baptist," was Baker's but all stressed that the Supreme Court subsequent to her retirement proved she was ahead of her time.

[87] Interviews with Griffiths, Romeo, January 7, 1978, and April 15, 1978.

[88] Interview with Griffiths, Romeo, April 15, 1978.

[89] "I am a free-trader," Martha wrote C.D. Smith, Executive Vice President for International Operations of Parke, Davis, November 13, 1967 (in Griffiths Papers, Bentley Library).

[90] Mark Ethridge Jr., "Another Wall Worries the U.S.," Detroit Free Press, April 1, 1962, clipping in MWG Scrapbooks, Griffiths Library.

[91] U.S., Congress, House, Committee on Ways and Means, Trade Expansion Act of 1962, Hearings before the Committee on Ways and Means, 87th Cong., 1961-62, vol. 1, Foreign Economic Policy for the 1960's, Report of the Joint Economic Committee, 87th Cong., 2d sess., January 17, 1962, 610-11; George Meany to Griffiths, May 29, 1962, in Griffiths Papers, Bentley Library.

[92] Griffiths, "My First Two Years on Ways & Means," p.100.

[93] "Facing Trade Wisdom from Mrs. Griffiths," Detroit Free Press, March 30, 1962, clipping in MWG Scrapbooks, Griffiths Library.

[94] Griffiths, speech to the Detroit Economic Club, November 15, 1965, in Griffiths Library; U.S., Congress, House, Committee on Ways and Means, United States—Canada Automotive Products Agreement, Hearings before the Committee on Ways and Means. 89th Cong., 1st sess., April 27-29, 1965 (1965), 139-40 and 302; U.S., Congress, 88th Cong., 2d sess., August 18, 1964, Congressional Record 110:20156-7; U.S., Congress, 89th

Cong., 1st sess., August 31, 1965, Congressional Record 111:21557-8; Griffiths, Newsletters 1956-74 (May 1965). James Robinson suggested that Griffiths was the pact's only enthusiastic supporter on Ways and Means. ("U.S.-Canadian Car Pact Hits Snag in Congress," Detroit Free Press, June 13, 1965, clipping in MWG Scrapbooks, Griffiths Library.)

[95]U.S., Congress, Joint Economic Committee, The 1971 Midyear Review of the Economy, Hearings before the Joint Economic Committee. 92d Cong., 1st sess., July 7-8 and 20-23, 1971 (1971), p. 191; Interview with Griffiths, Romeo, April 15, 1978.

[96]U.S., Congress, House, Committee on Ways and Means, Tax Proposals Contained in the President's New Economic Policy, Hearings before the Committee on Ways and Means. 92d Cong., 1st sess., September 8-9 and 13-17 (1971) 1:135-8.

[97]U.S., Congress, House, Committee on Ways and Means, Social Security Amendment of 1970 (H.R. 17550), H. Rept. 91-1096, 91st Cong., 2d sess., May 14, 1970 (1970), p. 243.

[98]U.S., Congress, House, Committee on Ways and Means, Tariff and Trade Proposals, Hearings before the Committee on Ways and Means. 91st Cong., 2d sess., May 11-14, 18-22, June 1-5, 8-12, 15-17, and 25, 1970), 2:484; 7:2013-5; and 15:4613-6.

[99]Griffiths to Martin M. Switzer, November 30, 1970, and Richard A. Ryan, "Bill Asks Shoe, Textile Limit on Exports," Detroit News, April 26, 1970, letter and clipping in Griffiths Papers, Bentley Library.

[100]U.S., Congress, House, Committee on Ways and Means, Trade Reform Act of 1973 (H.R. 10710), H. Rept. 93-571, 93d Cong., 1st sess., October 10, 1973 (1973), pp. 3-4 and 13-17.

[101]Interview with Griffiths, Romeo, May 16, 1978; U.S., Congress, House Committee on Ways and Means, The Trade Reform Act of 1973, Hearings before the Committee on Ways and Means. 93d Cong., 1st sess., May 9-11, 14-18, 21-24, 29-31, June 1, 6-8, and 11-15, 1973 (1973), 2:394-6; 4:1137; and 10:3233-4.

[102]Congressional Quarterly Weekly, October 20, 1973, p. 2793, quoting Al Ullman.

[103] Hearings, Trade Reform Act of 1973. . ., 10:3233-4; Albert R. Hunt, "Congressional Outlook for Nixon Program is Cloudy, especially for His Trade Bill," Wall Street Journal, June 15, 1973, clipping in MWG Scrapbooks, Griffiths Library.

[104] Griffiths, speech to the University of Michigan, 1966, in Griffiths Library.

[105] Interview with Griffiths, Romeo, April 15, 1978.

[106] Griffiths to William H. Merrill, August 21, 1963, and Griffiths to Pam Kamito, February 25, 1974, in Griffiths Papers, Bentley Library; Interview with Griffiths, Romeo, April 15, 1978.

[107] U.S., Congress, Joint Economic Committee, January 1962 Economic Report of the President, Hearings before the Joint Economic Committee, 87th Cong., 2d sess., January 25-26, 30-31, February 2, 5-8, 1962 (1962), pp. 28-30; Heller to Griffiths, August 16, 1962, in Griffiths Papers, Bentley Library; "Kennedy Answers Mrs. Griffiths," Grand Rapids Press, February 1, 1962, in MWG Scrapbooks, Griffiths Library.

[108] U.S., Congress, House, 87th Cong., 2d sess., March 29, 1962, Congressional Record 108:5395; Interview with Griffiths, Romeo, April 15, 1978; Griffiths, videotape, "Time-Life Interview [on Tax Bill]," February 1962; and Griffiths to Joseph Leahy Jr., May 7, 1962, tape and letter in Griffiths Papers, Bentley Library; Griffiths, Newsletters 1956-74 (August 1963), in Griffiths Library.

[109] U.S., Congress, House, 87th Cong., 2d sess., October 2, 1962, Congressional Record 108:21822-3.

[110] Juan Cameron, "Tax-Cut Pros and Cons," Christian Science Monitor, February 1, 1963; also Joseph Alsop, "Congress Holds Little Sympathy for Tax Cuts Now," Washington Post, February 2, 1963, in MWG Scrapbooks, Griffiths Library; and George Gallup, "One Fourth of Tax Cut Would Not be Spent," Washington Post, August 4, 1962, in Griffiths Papers, Bentley Library.

[111] U.S., Congress, Joint Economic Committee, January 1963 Economic Report of the President, Hearings before the Joint Economic Committee. 88th Cong., 1st sess., January 28-31, February 1 and 4-6, 1963 (1963), 1:43-45.

[112] "Heller Weak on Mink Facts," *Detroit Free Press*, February 8, 1963; also Tom Joyce, "Opposition to Tax-Cut Hinted in Liberal Camp," *Detroit News*, February 3, 1963; "'Puritans' Ethic' of Deficit-Wary American Hinders Proposed Tax Cuts, Heller Says," *The Wall Street Journal*, January 29, 1963; "Tax Cut: 'Puritans' vs. the New Frontier," *Newsweek*, February 11, 1963, pp. 67-68; and Jack Manning, "Thank Goodness for Rep. Griffiths and Her Courage," *Detroit Free Press*, February 1, 1963, clippings in MWG Scrapbooks, Griffiths Library. Manning said, "Martha probably will be snubbed by most of her party pals. She should be hugged and kissed instead."

[113] Douglas to Griffiths, January 1963, in MWG Scrapbooks, Griffiths Library.

[114] U.S., Congress, House, 88th Cong., 1st sess., September 24, 1963, *Congressional Record* 109:16997-17005; Joseph W. Barr (Assistant to Secretary of Treasury) to Griffiths, September 9, 1963, in Griffiths Papers, Bentley Library.

[115] Rowland Evans and Robert Novak, "Reform's Second Wind," *Washington Post*, June 16, 1963; "Thanks to 'Strong-Willed' Congresswoman Oil Industry is Facing Tax Hike," *Washington Daily News*, June 18, 1963; and "Tax Crackdown: Rep. Griffiths' Stand Points to Higher Dividend Levies," *Grand Rapids Press*, June 18, 1963, clippings in MWG Scrapbooks, Griffiths Library.

[116] *Chicago Tribune*, August 18, 1963, clipping in MWG Scrapbooks, Griffiths Library; Griffiths to Charles Muehlstein, August 20, 1963, and Griffiths to W. E. Cuthbertson, December 2, 1963, in Griffiths Papers, Bentley Library; Interview with Griffiths, April 15, 1978.

[117] Griffiths to Frank E. Osborn, May 9, 1960, in Griffiths Papers, Bentley Library.

[118] U.S., Congress, House, 88th Cong., 2d sess., June 17, 1964, *Congressional Record* 110:4064-5.

[119] U.S., Congress, House, 89th Cong., 1st sess., February 16, 1965, *Congressional Record* 111:2713; William E. Hamilton to Griffiths, February 17, 1965; Lynn Townsend to Griffiths, February 19, 1965; and Arjay Miller to Griffiths, February 19, 1965, in Griffiths Papers, Bentley Library; "Martha Does it

Again," <u>Detroit News</u>, May 21, 1965, clipping in MWG Scrapbooks, Griffiths Library.

[120] Griffiths to Frank Permuy, September 17, 1965, in Griffiths Papers, Bentley Library; Tom Joyce, "U.S. Hails G.M. Price Cut; Chrysler Rollback Seen: Federal Probe Unlikely Now," <u>Detroit News</u>, September 23, 1965, in MWG Scrapbooks, Griffiths Library.

[121] James Robinson, "LBJ Seeks to Delay Tax Cuts," <u>Detroit Free Press</u>, January 14, 1966, clipping in MWG Scrapbooks, Griffiths Library; U.S., Congress, House Committee on Ways and Means, <u>1966 Tax Proposals of the President, Hearings before the Committee on Ways and Means</u>. 89th Congress., 2d sess., January 19, 27, and February 1, 1966 (1966), pp. 87-88.

[122] U.S., Congress, House, 92d Cong., 1st sess., August 6, 1971, and October 5, 1971, <u>Congressional Record</u> 117:30712 and 34889.

[123] Griffiths to W. Rowell Chase, May 31, 1966; and Griffiths to E.G. Brown, August 16, 1966, in Griffiths Papers, Bentley Library; Griffiths, Newsletters, 1956-74 (October 1967), in Griffiths Library; "'Guns and Butter' Held Too Costly," <u>(Lansing) State Journal</u>, March 14, 1966; and Tom Joyce, "Tax Boost Still Not Certain, LBJ Strives for a Way Out," <u>Detroit News</u>, March 31, 1966, clippings in MWG Scrapbooks, Griffiths Library.

[124] Griffiths to Robert T. Horner, November 14, 1967; and Griffiths to Robert E. Springer, February 16, 1968, in Griffiths Papers, Bentley Library; U.S., Congress, House, Committee on Ways and Means, <u>President's 1967 Tax Proposals, Hearings before the Committee on Ways and Means</u>. 90th Cong., 1st sess., August 14-15, 21-25, 28, and September 12-14, 1967 (1967), 1:167-8; U.S., Congress, House, Committee on Ways and Means, <u>Act Temporarily Continuing Surcharges and Excises, Repealing Investment Credit Etc.</u>, H. Rept. 91-321, 91st Cong., 1st sess., June 20, 1969 (1969), p. 48.

[125] U.S. Congress, House, 90th Cong., 2d sess., May 29, 1968 and October 4, 1968, <u>Congressional Record</u> 114: 15510 and 29716-9.

[126] U.S., Congress, House, Committee on Ways and Means, <u>Tax Reform Act of 1969, (H.R. 13270)</u>, H. Rept. 91-

413, 91st Cong., 1st sess., August 2, 1969 (1969), 1:1-2; "Minimum Tax on Rich Draws Fire," *Detroit Free Press*, April 4, 1969, in MWG Scrapbooks, Griffiths Library.

[127]U.S., Congress, House, Committee on Ways and Means. *Tax Reform, 1969, Hearings before the Committee on Ways and Means.* 91st Cong., 1st sess., February 18-21, 24-28, March 3, 10-12, 14, 17-18, 20-21, 24-28, April 1-3, 14, 22-24, 1969 (1969), 15:5598-5604.

[128]The *Detroit News* ("Martha's Mistaken!," June 27, 1969, clipping in MWG Scrapbooks, Griffiths Library) believed Griffiths should not have linked reform to the surtax.

[129]*Hearings, The 1969 Economic Report of the President . . .*, 2:567-9; U.S., Congress, House, Committee on Ways and Means, *President's Proposal to Repeal Investment Tax Credit and to Extend Tax Surcharge and Certain Excise Tax Rates, Hearings before the Committee on Ways and Means.* 91st Cong., 1st sess., May 20, 1969 (1969), pp. 74-77.

[130]Lee M. Cohn, "Embattled Oil Industry Faces New House Test on Taxes," *(Washington) Evening Star*, July 22, 1969, clipping in MWG Scrapbooks, Griffiths Library. Griffiths said she was the only one on Ways and Means willing to wipe out the depletion allowance completely. (Griffiths to O.C. Beckbisinger, January 23, 1968, in Griffiths Papers, Bentley Library.)

[131]Griffiths to Daniel J. Sublette, April 29, 1969; and Griffiths to Andy Farkas, July 31, 1969, in Griffiths Papers, Bentley Library; *Hearings, Tax Reform, 1969, . . .*, 15:5598-5604; U.S., Congress, House, Committee on Ways and Means, *General Tax Reform, Hearings before the Committee on Ways and Means.* 93rd Cong., 1st sess., March 5-9, 12-16, 19-23, 26-30, April 2-6, 9-13, 16-18, 30, and May 1, 1973 (1973), 10:4315; "Martha Aims at Wrong Target," [ ], July, 1969, clipping in Griffiths Papers, Bentley Library.

[132]Laurence Stern and Richard Harwood, "Ford Foundation; Its Works Spark a Backlash," *Washington Post*, November 2, 1969, clipping in MWG Scrapbooks, Griffiths Library.

[133]U.S., Congress, House, Committee on Ways and Means, *Treasury Department Report on Private Foundations*,

89th Cong., 1st sess., February 2, 1965, pp. 5-10.

[134] Griffiths, transcript of remarks at Michigan Foundations Conference sent from Foundation News, April 9, 1974, in Griffiths Papers, Bentley Library. During the hearings, Griffiths told Bundy: "I would think that there could come a day when a foundation could go out of existence." (Hearings, Tax Reform, 1969 . . ., 1:379-84).

[135] J. G. Harrar to Wilbur D. Mills, July 9, 1969; Merrimon Cunninggion to Wilbur D. Mills, June 25, 1969; and William H. Baldwin to Wilbur D. Mills, May 8, 1969, copies to Griffiths in Griffiths Papers, Bentley Library; Hearings, Tax Reform, 1969 . . ., 1: 90-95.

[136] Griffiths to (Mich.) Attorney General Frank J. Kelley, September 11, 1969; and Jacob M. Rice, June 2, 1969, in Griffiths Papers, Bentley Library; Hearings, Tax Reform, 1969 . . ., 1: 95-97, 130-33, 304-307, and 379-84.

[137] McGeorge Bundy to Wilbur D. Mills, May 9, 1969, copy to Griffiths in Griffiths Papers, Bentley Library. Bundy wrote: "These grants did not appear to others as they did to us."

[138] Interview with Griffiths, Romeo, April 15, 1978; Hearings, Tax Reform, 1969 . . ., 1:383-4. Griffiths later served on an advisory panel on fiduciary responsibilities for the Council on Foundations.

[139] According to Ways and Means Counsel J. P. Baker this adjustment of the code was Griffiths' effort. (Interview, Washington, D.C., January 25, 1978). In speaking to "Parents without Partners," June 20, 1967 (speech in Griffiths Library), Griffiths joked: "In many cases . . . each person honestly believes that it was _he_ who contributed more than half."

[140] Griffiths wrote Esther Wilkins, June 11, 1964 (in Griffiths Papers, Bentley Library), "One of my pet peeves in the area of taxes is that the person who maintains his home pays more taxes than the one who lets his property run down. Of course this is a local matter."

[141] In 1971 she co-sponsored a bill with James C. Corman for child-care deductions for unmarried men. The case had arisen when a single man who was a foster

parent could not claim the dependency privilege. Regarding underpaid single women she told Ways and Means: "The thing that annoys me most is the single woman making less than $4,000 a year who is supporting a woman with three children on welfare. Now, I really don't think this is quite fair. I am interested in not only hearing this. I have been angered by hearing it." (U.S., Congress, House, Committee on Ways and Means, Tax Treatment of Single Persons and Married Persons where Both Spouses are Working, Hearings before the Committee on Ways and Means. 92d Cong., 2d sess., April 10 and May 1, 1972 [1972], pp. 90-94).

[142] Hearings, Tax Reform, 1969 . . ., 5:1984; Hearings, Tax Treatment of Single Persons, 1972 . . ., pp. 90-94.

[143] This was a 1971 amendment to the Social Security Act.

[144] U.S., Congress, House, 93d Cong., 2d sess., March 4, 1974, Congressional Record 120: 4962-3; Mondale to Griffiths, March 7, 1974, in Griffiths Papers, Bentley Library. Griffiths' welfare proposal was also based on a tax-credit concept.

[145] U.S., Congress, House, 93d Cong., 1st sess., December 13, 1973, Congressional Record 119:41290; U.S., Congress, House 93d Cong., 2d sess., June 30, 1974, Congressional Record 120:38237; Griffiths to David Tankard, August 2, 1974, in Griffiths Papers, Bentley Library.

[146] U.S., Congress, House, Committee on Ways and Means, Tax Treatment of Recycling of Solid Waste, Hearings before the Committee on Ways and Means. 93d Cong., 2d sess., March 20-21, 1974; U.S., Congress, House, 92d Cong., 2d sess., June 30, 1972, Congressional Record 118:23782-3; Griffiths to "Dear Colleague," August 7, 1972, in Griffiths Library.

[147] U.S., Congress, House, Committee on Ways and Means, Administration Request to Increase Debt Ceiling accompanied by a Spending Ceiling, Hearings before the Committee on Ways and Means. 92d Cong., 2d sess., September 18-19, 1972 (1972), pp. 104-106. The budget control committee recommended a standing committee on the budget for both Houses and improved appropriation policies and procedures. (U.S., Congress, Joint Study Committee on Budget Control, Preliminary

Draft of Recommendations for Improving Congressional Control over Budgetary Outlay and Receipt Totals, 93d Cong., 1st sess., April 6, 1973 (1973). The commission on economic efficiency was the result of the JEC recommendation for an action program to reduce inflation and restore economic growth. (See A Bill to establish a Commission on Economic Efficiency to Study barriers to an efficient market economy [H.R. 17283], 93d Cong., 2d sess., October 10, 1974.)

[148] Griffiths to John Cumming, October 7, 1974, in Griffiths Papers, Bentley Library.

[149] Griffiths, "Congressional Action for Health Care," speech presented at the Second Annual Civil Rights Conference, Notre Dame, Indiana, April 1975, in Griffiths Library.

[150] Griffiths' note on Geoffrey C. Harrison to Griffiths, April 10, 1961, in Griffiths Papers, Bentley Library.

[151] U.S., Congress, House, 87th Cong., 2d sess., October 13, 1962, Congressional Record 108:23634-5; Governor John Swainson, "Message from Executive Office," February 27, 1962; Griffiths to Rose B. Anthony, March 9, 1962; Griffiths to Carol Platz, July 30, 1959; and Griffiths to C. E. Wright, May 19, 1959, in Griffiths Papers, Bentley Library.

[152] U.S., Congress, House, Committee on Ways and Means, Medical Care for the Aged, Hearings before the Committee on Ways and Means (H.R. 3920). 88th Cong., 1st and 2d sess., 1963-1964 (1964), 2:799, 844-9, and 860-61.

[153] Griffiths to Paulette Wyman, February 22, 1965, in Griffiths Papers, Bentley Library.

[154] U.S., Congress, House, 89th Cong., 1st sess., April 8, 1965, Congressional Record 111:7390-1; James Robinson, "Women Should 'Keep Demanding Equal Treatment'" Des Moines Register, April 10, 1965, in MWG Scrapbooks, Griffiths Library; Griffiths to Henry T. Bodman, March 9, 1965, in Griffiths Papers, Bentley Library.

[155] Griffiths, "Social Security and Medicare Legislation," speech to the Conference on Public Employee Retirement, April 12, 1965, in Griffiths Library. In 1957 Griffiths was one of several co-sponsors with Senator

Humphrey and Representative James Roosevelt of an old-age rights act barring difference of benefits because of sex. (For her bill, see, <u>A Bill to amend the public assistance provisions of the Social Security Act to eliminate certain inequities and restrictions and permit a more effective distribution of Federal funds</u> (H.R. 7093), 85th Cong., 1st sess., April 30, 1957.

[156] U.S., Congress, Committee on Ways and Means, <u>Basic Facts on the Health Industry, prepared for Use of the Committee on Ways and Means by the Staff of the Committee on Ways and Means</u>, 92d Cong., 1st sess., June 28, 1971.

[157] Interview with Griffiths, Romeo, February 22, 1978; "Mrs. Griffiths Speaks: GOP Bungled Salk Shots, Dem Charges," <u>Detroit Free Press</u>, August 15, 1956, clipping in MWG Scrapbooks, Griffiths Library; and Griffiths, "Nutrition and Human Needs," speech to the Fifty-third Annual Meeting of the American Dietetics Association, Cleveland, Ohio, October 6, 1970, in Griffiths Library; Griffiths to Roy L. Reuther, May 25, 1955; and Griffiths to Governor G. Mennen Williams, February 25, 1958, in Griffiths Papers, Bentley Library. In his letter to Griffiths, May 20, 1955 (Roy Reuther Papers, Wayne State University, Labor History Archives), Roy Reuther congratulated Griffiths for "the real contribution you have made in connection with the Salk Vaccine program."

[150] U.S., Congress, House, 91st Cong., 2d sess., February 9, 1970, <u>Congressional Record</u> 116:2783-5. The announcement of the health bill was one of the few occasions in which Griffiths held a press conference. U.S., Congress, House, Committee on Ways and Means, <u>Social Security and Welfare Proposals, Hearings before the Committee on Ways and Means</u>. 91st Cong., 1st sess., October 15-16, 21-24, 27-28, 30-31, November 3-7, and 10-13, 1969 (1970), 4:1083.

[159] Interviews with Griffiths, Romeo, July 31, 1977, February 22, and April 15, 1978; Corman, Washington, D.C., January 26, 1978. For labor's support, see Meany's 1970 Labor Day Message (U.S., Congress, House, 91st Cong., 2d sess., September 22, 1970, <u>Congressional Record</u> 116:33176-7). In 1971 Bert Seidman, AFL-CIO Social Security Director, said, "The AFL-CIO intends to spare no effort whatsoever to secure enactment of the Kennedy-Griffiths bill." (U.S., Con-

gress, 92d Cong., 1st sess., June 24, 1971, Congressional Record 117:22247.)

[160] "Is It a Gravy Train?" Detroit News, February 14, 1970; Saul Friedman, "How State Democrats in Congress Size Up Outlook on Key Issues," Detroit Free Press, February 14, 1970, clippings in MWG Scrapbooks, Griffiths Library. Also "Who'll Pay for Health?" Dallas (Texas) Morning News, February 1, 1970; Fred L. Zimmerman, "Health Care Drive," Wall Street Journal, April 1, 1970; James Kilpatrick, "A 'No' on National Health Insurance," Detroit Free Press, December 11, 1970, clippings in MWG Scrapbooks, Griffiths Library.

[161] Cohen to Griffiths, April 14, 1970, in Griffiths Papers, Bentley Library.

[162] U.S., Congress, House, 91st Cong., 2d sess., July 7, 1970, Congressional Record 116:23071.

[163] Spencer Rich, "Health Care Battles Shaping Up," Detroit News, February 14, 1971, in MWG Scrapbooks, Griffiths Library.

[164] U.S., Congress, House, Committee on Ways and Means, National Health Insurance Proposals, Hearings before the Committee on Ways and Means. 92d Cong., 1st sess., October 19-20, 26-29, November 1-5, 8-12, and 15-19, 1971 (1972), 1:139; U.S., Congress, House, 92d Cong., 1st sess., June 24, 1971, Congressional Record 117:22246-8.

[165] Griffiths, tape of interview by Robert Barrie, United Mine Workers, May 9, 1974, in Griffiths Papers, Bentley Library; Hearings, National Health Insurance, 1972 . . . , 2:367.

[166] Griffiths, "Health Care and Its Distribution: The Right to Health," transcript of panel discussion, [c. 1974-75], in Griffiths Library.

[167] Hearings, National Health Insurance, 1972 . . . , 9: 1989; 1:50 and 148; Griffiths, speech to the Seventh Annual Conference on Employee Benefits, [c. 1974], in Griffiths Library.

[168] "Daily Summary—23rd Constitutional Convention of the UAW, April 25, 1972," [ ], clipping in MWG Scrapbooks, Griffiths Library; U.S., Congress, 92d Cong., 2d sess., May 3, 1972, Congressional Record 118:15716-8.

[169] *Congressional Quarterly Weekly Report*, September 15, 1973, p. 2425, quoting Griffiths.

[170] See *A Bill to establish a Department of Health (H.R. 14201)*, 92d Cong., 2d sess., March 29, 1972.

[171] Griffiths et al., "The Proceedings of 'Meet the Press,'" 18 (August 11, 1974), in MWG Scrapbooks, Griffiths Library.

[172] U.S., Congress, House, Committee on Ways and Means, *National Health Insurance, Hearings before the Committee on Ways and Means*. 93d Cong., 2d sess., April 24-26; May 3, 10, 17, 23, 31; June 7, 14, 21, 28; July 1-2, and 9, 1974 (1974), 2:610 and 620.

[173] U.S., Congress, House, 93d Cong., 2d sess., April 25, 1974, *Congressional Record* 120:11944-5.

[174] *Hearings, National Health Insurance, 1974 . . .*, 2:794-6; Griffiths to Kenneth Rankin, statement for *Physicians Management*, [n.d.], in Griffiths Papers, Bentley Library; Griffiths, "A Review of the Health Care Picture: An Interview with Martha W. Griffiths of the House Ways and Means Committee," reprinted from *Investor-Owned Hospital Review*, [n.d.], clipping in MWG Scrapbooks, Griffiths Library.

[175] *Hearings, National Health Insurance, 1974 . . .*, 2: 610-12, 614-6; and 620-23; Griffiths, tape of Interview by Robert Barrie . . . .

[176] *Congressional Quarterly Almanac*, 1974, p. 391, quoting Ford; "Mills Panel Lags on Health Plan," *Detroit Free Press*, August 22, 1974, clipping in MWG Scrapbooks, Griffiths Library. Griffiths joined the Ways and Means opposition against two attempts to make national coverage voluntary. (Stuart Averbach, "Mills' Insurance Plan Bogs Down in Panel," *Washington Post*, August 21, 1974, clipping in MWG Scrapbooks, Griffiths Library).

[177] Griffiths, "Congressional Action for Health Care," in Michael B. Wise (ed.), *Beyond Civil Rights: The Right to Economic Security* (Notre Dame Press: Notre Dame, Indiana, 1976), pp. 130-35; Griffiths, speech to Seventh Annual Conference on Employee Benefits . . . .

[178] Interviews with Filson, Washington, D.C., January 26,

1978; Conable, Washington, D.C., January 27, 1978; Ball, Washington, D.C., January 30, 1978; and Phineas Indritz, Washington, D.C., January 27, 1978.

[179] Interview with Griffiths, Romeo, April 15, 1978.

[180] Beginning in the mid-60s, Griffiths asked Congress to cure once for all the difficulty of declining veterans' pensions with each Social Security increase. It was her contention that veterans could not adequately live even with their social security and veteran pensions, both having been earned. (See, for example, her "Statement in Support of H.R. 4535—Committee on Veterans' Affairs, July 15, 1966," and her "Statement in Support of H.R. 647 before the House Committee on Veterans' Affairs, September 21, 1967," in Griffiths Papers, Bentley Library; also, U.S., Congress, House, Committee on Veterans' Affairs, <u>Bills to Increase Compensation Rates and to Increase Pension Income Limitations and Rates, Hearings before the Subcommittee on Compensation and Pension</u>. 91st Cong., 2d sess., May 26-27, and June 3, 1970 (1970), pp. 2829-30.) Griffiths offered a pension bill for World War I veterans and their widows and was upset when former GI members of Congress who had benefited from the lobbying efforts of the veterans voted the legislation down. (Interview with Griffiths, Romeo, April 15, 1978.)

[181] Interview with Griffiths, Romeo, April 15, 1978.

[182] Interview with Griffiths, Romeo, January 6, 1978.

[183] Griffiths to Katherine Alessi, January 16, 1969, in Griffiths Papers, Bentley Library; U.S., Congress, House Committee on Ways and Means, <u>President's Proposals for Revision in the Social Security System (H.R. 5710), Hearings before the Committee on Ways and Means</u>. 90th Cong., 1st sess., March 1-3, 1967 (1967), 1:239-49.

[184] U.S., Congress, Joint Economic Committee, <u>Income-Maintenance Programs, Hearings before the Subcommittee on Fiscal Policy</u>. 2 vols. 90th Cong., 2d sess., June 11-13, 18-20, and 25-27, 1968 (1968), 1:283; U.S., Congress, House, Committee on Ways and Means, <u>Increase in Public Debt Ceiling, Hearing before the Committee on Ways and Means</u>. 91st Cong., 1st sess., March 5, 1969 (1969), pp. 55-58; Griffiths to Josephine P. De Lorenzo, February 1, 1967; and Griffiths

to Mrs. Roger Schmill, October 7, 1968, in Griffiths Papers, Bentley Library. Griffiths loathed "wasteful" expenditures such as the supersonic transport plane and a plethora of federal highway signs.

[185] Griffiths, taped speech to the Association of Credit Bureau Conference, Washington, D.C., May 1973, in Griffiths Papers, Bentley Library; U.S., Congress, House, Committee on Ways and Means, Social Security and Welfare Proposals. Hearings before the Committee on Ways and Means. 91st Cong., 1st sess., October 15-16, 21-24, 27-28, 30-31, November 3-7, 10, and 12-13, 1969 (1970), 5:1797-9. A 1967 Ways and Means report on the dependency test noted: "Because men are not ordinarily dependent on their wives, it seems reasonable to retain the requirement that a husband must show that he was dependent on his wife." (U.S., Congress, House, Committee on Ways and Means, Social Security Amendments of 1967 (H.R. 12080), H. Rept. 544, 90th Cong., 1st sess., August 7, 1967 (1967), p. 57.

[186] Nettie Jemison to Griffiths, February 27, 1967; and Mrs. Lecha Fries to Griffiths, February 23, 1967, in Griffiths Papers, Bentley Library. These are only a few of several letters on this subject.

[187] Hearings, President's Proposals for Revision in the Social Security System . . . , pp. 234-49; Griffiths, transcript of "CBS Commentary, Martha W. Griffiths," February 1975, in Griffiths Library.

[188] U.S., Congress, House, 90th Cong., 1st sess., March 16, 1967, Congressional Record 113:6953-5.

[189] Sims Embler to Griffiths, September 8, 1967; and Edward A. Harace to Griffiths, November 27, 1967, in Griffiths Papers, Bentley Library; Interview with Griffiths, April 15, 1978.

[190] Interview with Filson, Washington D.C., January 26, 1978.

[191] Weinberger v. Wiesenfeld, 420 U.S. 636 (1975).

[192] U.S., Congress, Senate, Special Committee on Aging, Future Directions in Social Security Hearings before the Special Committee on Aging. Part 18, "Women and Social Security," 94th Cong., 1st sess., October 22, 1975 (1975), p. 1673.

[193] *Gruenwald v. Gardner*, 390 F. 2d 591 (C.A. 2, 1968), cert. denied, 393 U.S. 982.

[194] Hearings, Private Pension Plans . . . , 2:387; U.S., Congress, House Committee on Ways and Means, Social Security Amendments of 1970 (H.R. 17550), H. Rept. 91-1096, 91st Cong., 2d sess., May 14, 1970 (1970) p. 15; Sharon Galm to Griffiths, "Reasoning of the Second Circuit in Upholding Discriminatory Criteria for Computing Social Security Benefits at Age 62," September 24, 1970, in Griffiths Library.

[195] Griffiths, taped speech to the Association of Credit Bureau Conference . . . .

CHAPTER IV

History has an uncanny way of repeating itself. In 1848 Martha Wright joined her sister Lucretia Mott and a coterie of feminists in launching the first women's rights convention. A little more than a century later, another Martha Wright—Martha Wright Griffiths—spearheaded a drive for equal rights. Because of her leadership, the Civil Rights Act of 1964 extended equal employment opportunities to women, and the Equal Rights Amendment was forced out of the House Judiciary Committee where it had languished for nearly fifty years. Martha Griffiths did not, of course, battle alone. She would have been the first to admit it. But without her influence, sex discrimination in employment would not have been outlawed in the early 60s as a civil rights violation; the ERA would not have passed Congress; and the quest for legal equity would not have gained its current momentum.

Sex discrimination in the United States—indeed world-wide—has had a long, pervasive history. Only very recently have shifting attitudes begun to make noticeable fissures in the wall of prejudice. Women's rights—civil, property, and political—as derived from English common law, were substantially less than they were for men; for married women they were practically nonexistent. Paraphrasing Blackstone's famous dictum that "the very being or legal existence of the woman is suspended during the marriage, or at least is incorporated and consolidated into that of the husband," it could be said that under this legal theory the two became as one and he was the one.[1] The legal subordination of women so prevailed into contemporary times that normally reasonable persons did not recognize it for what it was. Speaking about his colleagues after the passage of the Civil Rights Act of 1964, a leading member of the House Judiciary Committee confessed:

> This was the first example, the first instance, the first time that most of us got an indication of sex discrimination in this country. We really hadn't heard about it before. We'd heard about what they—white people—did to Indians, to black people, and so forth, but not to women and, if you think about it, it's a relatively new concept that discrimination against sex should be protected by law.[2]

In 1969 Presidential Counselor Arthur Burns told a group of reporters that he was "not aware of any discrimination against the better half of mankind." Asked if he was really serious, he replied, "Oh yes," but indicated that if there was any bias, it had to be of "the unconscious variety."[3] Griffiths also believed that much sex discrimination was the product of "simple and habitual lack of thought," yet she did not excuse the perpetuation of legal inequality. As she repeatedly told the men of Capitol Hill, whether they liked it or not, it was "really a new world."[4]

Just how new can be seen from the dramatic changes in the life-style of American women during the 60s.[5] The number of white women in their twenties completing high school or with some college education rose from 66 to 80 percent; among black women, the corresponding percentage climbed from 43 to 63 percent. In that decade, the number of women with some college education increased 160 percent, 60 percent more than that of men. The number of women living alone or with an unrelated adult jumped 50 percent—about 10 percent of all women —with the largest and fastest growing number between the ages of 20 and 34. By 1970 the percentage of single women between 20 and 24 leaped from 28 to 36 percent and, correspondingly, the number of children born to women under 25 declined appreciably. The delay in marriage and family kept women free for college and for work.

By 1970, 43 percent of adult women worked outside the home as compared to 37 percent in 1960. Working women of the early 70s comprised 38 percent of the professional and technical labor force, a 10 percent increase in two decades. Two-thirds of the employed were either single, divorced, separated, or had husbands who earned less than $7,000 a year, a fact which disproved the notion that a wife's check bought superfluities. That more than 10 percent of all American families by 1970 were headed by women also weakened the myth that women were "secondary" workers. Forty-three percent of poor families were headed by women, a figure almost doubled since 1960; and among poverty-level black households, 64 percent had female heads. These employment and family trends pointed to what Griffiths perceived as the prime evil of sexism: almost every distinction in the law carried a financial loss to the woman.[6]

Griffiths never tired of repeating this fact.[7] As stated earlier, she was particularly exercised about discrimination in Social Security. Before her amendment of 1967, children of a deceased mother had no survivors benefits if she was out of work a year and a half before her death. No such test, however, was required of a man. And not until <u>Weinberger v. Weisenfeld</u> (1975)[8] did a dependent widower automatically have entitlement to his spouse's benefits, while a woman had always been entitled to her deceased husband's benefits. A working woman could not claim both her earned Social Security and her entitlement as a wife, which meant that many non-working wives received greater benefits than working wives. A working widow, irrespective of the number of children she had to support, lost her mother's rights if she earned more than the sum stipulated by law; and a divorcee had no wife's benefits unless she was both married twenty years (ten years beginning in 1979) and, until 1972, received half of her current support from her former husband. A homemaker could earn no Social Security benefits of her own, although it would have cost her husband a considerable sum to pay someone to keep the home and care for the children. Moreover, if a husband had a private pension, the survivorship benefit depended on his good graces: a divorced and remarried retiree could totally disregard his wife of forty years and leave his pension to a young bride of even a few days.

Griffiths excoriated the taxing structure as no less inequitable than Social Security. Singles—mostly women—were taxed more than heads-of-households, whether or not they were responsible for elderly parents or for the upkeep of a home, whether or not they were widows or divorcees. After 1969, a working couple was taxed more than two singles earning the same aggregate income. The tax code also favored males. The law permitted a surviving husband and wife to continue income splitting two years after the spouse's death—a provision benefiting the higher earner—generally the man—because taxes were based on the couple's combined income. The law also allowed deductions for business entertainment but not domestic help, and the benefits derived from the child-care deduction were basically too small to be of use to the mass of working women.

In addition to encountering Social Security and tax inequities, women living in the eight community-property states were faced with another unique set of distinctions. Only the husband had the legal right to manage family property. In four of these states—Arizona, Louisiana, Nevada, and New Mexico—a wife had no right to control even her own earnings. Yet, a woman separated from her husband and without an interest in the community assets could be held liable for half of the indebtedness from her personal income. What was worse, by law she had no right to know how her husband managed the estate. If community-property states were unfair to women, so was the world of loans, insurance and credit. A woman paid higher premiums as a way of life. Mortgage lenders generally discounted some or all of a wife's earnings in granting a loan and required that young couples be on birth control. A married woman could not take out a loan or obtain credit in her own name, even though she was economically independent and personally liable for her debts; at times a father had to sign for his mature self-supporting single daughter. Discrimination such as this demonstrated one fact: in the financial market, a woman's dollar was valued less than a man's.

A woman's service was also worth less than a man's in federal employment and in the armed forces. Pension benefits for a federally employed woman were substantially fewer than for her male counterpart. Likewise, a military woman did not receive the usual fringe benefits for herself or for her husband and children, unless they were dependents. Furthermore, a female veteran and her husband did not qualify for the loans, educational assistance, death or disability compensation on the same basis as male veterans and their wives.

State protective laws were also among the most oppressive and inequitable because of the many women affected. Some states barred women from specified occupations and from owning and operating businesses. Many limited hours and times of employment, thereby practically excluding women from executive positions and other higher paying employment. Laws forbidding admission to public colleges and universities offering specialized training, such as engineering, also worked against a woman's economic well-being. So did welfare regulations. The benefit-loss rate of Aid to Families with Dependent Children, for example, discouraged recipients from entering the labor force, thus deepening the poverty cycle for themselves and their offspring. In sum, legally enshrined sex differentiation created a not-too-subtle form of economic bondage for most American women. "When a widow watches her husband's casket being lowered into the grave," Griffiths told a California audience in 1972, "she ought to weep—even if he used to beat her—because in terms of economic rights and power she is losing a lot . . . . The laws do not enable women to be the economic equals of men."[9]

During the 60s, Congress made two major attempts to bring women into the economic mainstream. The first was the Equal Pay Act of 1963; the second, the Civil Rights Act of 1964. In amending the Fair Labor Standards Act of 1938, the Equal Pay bill prohibited sex discrimination in wages and provided for collecting back pay where violations had occurred. The statute also stipulated that in equalizing compensation between men and women, employers had to use the going rate for men in adjusting wages for women. It further forbade labor unions to pressure employers to engage in discriminatory practices.

Although equal pay bills had consistently been before Congress since 1945 (Griffiths first became a co-sponsor in 1957) the federal government was a Johnny-come-lately to the equal pay scene.[10] Between 1945 and 1963, 38 nations belonging to the International Labor Organization had ratified an equal pay accord. Common Market participants had agreed to institute equal pay laws in their own jurisdictions, and 22 states (Michigan in 1962) had legislated fair pay measures of varying force.

The federal act of 1963 was originally embedded in the fair employment practices bills of 1961 and 1962. In 1962 concerned members of Congress, led by Representatives Edna F. Kelly and Edith Green and Senator Patrick McNamara, extracted the pay section from the doomed antidiscrimination measure to test its viability. The Kennedy Administration supported the move on the grounds that, in a modern age, sex-based wage differentials were "indefensible from every standpoint."[11]

Griffiths joined the chorus of advocates, her contribution foreshadowing her work for the civil rights statute the next year. She argued that if moral considerations did not move Congress to legislate equal pay, then the growing number of deserted and divorced women should. Women who were already supporting 10 percent of all American families needed legal leverage to keep themselves and their children off welfare. She also reasoned that, given any fair employment practices act which barred discrimination on the basis of race, the only persons against whom there could be discrimination without a civil rights act would be white women. Finally, she pleaded with Congress to put its own house in order and recognize the wage inequalities among federal personnel.[12]

One of the most interesting discussions on the bill concerned the amendment of Katherine St. George of New York proposing to substitute the word "equal" in reference to the work performed for the original term, "comparable."[13] According to St. George, "'comparable' opened great vistas." Men and women, she said, did not wish to be compared to each other. Griffiths opted for the original wording. She argued that if "equal" were used it would not be possible for two members of Congress to draw the same pay. Edith Green picked up on Griffiths' inference, remarking that everyone knew that Congressional responsibilities were not "equal" nor treated as such; members of Congress, therefore, could only claim the same compensation for "comparable" work. A further argument advanced against "equal" was that it could become a "monstrosity" in attempting to prove what it meant. Catherine May, however, said that legislative intent was more important than terminology, and St. George pointed out that quibbling over "equal" would ultimately lead to amending the Declaration of Independence. Thus ended the debate, a debate to be heard again during passage and ratification of the Equal Rights Amendment.

When the Equal Pay bill finally cleared both Houses in 1963, President Kennedy remarked that it was "a significant step forward." He was nevertheless dismayed that despite the labor advances made since the New Deal the average working woman still earned only 60 percent of a man's wage.[14] Congress took up the challenge in 1964 and enacted Title VII of the Civil Rights bill.

Title VII differed from the Equal Pay Act as a comprehensive equal employment opportunity statute. Included were provisions for hiring, discharge, promotion, seniority, job advertising, and conditions of employment. The bill affected not only employers but also public and private employment agencies, labor unions, and labor-management programs. Moreover, to prevent or eliminate prejudice on account of sex, as well as race, color, religion, and national origin, Title VII established a five-member Equal Employment Opportunity Commission (EEOC). Reflecting its own time, the bill did not protect atheists, Communists, nor the aged from job discrimination. Despite these limitations, the 1964 statute was the most far-reaching piece of civil rights legislation since Reconstruction.

Prior to 1964, fair employment practices had been written into government contracts by Executive order.

Congress, however, had failed to pass a federal equal employment bill both in 1961 and 1962, although several states had had them since World War II. (G. Mennen Williams had made an FEPC part of his first gubernatorial campaign.) In the summer of 1963, Kennedy publicly announced that he would press the Eighty-eighth Congress for an EEOC. Though he did not live to see the realization of his dream, his successor forced through a compromise measure in 1964. That the Senate was able to end a filibuster on the act, the first on any civil rights measure, attested to the temper of the new Executive and the mood of the country.

Before Title VII cleared the House early in 1964, eighteen attempts were made to amend it, the most important being the inclusion of "sex" among non-discriminatory classifications. Although Howard W. Smith, Chairperson of the Rules Committee, introduced the sex provision, Griffiths is generally considered its author.[15] Smith's role in the maneuver will ever remain an enigma. Some saw it as Southern deference to the women in the House. Others, such as organized labor, thought it a Southern ploy to sabotage the entire civil rights effort.[16] The AFL-CIO, for example, argued that the act pertained explicitly to blacks and thereafter urged Griffiths to forego her amendment,[17] as did Assistant Secretary of Labor Esther Peterson.[18] Even Edith Green, long-standing equal rights champion, opposed adding "sex" for fear it would jeopardize the entire act.[19] Griffiths, thinking otherwise, forged ahead:

> When I looked at the bill, I realized that the [Judiciary] committee had never really considered the rights of Negro women at all, or, if they had, they had simply believed that they would get approximately the rights of white women. I made up my mind that all women were going to take one giant step forward, so I prepared an amendment that added "sex" to the bill. Then I learned that a woman newspaper reporter had asked Howard Smith of Virginia to offer such an amendment and he had agreed. Judge Smith was the Chairman of the Rules Committee and the leader of the conservative bloc, who would, if they could, have killed the bill. I realized that Mr. Smith would get more than a hundred votes just because he offered the amendment. I needed, if everyone voted, 218 votes to win. Without saying anything to anyone, I decided to let him offer it, and use my powers of

persuasion to get the rest of the votes.[20] To sum up this part of her strategy in her own words: "I used Smith."[21]

In introducing the sex amendment, octogenarian Smith said he was about setting aright "the imbalance of spinsters."[22] Chanting "'Vive la différence,'" the 75-year-old Chairperson of the Judiciary Committee, Emmanual Celler, immediately took up the debate, which he turned into a charade. He pointed out that in his home women were not a minority and he thought it anomalous that two old men should be at odds over women. Smith assured him they were not. Celler retorted that the amendment was "illogical, ill timed, ill placed and improper," to which Smith replied that he was chagrined over his colleague's opposition. Celler responded that the absence of data made a sex amendment premature. At this juncture, Frances P. Bolton interjected her proposal that "sex" be placed under the bill's miscellaneous title, but Smith thought women deserved better than that.

Unable to abide the laughter any longer, Griffiths went to the well. "Before I spoke," she recalled several years later, "I had given the whole idea very careful consideration. It was my judgment that a bill could not be constitutionally drafted which gave to black men the rights of white men, and to black women the rights of white women. Such a bill would have been too vague. Nobody knew what the job rights of white women, if any, were." Returning to the argument she had used in the equal pay debate, she pointed out that without a sex clause white women would not be protected by the law, whereas black women could claim equality because of color. "She [the white woman]," Griffiths reasoned, "will continue to work in the greasy spoon, drive the schoolbus, and do the other underpaid jobs."

She reviewed for her colleagues why this was so. Under the Constitution women had no legal recourse. The Supreme Court had ruled in the 1970s that the Fourteenth Amendment did not guarantee their suffrage or right to practice law and, as late as 1948, it had upheld a Michigan statute prohibiting a woman from bartending unless her husband or father owned the establishment.[23] That a modern Court could still call to mind Shakespeare's "alewife, sprightly and ribald" in maintaining that a law need not reflect social change was, in Griffiths' opinion, "arrogant prejudice," and she was impatient that this continue. "Your great-grandfathers were wiling to be prisoners of their own prejudice to permit ex-slaves to vote, but not their own white wives," she reminded her basically white male colleagues. "A vote against this amendment today by a white man is a vote against his wife, or his widow, or his daughter, or his sister."

Although most who followed Griffiths to the podium supported her view, passage hung in the balance. An hour before the vote, James Roosevelt, who said his mother would not have backed the amendment, told *Time* and *Life* reporters that "sex" would never be added because no one saw it as a basis of discrimination against white women.24 That the House voted 168 to 133 for passage attested to the polarity of opinion on the issue and to the persuasiveness of one woman.

Griffiths continued to monitor the amendment's progress in the Senate. She called on Liz Carpenter, press secretary for Lady Bird Johnson, to tell the President that if "sex" was removed by the Senate or in conference committee she would send her speech to the constituents of every opponent. The Business and Professional Women Clubs also mounted a campaign against Senator Everett M. Dirksen's initiative to strike the clause, and Margaret Chase Smith supported the amendment in the Repbulican caucus.25 "Sex" remained.

Women, individually and collectively, thanked Griffiths "for winning a place" for them, and particularly for their working sisters.26 Myra K. Wolfgang, Secretary-Treasurer of the Hotel, Motel, and Restaurant Employees Union Local 705 and later one of ERA's primary critics because of its ban on protective legislation, concurred from experience that the first employees to be let go in hard times were white women. Immediately after the passage of the amendment, she wrote Griffiths that she would have opposed the civil rights bill had it excluded women.27 Griffiths' response was politically shrewd:

> Myra, I would not be sitting in this seat today if it were not for the women who went to jail so that all of us could vote, and for women who have worn their shoes out helping me get elected. I will be darned if I am going to sit there and let the one bill in a hundred years pass when a woman could stand up and say that women also have been discriminated against. I will be further darned if I am going to sit there while

white women come in last at the hiring gate. It was a glorious victory!28

The story that Griffiths liked best about the impact of her amendment concerned a high-level black professional on Johnson's Civil Rights Commission. Not totally convinced of the necessity of having added "sex" to the Civil Rights Act, he changed his mind when a manufacturer, who had called him on the phone and was unaware that he was black, confessed that he would rather have "niggers" working for him than women.29 The anecdote confirmed Griffiths' belief that, in its original form, the civil rights act had little to do about equality for any woman—black or white.

Sitting in the House gallery the day the vote was taken on the sex amendment was soft-spoken Washington attorney, Phineas Indritz. Having known Griffiths when he served as staff to the Government Operations Committee, Indritz, then chief counsel for the House Subcommittee on Conservation and Natural Resources, recognized a kindred spirit and from that moment contributed to Griffiths' battle with the EEOC, Title VII's enforcement arm.30 Until 1972, when Congress extended the jurisdiction of the Civil Rights Commission to include sex discrimination, the EEOC was the most important vehicle for eliminating bias in employment.

Griffiths and Indritz gave the EEOC a year to put its house in order. In June 1966 the two struck, Griffiths delivering on the floor of Congress a text carefully prepared by Indritz which outlined the Commission's failures. She castigated Herman Edelsberg, EEOC Executive Director, for having brought ridicule on the sex provision by calling it "'a fluke. . . conceived out of wedlock,'" and she accused Acting Commissioner Luther Holcomb and his Commission of having furthered the contempt in raising oddities as male "bunnies" and men housemothers. She likewise indicted the Commissioner for "legal schizophrenia" in applying a different set of advertising guidelines to racial groups than to the sexes. "The whole attitude of the EEOC toward discrimination based on sex," she protested, "is specious, negative, and arrogant." She was tired of the Commission's "shilly-shallying and wringing of hands" and its "whining" that antisex discrimination was never intended by Congress, was too difficult to enforce, and interfered with the agency's main work of eliminating racial prejudice.

Griffiths pointed out that the Commission had much to do as wage differentials and unemployment statistics widened between men and women, especially between men and black women. She recommended that EEOC revise its guidelines on job advertising and begin hearing cases of aggrieved women like the women airline flight attendants. She suggested further that the President appoint only serious-minded persons to the Commission and that newspapers voluntarily comply with the law. Finally, she urged organizations and individuals at odds with the EEOC to protest to the President and, if all else failed, to sue.[31]

Reaction to the speech was immediate and widespread. The CIA informed Griffiths that the Russians took her remarks as evidence of America's brutality to women. Griffiths responded that the CIA ought to thank the Kremlin for its interest in women, though misguided; she was more anxious, however, to hear from the White House than from Moscow.[32] The solitary "'Bravo!'" from former EEOC Commissioner Aileen C. Hernandez captured the sentiment of many.[33] A by-product of the enthusiasm Griffiths generated by her speech was the founding of the National Organization of Women (NOW).[34] Designed to move quickly against legal sex barriers, NOW brought the first suit against discriminatory labor practices. Asked in 1966 to serve as honorary president, Griffiths declined because of campaign pressure, but she subsequently served on NOW's advisory council and more importantly, always identified with the organization's key concept of equity before the law.

In her EEOC speech, Griffiths had raised two specific criticisms against the Commission: first, its interpretation of the advertising provisions of Title VII; and, second, its handling of the so-called "stewardesses cases." The Civil Rights Act had outlawed the printing of any sex preference in classified ads unless a BFOQ, a bona fide occupational qualification, was involved, that is, where being male or female was necessary to the work performed. The Commission interpreted nonsexist advertising to permit gender-labeled columns because of the reading habits of job seekers. Acting Chairperson Holcomb noted that in those instances where sex headings were omitted reader response had dropped off. "My answer is," Griffiths told Congress, "I have never entered a door labeled 'men' and I doubt Mr. Holcomb has frequently entered the women's room. The longstanding custom that women do not enter a men's washroom, and men do not enter a women's washroom, is an effective barrier in almost all instances. The same principle operates in the job seeking process." It was the EEOC's business to achieve economic equality even if it meant changing the public's reading habits and, thus, by its private interpretation, the Commission was not faithful to the law as far as Griffiths was concerned.[35]

Holcomb responded to this particular charge by launching a probe of seventy-five help-wanted advertisers without, however, altering the stance of the EEOC on sex-segregated columns.[36] Griffiths continued to press for revision. In December 1966, NOW filed a petition requesting either a change of the regulations or a public hearing, the latter which was held in May 1967. The following October, President Johnson issued an Executive order prohibiting sex-differentiated advertising by federal contractors and subcontractors.[37] Unable to withstand further opposition, the EEOC capitulated.

The newspapers were not altogether happy. The Washington Star labeled the revised regulation "a nuisance. . . [and] nonsensical outrage." Life raised the bogey of unisex, a suggestion Griffiths dismissed as "grisly, unhumorous, thoroughly confused, a complete nonsequitur." The American Newspaper Publishers Association brought suit on the basis that a change in practice would confuse the reader and be costly to advertisers.[38] But single listing was accomplished. Griffiths and Indritz then moved on to convince the Census Bureau that revising its stereotypic job classifications would be in the spirit of Title VII. "Clergy," they argued, was preferred to "clergyman," "flight cabin attendant" to "stewardess," and "homemaker" to "housewife." Laugh, as some might, language shaped identity.[39]

The second major concern raised by Griffiths in her June 1966 EEOC speech was the sex bias promoted by the airlines. Griffiths had already demonstrated interest in airline policies. In 1961 she had a bill requiring that flight attendants be licensed both to promote air safety and to dignify their traditionally low-paid position. Passage of Title VII gave her the impetus to renew her struggle from the standpoint of economic manipulation. That the airlines required their female cabin attendants to resign when they married or reached their early thirties were problematic requirements for Griffiths. Because their situation was one to elicit public sympathy—although the attendants did not always think of themselves as oppressed—Griffiths capitalized on the sexist policies to drive home many years of injustice and irrationality. She also encouraged the aggrieved parties to fight their cases as far as the courts if they received no support from the EEOC.[40]

The previous April, United Airline officials had defended their sex-determined requirements before the EEOC on the grounds that the duties of a flight attendant made it "a girl's job." Men could deliver trays and hang up coats, they argued, but only "attractive, young females . . . [could] create for the passenger the psychological impression of a memorial occasion. . . [and] by their presence, their appearance, their grace or their warmth, add to the pleasure of the trip, the loveliness of the environment or the ego of the male passenger."[41] American Airlines bolstered United's contention by a survey of both its clients and former female attentants. Ninety percent of the retirees agreed that the profession should remain a women's preserve, that being female, in other words, was a BFOQ for holding the position. "After all," wrote one retiree, "How many men can burp a baby?"[42]

In the fall of 1966, Griffiths leveled an all-out attack on United.[43] She wanted to know how that airline could fire an employee of eight years for "misconduct" when her secret marriage came to light. United Vice President Charles M. Mason replied that the former employee had known at the time of hiring the "singles only" policy, which he said was of long tradition and universal acceptance. Griffiths' widely publicized retort was unambiguous: "You point out you are asking a bona fide occupational exception that a stewardess be young, attractive and single," she wrote. "What are you running, Mr. Mason, an airline or a whorehouse?"

"Shocked" by Griffiths charge, Mason protested for his company and its thousands of flight attendants and their families. "There are two sides to every discussion," he asserted. In limiting the position to women, United was exercising "legitimate business judgment." Griffiths termed the reply "brazen" for defying national policy which prohibited marriage restricitons in employment contracts. She knew why the service of unmarried women was so profitable to the airlines—what was really at the heart of the "legitimate business judgment." By keeping the job short-term, the airlines realized sizable corporate savings in fringe benefits like vacations and pensions. She intended to ask the Justice Department to bring suit against the companies and to intervene in pending cases.[44]

Griffiths' judgment upon United jolted the public. Her blunt language, coming on the eve of an election, raised some eyebrows including Hicks'. The mail, however, ran heavily in Griffiths' favor and the press was delighted that someone had taken on the barons of the air. A number of individuals, notably former flight attendants and their families, nevertheless, felt Griffiths had demeaned them and their occupation.45 This Griffiths chalked up to ignorance of what the airlines were getting away with at the expense of their female employees. She also lamented the Supreme Court's lack of sensitivity in refusing to deal with the unconstitutionality of the marriage regulation.46 In the spring of 1967, Griffiths pleaded with President Johnson to force the EEOC to take up the cases of aggrieved women. "I have appealed everywhere," she lamentably told one, "to no avail."47

Nevertheless, times were changing. In October 1967, Johnson, acting on Griffiths' advice, included sex as a discriminatory classification in federal contract compliance, and the following February the EEOC issued guidelines bringing age and marital status under the ban. Conceding to the inevitable, the airlines began voluntarily to eliminate marriage restrictions from their contracts and within a few years the courts ruled that the "no marriage" policy violated Title VII.48 What was important to Griffiths in this long struggle was that women were taking up their own cause wherever they were. That was her spirit. "She was very, very vocal and a strong advocate of women's rights at a time when others were not speaking this way," recalled a former Congressional colleague. "I remember her fight for the stewardesses. . . . And whenever I see an older stewardess, I think of Martha."49

In pressing for economic equality for women, Griffiths looked to Title VII to eradicate protective legislation. In combating the deplorably inhuman labor practices against women at the turn of the century, the states had enacted laws restricting women's hours and times of work, places and manner of rest, maximum weights and the like. Griffiths claimed that by the mid-twentieth century these regulations had become job barriers and women were left to low-paying, sex-typed work. She further argued that protective legislation continued to reinforce the national schizophrenia that a woman's virtue had to be secured at any price—as long as the woman paid. For example, Griffiths knew of no law that protected a woman from holding two or three ill-paying, demeaning jobs to keep her family together. For years Griffiths had wondered why women could not be hotel night clerks while down the street their sisters danced at the burlesque shows or scrubbed executive suites at two in the morning. "Then it came as a bolt of lightning," she recollected. "Men would want to know from the clerk where the girls were!"[50]

Griffiths was not against restrictive legislation that protected both sexes; rather she opposed sex as a category for determining employment differences. In 1941 the Supreme Court supported this view in sustaining the federal government's right to apply universal norms for wages, hours, and working conditions, but seven years later backtracked by making sex a determinant for tending bars.[51] Griffiths saw Title VII as the means to end all employment restrictions. The EEOC, reluctant to concede so far-reaching an interpretation, proposed guidelines for protective legislation deemed nondiscriminatory, which to Griffiths' thinking simply "rob[ed] Polly to pay Pauline."

What was more, the EEOC hesitated to pass judgment when it discovered protective enactments at variance with Title VII. Less ambivalent than the EEOC, Griffiths was elated when in 1968 the Los Angeles federal district court struck down the first protective law as being in conflict with the civil rights statute.[52] The following year, the EEOC strengthened its antidiscriminatory guidelines but, lacking enforcement authority, the agency continued to threaten no one. Coterminously, the Supreme Court struck down the policy of the South Central Bell Telephone Company excluding women as commercial representatives.[53] Bell's arguments that women might be exposed to danger and harrassment while traveling to their clients or be harmed by lifting 90-pound coin boxes greatly amused Griffiths. Who, she wondered, lugged infants around the house all day and who had to be ready for the everyday exigencies of homemaking? She therefore thought the Supreme Court progressive when it ruled against the utility, requiring that every job applicant be assessed on individual merit.[54]

Despite the technological explosion, the onslaught of civil rights legislation, and the momentum of the women's movement, restrictive legislation continued to linger on the books throughout the 60s. Advocates for retention, particularly among labor leaders, argued that without protection, all women, including the few who were organized, would be returned to the Dark Ages.

For their part, anti-protectionists like Griffiths and the proponents of an equal rights amendment were convinced from their reading of history that as long as legal distinctions were tolerated, discrimination would continue. Given this impasse, women's rights supporters began to consider other strategies to activate their goals.

The weaknesses of the EEOC, as evidenced by a succession of three chairpersons in two years, prompted concerned women to take charge of their own lives and in 1968 they founded the Women's Equity Action League (WEAL) to remedy sex-biased inequities in education, employment, and taxation. For some time Griffiths had advanced such a coordinating body on the basis that challenging the system was beyond the human and material resources of individual persons and groups. In early spring 1968, Elizabeth Boyer, special counsel to the Attorney General of Ohio, suggested that NOW set up a legal unit. Griffiths, however, advised an independent association, fearing that NOW's recently proclaimed pro-abortion stand would alienate a large number of women. Accordingly, Boyer changed her strategy and invited several professionals to Cleveland in March to what she dubbed her "Martha Griffiths' Meeting." Griffiths not only provided the content for the session but also, encouraging the participants, explained why it took a "major miracle" to get such an endeavor going. She told them that some very professional women were afraid to take a public stand on women's rights lest they be laughed at, be called feminists, or, what was worse, lose their jobs. By summer—and despite an apparently timorous beginning—Boyer wrote Griffiths that because of "the impact of your appearance here [in March]. . . we seem to be off with a bang."55 In November WEAL incorporated, Griffiths serving on the first advisory board. Once over its initial hurdle, WEAL established itself as an effective women's legal rights organization.

Though efforts such as WEAL claimed Griffiths' time, she continued to focus steadfastly on the lawmaking process. Since her JEC pension-study days, she had been concerned about the difference of treatment for men and women in private retirement plans. The 1964 Civil Rights Act and Johnson's 1967 Executive order barring sex discrimination in federal contracts provided Griffiths leverage for attacking pension distinctions in age, vesting, rates, and survivor benefits. The principle she enunciated was that women wanted to be the legal equals of men, even if it meant surrendering the few privileges they ostensibly had, such as earlier retirement than men. But the struggle for equality was slow and often unrewarding.

In February 1968 the EEOC issued guidelines forbidding sex-based differences in optional and mandatory retirement ages. On hearing this, Senator Everett Dirksen of Illinois proposed to amend a pending tax bill so that women could retire at an earlier age than men. (Senator Javits proposed a similar amendment to the Civil Rights Act.) Indiana's Vance Hartke and Michigan's Philip Hart led the Senate fight against what Louisiana's Russell Long styled "the Dirksen-chivalry-for-ladies-is-not-dead amendment."[56] Armed with Griffiths' legal analysis, Hartke argued that the Illinoisan's proposal emasculated Title VII and that, despite its apparent beneficence, the age differential gave industry the excuse for forcing women out of the labor market. Dirksen justified his move against the EEOC guidelines on a colloquy held between Senators Hubert Humphrey and Jennings Randolph during the Title VII debates which seemed to indicate that pensions were exempt from the sex provision. Despite the problematic weight of this earlier conversation, Hartke and Hart could prevail on only ten senators to support their opposing view. One, William Proxmire, wrote Griffiths shortly after the vote explaining why he had joined the minority. "First," he noted, "you had alerted me to the significance of this amendment; and, secondly, in the years we have spent on the Joint Economic Committee together, you have educated me on the injustices of sex discrimination."[57] Fortunately for Griffiths, the tax bill and its amendment died with the adjournment of the Ninetieth Congress.

The issue, however, was not dead. In 1970 Michigan Representative Marvin L. Esch attempted to amend Title VII by a comprehensive package of sex-based pension distinctions. Aroused, Griffiths argued that the amendment directly violated Title VII, that it was not needed as evidenced by the overwhelming percentage of pension plans without sex discriminations, and that it was not supported by the largest women's organizations that traditionally championed their working sisters. Finally she pleaded with Congress to be done with the "adult child" myth.[58] The bill incorporating the Esch Amendment never got out of the Rules Committee; but, if it had, Carl D. Perkins, Chairperson of the House Committee on Education and Labor, assured Griffiths that, having made her case, his Committee would have fought to excise the discriminatory proposal.[59] ERISA did much to equalize benefits between the sexes, although it still excluded from survivorship rights husbands who could not prove dependency. By the mid-70s Griffiths looked to the ERA as the only strategy that would eliminate sex distinctions all together.

While she spent a good deal of her energy fighting sex bias in the workplace, Griffiths was concerned that sex distinctions be eliminated wherever they existed. Accordingly, she asked the House to require from its standing committees a full investigation of the status of women in all the laws and regulations under their respective jurisdictions.[60] She further pressed the FBI to admit women as special agents and protested to the Attorney General sex-segregation in the public schools.[61] Angered by sex disparities in criminal justice and by the lack of benefit equity for federal women employees, she moved systematically and persistently for changes in the law.

Griffiths was particularly agitated to discover that some jurisdictions applied criminal law differently because of sex. Instances of this included the policy of trying girls as adults at a younger age than boys in some of the states where girls were accorded their majority status earlier. Disconcerting, too, was the practice of meting out longer sentences to women than to men guilty of the same crime on the grounds that women, being more malleable than men, would benefit by a more extended period of rehabilitation. Griffiths termed the reasons behind these legal differences as "pure witchcraft, a belief that women—like Eve—are responsible for any evil that befalls. Has any real guilt," she asked, "ever been attached to Adam for being such a fool?"[62] In 1968 Griffiths joined the other women of Congress as amicus curiae protesting a Connecticut statute that mandated more stringent punishment for women than for men. In their brief these lawmakers noted that as "a special class" they had "a special duty" to speak out where women were discriminated against solely because they were women.[63]

Another area of criminal justice where sex made a difference was in the selection of state jurors.[64] In <u>Hoyt v. Florida</u> (1961), the Supreme Court held that Florida's automatic exemption of women from jury duty, unless they registered for that service, did not violate the Fourteenth Amendment.[65] Based on the argument that a woman's primary place was in the home, the decision elicited a strong protest from Griffiths. The Court, she said, "protected the dream—the child-bearing duty of women—to the exclusion of all other duties of women as citizens and . . . as defenders. If the theory of Hoyt vs. Florida were carried to its true logical conclusion, . . . trial by jury would be outmoded. . . . We would doubtless go back to trial by fire or trial by water," she pointed out cynically.[66]

In 1966 Griffiths and New Jersey Congresswoman Florence Dwyer successfully prevailed on the House to include in a pending civil rights bill a provision outlawing sex-based distinctions in the selection of state jurors. The measure unfortunately died in the Senate. In testifying before the Senate civil rights subcommittee, Griffiths emphasized that had the Supreme Court applied the Fifth and Fourteenth Amendments to women, the issue would have been resolved years ago. The Court's failure more than ever underscored the need for an equal rights amendment which would bring all persons under the Constitution.[67] She also sought to include sex discrimination within the jurisdiction of the Civil Rights Commission, regretting that this had not been done by the 1964 Civil Rights Act.[68] Her goal was realized in 1972 when Congress empowered the Commission to review all federal laws and policies regarding sex bias and report its findings to both the President and Congress.

While working to bring women within the whole gamut of civil rights, Griffiths took up the fight for federally employed women, including those in the foreign and armed services. As a civil servant her interest was a natural one. But she did not get into the enormity of the inequities, particularly those facing married women, until she began to look at the Social Security program. She then investigated the civil service pension fund into which she had been paying to discover that if she dropped dead her husband, unless dependent on her, would get only what she had contributed. Were she a man—say an independently wealthy Senator—her spouse would receive full survivor benefits. "I think you do not understand that I am paying the same amount of money for a lesser pension right now than you are paying," she informed John W. Macy Jr., Chairperson of the Civil Service Commission, and she asked him what he intended to do about it.[69] The response was always the same, to her and to the many women she had induced to besiege the Commission. "In our society the husband is the provider," wrote a Commission official to one of the enquirers.[70]

Griffiths held to the notion that the so-called fringe benefits accompanying a base salary—survivorship annuities, overseas quarters allowances, veterans pensions—were really compensation and thus came under the principle of equal pay for equal work.71 Moreover, she could find no justification in requiring more education from a female air force applicant than for a male applicant, nor could she see the reason why women with children were not accepted for overseas employment or why women air force officers were disallowed the custody of their children for more than thirty days a year. "The Federal Government should be the fairest employer of all," Griffiths told President Johnson in a private interview in 1967. "And," she lamented, "the truth is that it is probably the least fair." On behalf of all federal workers, she asked Johnson to press Congress for an equity statute.72

Because of their minority status, women in the armed forces were particularly vulnerable to discriminatory practices. From the moment they applied for service, more was required of them than of men; but, once enrolled, military women received less than men.73 For example, they had no overseas quarters allowance or transportation for their spouses and children, no free medical and dental care or commissary privileges for their spouses, and no free schooling for their children. Likewise, only dependent husbands were covered by the survivor annuity. Women veterans, moreover, were not eligible for the same educational assistance as men veterans and, if they were married, their spouses did not have the benefits available to those of male veterans.

Through persistence Griffiths saw changes effected to the benefit of federally employed women. In January 1971, Nixon signed a survivor-annuity bill for all civil service personnel. Two factors in particular had helped remedy what Griffiths considered as "the most inequitable practice of the pension system."74 First, the men in Congress had awakened to the realization that under the prevailing system other _men_ were being deprived survivorship privileges. Second, members of Congress were shamed into granting full pension rights to women civil servants, especially their colleagues, once they passed the so-called "widowers' bill" that gave retirement benefits to the women who married widowed, retired Congressmen.75

In December Congress amended the Civil Service code

to equalize treatment for all families of civil service employees. Included in the act were veterans preference employment benefits for the spouses of deceased and disabled veterans. Also enacted on behalf of government workers stationed abroad was a separate maintenance allowance for their spouses and children who continued to reside in the United States.[76] The previous August, the State Department had changed its placement regulations to apply equally to men and women, and, in cases where both spouses were members of the foreign service, the Department pledged to do what it could to assign them to the same location. Furthermore, a woman was permitted to take her husband, children and/or dependents abroad without losing her career choices.

Passage of the Equal Employment Opportunity Act of 1972 capped the drive for legal equity for the nation's female civil servants. In giving substance to the governmental drive against sex discrimination, the law made it possible for women to seek redress in the federal courts. That same year Congress adjusted the veterans educational assistance to include women and in 1973 enacted an equality of treatment bill for all married military personnel, their spouses, and their children.[77]

Although it might have been social enlightenment that brought the lawmakers along, throughout 1973 a suit was pending before the Supreme Court testing the dependency qualification for husbands of women serving in the armed forces. In the spring, four of the Justices held that Joseph Frontiero was a presumptive dependent of his wife, Air Force Lieutenant Sharron Frontiero, and was therefore eligible for the same benefits and privileges as the wives of male personnel. Griffiths was delighted with the decision but disturbed that three of the other Justices had begged off rendering an opinion pending the ratification of the ERA. "Are they waiting for the people to vote on how to interpret the Constitution?" she asked. Nevertheless, the implications of the case did not escape her. <u>Frontiero v. Richardson</u> was "a clear bell ringing in quiet air, . . . a summons to legislatures to step into the 20th century." She regretted that women had to bring case after case to secure their rights. But she was sure they would do it.[78]

At the time Griffiths worked to effect sex equality among governmental agencies outside of Congress, she fought for changes within. Joining Ways and Means during the civil rights decade, she was particularly attuned to discriminatory practices in the Social Security system. Without her persistent intervention on that issue during that critical juncture, American women would not have had a voice in security-benefit legislation.[79] Not all of Griffiths' colleagues were calloused —they were not—but nearly all tended to read the law from a man's point of view. Griffiths' review of Social Security revealed how stacked it was against all women, especially working women.[80] She also saw how Social Security distinctions adversely influenced other legislation. For example, one of the strongest arguments supporting gender distinctions in private pension systems was that Social Security had them.

Griffiths' attack on the discriminatory features of Social Security did at least three things. First, it provided the environment for amendatory legislation. Second, it eventually aroused both Congress and the Executive branch to deal in some depth with sex-based inequities. And third, it won for Griffiths a name as a recognized authority on the Social Security system. She often noted humorously that all it took to become an expert on anything in Ways and Means was to have persevered through committee meetings.[81] The truth was she always did her homework.

Underlying the seeming immutability of Social Security enactments was the attitude that the man was the "primary worker," despite the fact that by the mid-60s women comprised nearly 40 percent of the labor force. Griffiths believed that as long as lawmakers and bureaucrats refused to recognize how socio-economic changes, like rising divorce rates and accelerating inflation affected income patterns, there could be little hope of revising the law. In her many debates on this issue she often made her point by asking the men to define "a primary worker." She had already arrived at her own definition. "Since most women are working for money to supply the necessities of life or to assist in educating their children," she said, "it would certainly be more realistic to define a primary worker as the one whose salary paid the grocery bill, bought the childrens' books and clothes; and a secondary worker as the one whose salary paid for the outboard motor, the fishing tackle, the booze . . . . As a rose is a rose is a rose, a worker is a worker and should receive exactly the same consideration as any other worker." Griffiths was also quick to point out that in many instances the primary worker and _her_ family were among the nation's poorest.[82]

Griffiths anguished most over the Social Security

inequities of working women.[83] The vagaries of the law often resulted in higher retirement and widowhood benefits for homemakers since they could draw on their spouses' Social Security. In contrast, the working wife, frequently employed in a low-paying job to supplement her husband's inadequate salary, had to choose between her own Social Security benefits or her husband's, but could not have both. Griffiths thought it basically unjust that a federally legislated retirement system should allow greater coverage for a one-earner family than one in which both spouses paid into the pension fund.

The Social Security law was not only inimical to a working wife's retirement income and widow's benefits but drastically limited earned survivorship rights. There was no insurance for a self-sufficient husband nor mother's benefits for children unless the deceased was in the work force within a year and a half of death. In contrast, a man's annuity contained no tests whatever.

Lack of benefit guarantees for single women—the unmarried, widowed, separated, and divorced—were especially unfair since single women were among the nation's poorest. Because of the family-benefit concept, the unmarried, who were often responsible for the care of aged parents, paid high Social Security taxes along with steep income taxes. When they worked or remarried, widows lost their survivor benefits, a particular hardship on young widows with children. Young families with retired fathers also suffered the diminution of benefits when the mothers worked. Freedom from the conjugal bond left many older divorcees destitute since the law did not assure the benefits they had accumulated through their former spouses' Social Security. It was the bitterest of legal ironies that a remarried husband could endow his new bride with the anticipated retirement income of a spouse who had kept his home and family for twenty, thirty, even forty years.

Because of Griffiths' influence, Congress amended the Social Security Act in 1965 to provide wife's and widow's benefits to a divorcee who had been married twenty years to her former husband. Without Griffiths' knowledge, however, a dependency test was added requiring that the divorcee receive at least half of her support from her former husband.[84] In 1972 Griffiths succeeded in removing this qualification which she was convinced restricted benefits to only those wealthy enough to hire an attorney at the time of their divorce. She surprised many later when she did not join in efforts to lower to ten years the twenty-year guarantee of benefits. For her the issue had been to assist middle-aged women who lacked marketable skills because they had spent their lives caring for their families. Conversely, it was not to her liking that working women be taxed to support young, employable divorcees.[85] In 1967 Congress enacted another Social Security amendment that Griffiths had advocated for years: automatic survivor rights to minor children of deceased working mothers; eight years later the Supreme Court guaranteed the same benefits to widowers.[86]

The inequities against working women which Griffiths decried most was the double tax on working couples. Two-earner families paid more income taxes than one-earner families and, after 1968, more than two singles. They also received less from their Social Security contributions because a working wife had to renounce her own Social Security benefits in claiming her wife's benefits. Even before Griffiths joined Ways and Means she recognized this problem,[87] and, once on the Committee, labored doggedly to correct it. She would have working spouses draw on their combined Social Security credits thereby providing the couple as much income as if they were a one-earner family.[88] While many could not fault her analysis, they disagreed with her solution which would have cost about a billion dollars in 1965.[89] Griffiths, however, argued that savings could be made by cutting extraneous Social Security programs like college education for the children of deceased retirees and benefits for dependent grandchildren.[90] In her opinion the issue was not money but justice, and she was waiting for a "smart" Supreme Court to strike down the law as violating the equal protection clause of the Constitution.[91]

At times Griffiths admitted frustration in her attempts to achieve economic equity for working women. She told a Senate committee in 1975 that her arguments fell "on mighty deaf ears."[92] But she had planted the seed of change. Three years after she left Congress, a HEW task force was set up to review the treatment of women under Social Security. The group was specifically charged to recommend solutions: first, to the benefit disparities between one-earner and two-earner families and their surviving spouses; second, to the inequities affecting singles and homemakers and; third, to the gender-based differences still encumbering the law.[93]

In her optimistic moments, Griffiths predicted that

by the twenty-first century Social Security would be freed of all distinctions (the ERA would wipe them away) and every member of a family would be insured: workers—men and women—by their retirement contributions; traditional wives by a homemaker's guarantee, an idea proposed in 1974 by Griffiths and Texas Representative Barbara Jordan;[94] and children by support from both parents. She foresaw that changing family roles would bring about a greater appreciation for every person's work—whether in the home or outside of it, whether performed by men or by women. "It is really a world that has existed for a long time, but now the law will recognize that world. It will be a world," she told a gathering of corporate managers, "with a little more justice for everybody."[95]

In the struggle for universal equality, Griffiths often said that the promise would be realized the day the Supreme Court acknowledged that a woman deserved the protection of law simply because she was human.[96] Despite the many gains made by women in the fifty years since the Nineteenth Amendment, the equal rights "fact" was at best ambiguous. State and federal courts could not agree whether or not the Fourteenth Amendment prohibited the exclusion of women from certain occupations or state-supported universities. The courts equivocated over the right of women to sue for consortium or to be served at bars. Confusion reigned over the legality of school-board regulations forbidding women to teach during pregnancy and there was as yet no consensus on sex-based differences in laws governing the selection of state jurors.

Despite Title VII, fair employment for women also remained problematic since only one case was filed in the first five years of the EEOC and it did not address the constitutional issue. Sexism in credit and insurance was so pervasive that most persons did not see injustice in the fact that in these areas women were not recognized as Social Security contributors, civil servants, and military personnel. In sum, as the United States approached its bicentenary, the legal status of women was still part of the nation's unfinished business.

It was not that efforts had not been made. Since 1923 an equal rights amendment (ERA) had been before Congress annually, and by 1945 both political parties had endorsed it. In 1950 and 1953 it passed the Senate and did so again in 1960 when it died upon being returned to committee. The ERA had never been presented to the full House, however, until Martha Griffiths accomplished this feat in 1970.

The contemporary equal rights movement, like its nineteenth century predecessor, aroused controversy from its inception. Suffragettes themselves were split between those who believed in working through the states and those, who, like Alice Paul's National Women's Party, looked to Congress for the advancement of their cause. In 1923, buoyed up by recent enfranchisement, the NWP introduced the so-called Lucretia Mott Amendment. Opposition outside suffragette ranks immediately centered on the contention that the ERA was anti-American. A minority of the Senate Judiciary Committee conducting the first hearings on the amendment charged that it was "another long step toward totalitarianism" and a later critic warned that it "could bring this nation to the brink of hell." Who, he asked, would dare utter those twenty-four "terrifying" words: "Equality of rights under the law shall not be denied or abridged by the United States or by any state on account of sex?" 97

Although she has been called the "Mother of the ERA," and although the ERA had been dubbed by former President Ford, "a monument to Martha,"98 Griffiths initially felt that the best way to bring women within the comprehension of the Fourteenth Amendment was through the Supreme Court rather than by a constitutional amendment.99 Yet, as an earnest Democrat, she supported the ERA from her earliest days in politics. In her first successful Congressional campaign she went on record as being "unequivocally" for passage, and beginning with her second term, she introduced the ERA resolution with each succeeding Congress.100 Coming to the conclusion by the mid-60s that the Supreme Court was immovable on women's rights, she became one of ERA's most important exponents, if not its chief sponsor.101 From the outset Griffiths emphasized that ERA's one aim was to bring women under the protection of the law. Holding fast to this goal, she never allowed herself to be sidetracked by secondary issues such as abortion.

As the fiftieth anniversary of women's suffrage approached, enthusiasm for the ERA mounted. In asking Griffiths to sponsor the amendment in 1969, NWP President Emma Guffey Miller noted optimistically that the cause was "growing daily." She estimated that 71 Senators and over 200 members of the House would back the proposal.102 Having concentrated all its energies on Congress, however, the NWP had not kept pace with other legislative developments affecting women nor had it done anything significant toward educating the public to the issues.103 Griffiths was sure she would need more than NWP backing to convince Emmanuel Celler, Chairperson of the House Judiciary Committee, that he should put the ERA on the floor after having kept it bottled up for nearly fifty years.

Meanwhile, the President's Task Force on Women's Rights and Responsibilities, headed by Michigan Business Executive Virginia Allan, recommended that the amendment be discharged from the Judiciary Committee, a procedure requiring 218 signatures. Subsequently, two of Allan's close associates converged on Griffiths: Catherine East, Executive Secretary of the Citizens' Advisory Council on the Status of Women, and Washington Attorney Marguerite Rawalt who had just retired from the President's Commission on the Status of Women and the Citizens' Advisory Council. The three women agreed that Griffiths was to secure a hearing from Celler, and if that failed, she should then file a discharge petition.104

Griffiths' personal resolve was prompted by the sober realization that it would take the courts two hundred years to grant legal equity to women. In 1961 the Supreme Court had ruled that sex was a reasonable classification for relieving women of jury duty; yet, five years later a federal district court struck down an Alabama statute banning women as jurors.105 In 1969 the Fifth Circuit Court of Appeals ruled that refusing to hire mothers with preschool children was not unconstitutional, a case so blatantly in violation of the 1964 Civil Rights Act that the Justice Department urged the Supreme Court to hear it.106 Further, it seemed as though no amount of prodding could move the Court to review the sex-based distinctions in Social Security or the tax differentials affecting so many women, especially the single and widowed. "It is Supreme Court decisions that have made us 'unequal,'" Griffiths noted with feeling.107

In early May 1970, Senator Birch E. Bayh, Chairperson of the Subcommittee on Constitutional Amendments, pledged to the Business and Professional Women, of which Allan and Rawalt were past presidents, that he would sponsor the ERA in the Senate and call for hearings.108 The renewed Senate activity revived Griffiths' hopes that something might be done in the House. Testifying before Bayh's Subcommittee, she spoke of the Court's ambivalence on equal rights and pointed out that an amendment would awaken "the nine sleeping Rip Van Winkles" to a fast approaching twenty-first century. She underscored the debilitating effects that discrimination had on women and their families. Speaking for all the women of Congress and working women in general, she said she was tired of supporting non-working wives and rich widows. She looked to the ERA to rationalize these inequities, although there would be "the usual snickering, the usual obscenities, and . . . a good many court cases." However difficult, the struggle was worth the candle. "I seek justice—not in some distant tomorrow, not by some study commission," she concluded, "but now while I live."[109]

Despite Griffiths' hope that Celler would take his cue from Bayh and summon up the ERA for consideration, the New Yorker intended to hold fast. Therefore as planned, on June 11 Griffiths delivered to the clerk of the House a petition to discharge the amendment from committee. It was "well past time," she said in presenting it, for both the Supreme Court and Emmanual Celler to face up to the modern world.[110]

Griffiths had her votes counted and her strategy in place. Many colleagues owed her support. Southerners in particular liked Griffiths as much as they disliked the czar of the Judiciary Committee.[111] Taking the advice of Pennsylvania Representative James A. Byrne that the best way she could get enough signatures for discharge was through personal contact, Griffiths applied the direct approach.[112] During each roll call she accompanied her colleagues to the well, an experience some could not forget. One recalled this experience years later:

> One day, (it was when she was getting near the number [of votes] she needed), . . . I was in the gallery with some guests from home and they said to me, 'Do men have to go down with that woman and sign something before they can vote?' I had not been paying attention, and I said, 'What do you mean?' They said, 'See that lady down there. She is taking those men down and having them sign something.' I watched for a few minutes and she must have taken ten members down, . . . almost by the ear and had them sign the ERA discharge petition.[113]

Midway through the signing, Griffiths received a tremendous boost from the 7,000 Business and Professional

Women meeting in Honolulu. Heartened by the prospect of the amendment's release from committee, the BPW put Marguerite Rawalt and Virginia Allan before the convention as "RA for ERA." Each night Griffiths called the two activists to let them know who had signed that day.[114] As a result, recalcitrant representatives were deluged with telegrams.

As the signatures edged toward 200, the stream of signers began to dry up. Reviewing the list carefully, Griffiths noted that the Democrats had outsigned the Republicans 3 to 1. According to her recollections five years after the event, she went to Gerald Ford, House Minority Leader, "and told him I felt sure I would get enough signers, and it would look very bad if there were not more Republicans." Ford recalled how "Martha came across the aisle . . . and sat down next to me and said, 'Jerry, we need 17 signers. I can't get my Democrats to do any more than what they are doing and I'm very disappointed. And unless we get some Republicans—more Republicans—we aren't going to get it on the floor.'"[115] Griffiths prevailed on Majority Whip Hale Boggs to sign as number 200 and Virginia Democrat John O. Marsh joined the 17 Republicans Ford had lined up to throw the petition over the top.

Barber Conable, one of those sitting with Ford the day Griffiths approached for more signatures, thought Ford's involvement in the discharge petition was neither generally known or understood. According to Ford, there was "no question" as to the importance of his intervention. He believed that without it the ERA would still be languishing in committee. For her part, Griffiths considered Ford's display of bipartisan friendship as "darn [sic] nice" as well as his offer to speak on the amendment when it reached the floor, "unless," he added, "you 'gals' object."[116]

Griffiths was "delirious with delight" over the progress she had made[117] but saved the jubilation until after the floor fight. She knew that while her supporters wished her well, few believed sixty minutes' deliberation could overcome forty-seven years of fruitless effort.[118] On August 5, Griffiths notified her colleagues in an "I-need-you. Justice-needs-you" letter that on August 10 she would seek to discharge the ERA from committee and, if successful, would immediately call for debate on the resolution itself.[119]

In an overwhelming 332 to 22 vote, the petition

passed, Celler pledging a final attack on the floor despite Griffiths' intention of directing the discussion to the advocates.[120] Celler's primary argument, reminiscent of the 1964 Civil Rights debates, was that nature created unalterable sexual distinctions which the law could not obliterate. "Neither the National Women's Party nor the delightful, delectable and dedicated gentlelady from Michigan can change nature," he insisted. "There is as much difference between a male and a female as between a horse chestnut and a chestnut horse—and as the French say, Vive la différence." His plea for time and a reworked statement brought Ford to his feet who said he was looking forward to conferring the full privileges of citizenship on his wife. Ford likewise told Celler that an equal rights amendment was mandatory in an enlightened age and had Celler wanted a better worded resolution he had had twenty years in which to draft one. Celler held his ground calling the ERA a "blunderbuss amendment," a favorite phrase with the opposition. He warned the House not to be deceived by ERA's apparent simplicity which was, he said, a web to ensnare Congress in domestic and marital relationships of all kinds.

The amendment's proponents, less colorful perhaps than the head of the Judiciary Committee, were no less firm. Speaker McCormack and Majority Leader Carl Albert insisted that the intent of the law was not to change nature but to change oppressive conditions like discrimination. Black Representative Shirley Chisholm noted that sex bias was the worst prejudice of all; for black women it cut two ways. Griffiths reiterated her argument that the real enemy of legal equity was the Supreme Court. Paraphrasing Sojourner Truth she asked, "'Ain't I a person'"? In Griffiths' reference both the <u>Washington Post</u> and the <u>Evening Star</u> caught the subtle but central issue of the ERA. "Actually the amendment doesn't mention women," observed the <u>Evening Star</u>, "it is a marvel of brevity guaranteeing equality for <u>both</u> women and men. This is all there is to it."[121]

In a last-ditch effort, House foes tried to recommit the bill to Celler's Committee. Joining the handful of 26, were Michigan Representatives John D. Dingell and Lucien Nedzi who maintained that the amendment was "mischievous" (another favorite term of ERA opponents), because it would undermine family relations and destroy the positive effects of protective legislation.[122] In a resounding affirmation, the House passed the ERA 350 to 15 (64 not voting). For the great majority of women leaders everywhere, August 10, 1970, was a red-letter day. That evening Griffiths dined at the National Lawyers Club with Marguerite Rawalt and a group of longstanding friends. When they entered the foyer, they playfully turned William Blackstone's bust to the wall.[123]

The victory dinner should really have been a rally of warriors preparing for battle. Even before the ink was dry on the House Journal, Sam J. Ervin Jr., was preparing his case for the Senate—aided by the AFL-CIO, several influential newspapers, and Professor Paul A. Freund of the Harvard Law School, who warned that the amendment, while noble in concept, would work "mischief" in application.[124] In a lengthy letter dated August 15, Ervin asked his colleagues to share his distress on three counts over the House's version of the ERA. First, it would nullify Congressional enactments exempting women from compulsory military service. Second, it would strike down state protective legislation such as minimum wage provisos for women. Finally, it would invalidate laws guaranteeing privacy to women. (Griffiths called this the "potty argument.") Common sense and tradition, the North Carolinian contended, recognized a sex-based classification when it was natural, reasonable, and favorable to women. He therefore proposed a substitute amendment with the goal of preserving the right of Congress and state legislatures over current and future protective enactments. He recommended, likewise, that the substitute be implemented within two years and ratified within seven.[125]

The Ervin amendment and subsequent Senate hearings touched off a vigorous debate. Griffiths found herself continually defending the House bill against conservatives who looked upon the ERA as "the contrivance of a gang of professional harpies." Opposition was upsetting and discouraging. "When it comes to prejudice," Griffiths told the American Bar Association in 1974, "nothing can beat the debates on the equal rights amendment."[126] Previously committed Senators began to change their minds; Ervin bombarded the September hearings with anti-ERA testimony; and in October, the Senate tacked the school-prayer amendment onto the ERA, a maneuver which Amendments Chairperson Bayh considered "a rather harsh blow" and the Washington Post, an "unprincipled act."[127] Griffiths meanwhile publicly kept her poise.

She repeatedly told opponents that the ERA had but one end: to bring women under the equal protection of law.[128] "The intent of the bill," she wrote in the fall of 1971:

> is to give women the same protection under the
> Constitution of the United States that men now
> have, and that has been gained by all other
> minority groups. Among other things, it would
> give a working wife's husband & her survivors
> the same right to draw on Social Security that
> a man's wife and his survivors now have. In
> community property States, it would give the
> wife the same control of the community property
> that the man now has. It would permit the
> court to decide the custody of children in all
> States. It would require that the marriageable
> age be the same for both boys and girls. It
> would prohibit any arm of the Government from
> making one law for men and another for women.
> In almost all instances such laws have worked
> to the women's disadvantage.[129]

While Griffiths held to a factual discussion of the ERA, Ervin suffused the debate with emotional rhetoric. He called attention to the House approach as a "self-defeating blunderbuss" and praised the Court for excluding women from jury duty. "An ounce of mother," he said, quoting a Spanish proverb, "is worth a pound of priest." On compulsory draft for women he lamented, "Father, forgive them . . . ." If the ERA was what Griffiths and the "militant" said it was, then he argued the constitutional rights "of millions and millions of women and millions and millions of little girls " stood in the balance.[130] While progress on the ERA ground to a halt, Griffiths set in motion an idea she had had since 1967 for a national legal women's defense system. She had come to the conclusion that individual women and small women's groups could not legally make their influence felt. A central legal staff that had the backing of several women's organizations could pursue every worthwhile sex discrimination case in the courts with greater hope that the law would eventually change.[131]

If Griffiths was dismayed by Senate reaction to the amendment, Bayh was equally embarrassed in having failed to harness pro-ERA sentiment. To save the amendment from total defeat, he and Marlow W. Cook of Kentucky offered a compromise in October that consisted principally in adding "sex" to the equal protection clause of the Fourteenth Amendment. Bayh contended that the new version would achieve legal equity for women and accomplish what the ERA proponents had in mind. He also argued that his measure retained the essential symbolic character of an equal rights bill.[132] Among those joining their Hoosier brother were Jacob Javits, Edward Kennedy, Robert Dole, and Robert P. Griffin.

Reaction was swift and decisive. Leading women's groups—WEAL, NOW, NWP, the National Federation of Republican Women, the Citizen's Advisory Council on the Status of Women, to name a few—were unwilling to accept anything short of the Griffiths' amendment.[133] They charged that Bayh's proposal not only would not achieve their goals but would actually impede their cause by acknowledging that the Fourteenth Amendment did not apply to women. Moreover, the use of Fourteenth Amendmend language—albeit a partial use—confirmed sex as a reasonable classification for legal distinctions, which was precisely how the Supreme Court had interpreted the equal protection clause for nearly two centuries. As one of Griffiths' assistants expressed it: "The Bayh amendment has not ended the battle, but merely changed the battlefield."[134] A number of ERA advocates also believed that, since a total revision would never pass Congress at the eleventh hour, it would be carried over to the next session to complicate the debate for those wedded to the Griffiths' bill.

Intent on pleasing the ERA proponents, Bayh announced that, although he did not see how his bill had in any way licensed the courts to uphold sex-based distinctions in the law, he would modify his resolution to incorporate the explicit language of the Constitution's due process and the privileges and immunities clauses.[135] ERA supporters informed the Senator that this substitute was no better than his first and therefore of little value to their cause. Surprised by this resistance, Bayh offered to meet with the women after the elections toward reconciling differences because, as he told Congress, he did not wish Griffiths' efforts to "go for naught."[136]

When the heads of thirteen organizations later met at Bayh's invitation, they told the Senator that his proposal continued to enshrine the reasonable classification doctrine. Marguerite Rewalt, spokesperson for the gathering, pointed out that legislative history had a greater bearing on judicial interpretation than Congressional intent. As each group presented its arguments against the substitute, the Senator became convinced he should drop it.[137]

Before they disbanded, the women asked Rawalt to explore the possibility of maintaining the organization liaison developed over the preceding weeks. A clearinghouse would be absolutely essential for the future. In May 1971 this project came to fruition when Griffiths urged Rawalt, Washington Attorney Margaret Lawrence, and syndicated writer Sara Booth Conroy to form a coalition that would both lobby for the ERA and administer the women's legal defense fund.[138] Women United was born. In the year and a half before passage of the ERA, Chairperson Lawrence and Vice Chairperson Rawalt worked feverishly to keep organizational leadership daily apprized of legislative progress. To this end, they frequently conferred with Griffiths on the best information to convey to the thousands of organized women they represented. When Women United dissolved in August 1972, the ERA Ratification Council took its place and in turn helped organize ERAmerica, ERA's national fund-raising and public relations effort.

Abandonment of the Bayh substitute marked the end of Congressional action on the ERA for 1970. Where had the debate gone wrong? <u>The Wall Street Journal</u> thought the answer was that the Senate had no Martha Griffiths.[139] Griffiths, however, blamed the women's groups themselves for assuming in an election year that the eighty-two Senators who had pledged their word would keep it. "When the moment of truth arrived," she observed, "Senators refused to vote for their own measure, caving in to the pressure of friends and betraying the trust which women's organizations had placed in them. . . . How phony can you get?" Moreover, organized women had not reckoned with strongly entrenched antagonists like some union chiefs affiliated with the AFL-CIO. The lesson to be learned for the future was that there could be no letting up until the ERA passed.[140]

The discharge petition, nevertheless, had afforded Griffiths too much hope to imagine that the cause would not eventually triumph. Because of that, she could banter about what had already transpired. In addressing the Gridiron Club in late November—the first woman to do so—she pointed out that when she had debated the ERA in the House, she realized "how Eve must have felt in the Garden of Eden surrounded by men, serpents, and apples." In the Senate the amendment "got about as much support as our braless young women liberationists," she quipped. Was she going to give up? By no means. The country owed it to "our foremothers" to see to it that the ERA became part of the Constitution. "Look at

Betsy Ross. She created our flag, but . . . neglected to take out a patent on it, and now it's been stolen by Spiro Agnew and the hardhats." Finally, she wanted to set the record straight about rumored arm-twisting during the signing of the discharge petition. "What's a scratch or two among friends?" she asked. "And no matter what you have heard, there will not be 14 new majority leaders. Oh! Promises, promises. Only votes count."[141] She was right: in the showdown only votes counted.

To secure the votes, Griffiths reintroduced the ERA in January 1971 with what she considered two "minor technical" changes borrowed from the Bayh and Ervin amendments: a seven-year ratification period and the extension of the effective date to two years after ratification.[142] When introducing the same measure in the Senate for himself and Cook, Bayh stressed ERA's symbolic value and refuted the contentious anti-ERA arguments pertaining to compulsory draft, domestic relations, and protective legislation.[143] Throughout the year, however, the Senate made little headway on the equal rights issue. Ervin filibustered the proposal and the Rules Committee refused Bayh's request to bypass the Judiciary Committee and place the bill directly on the floor. To show their further displeasure with their colleague's efforts, the Senate struck Bayh's anti-discrimination amendment from the Higher Education Act.[144] One had to look to the House in 1971 for progress.

In March and April, that body held its first hearings on the ERA since 1948. Griffiths was star witness. She told the Judiciary subcommittee that the Supreme Court had proved itself "a very poor legislator" in having forced numerous underpaid women to spend unconscionable sums in suing for their rights—and without a single success. The Court also did not know its own mind. How, for example, could it simultaneously uphold one law that gave a man precedence over a woman as administrator of the estate of an intestate and another that denied a natural father custody rights to his illegitimate children.[145] The Court, moreover, showed itself impervious to social change in continuing to countenance sex distinctions in jury duty, in admission to state-supported universities, and in school attendance of unwed mothers.[146]

How could the Court, she queried further, tolerate Social Security dependency tests and IRS category-based exemptions? Why did it never question discriminatory federal housing regulations, the exclusion of women as FBI agents, and higher admission standards for women entering the armed forces? In sum, how could this be called a system of justice as long as the law remained arbitrary and ambivalent?

Griffiths also had something to say regarding misconceptions raised about implementing the ERA. Of necessity, she pointed out, it would have to harmonize with other constitutional rights such as privacy. All sex-based statutes would be subject to judicial review, but, according to established procedure, the Court would invalidate only that portion of a law which violated the Constitution. Most likely the Court would require that gender-based provisions apply universally. Griffiths also noted that under certain rare circumstances sex was a reasonable basis for distinction "because there is not anything else you can do about it." Her point was that to date the Court had treated the exception as the rule.[147]

Griffiths' testimony and private conversations with Don Edwards so inspired the chairperson of the House ERA subcommittee that, despite Celler's displeasure, he brought a substantial majority of his membership to join him in supporting the original bill.[148] The full Judiciary Committee, however, was less inclined to pass the ERA unencumbered. Accordingly, a rider to exempt women from the draft and preserve state protective laws was introduced by Edwards' California associate, Charles E. Wiggins. Wiggins had incurred Griffiths' wrath during the previous hearings when he suggested that her bill would require the same license fee for a bitch as for a dog.[149] The Committee voted down the rider only to have Jack Brooks reintroduce it with a slight modification. Edwards objected, but Celler overruled the point of order to allow the Committee to approve the Wiggins amendment 19 to 16.

These events set the stage for a new battle. With Women United established and functioning, Griffiths scoured the country in the spring and summer of 1971, making four or five speeches a week. She asked her audiences to flood their representatives with mail and she requested all women state legislators to review the laws and regulations of their respective states for overt and hidden discrimination.[150] Meanwhile, the sixteen members of the House Judiciary Committee who had voted against the Wiggins amendment urged their colleagues not to "soil [the ERA] by qualification." As they had noted in the committee report: "The Equal Rights Amendment as proposed by Mrs. Griffiths embodies a moral value judgment that a legal right or obligation should not depend upon sex."[151]

In the final month before the floor debate, a flurry of ERA literature inundated Capitol Hill. With the collaboration of the BPW, Griffiths distributed a 14-page article from the Yale Law Journal, that Celler and ranking minority member William M. McCulloch seized as evidence of ERA's mischief. "'Equality' means absolute sameness, identical treatment in all cases," they wrote their colleagues in rebuttal. Even with the Wiggins' safeguard, they intended to vote against the amendment because it gave little thought to women as mothers. "As far as I know," affirmed Celler, "the Fallopian tube has not become vestigial."[152]

Fortunately for ERA advocates, the Wiggins' people had not maneuvered a clean bill from committee. To have left the rider for floor debate and possible excision from the main proposal was "pretty dumb," according to Edwards. "[We] defeated Wiggins overwhelmingly," he mused. "We all stood at doors. . . . Martha stood at one door and I stayed at another and said, 'Vote No! Vote No! Vote No!' And we won very nicely and, then of course, got more than two-thirds."[153] On Columbus Day, the House rejected the rider 265 to 87 and passed the Griffiths' resolution by 354 to 23 votes, 4 more than the previous year.

The following month, women won their first case under the Fourteenth Amendment when the Supreme Court invalidated an Idaho statute preferring a man over a woman as executor of the estate of an intestate.[154] Griffiths was only moderately pleased, however. The decision, rendered on very narrow procedural grounds rather than on the constitutionality of a sex-based classification, did not obviate the need for other burdensome proceedings. In Griffiths' opinion, the Supreme Court continued to be "a bottleneck" for women's rights. "They're just nine old idiots," the Washington Post reported her as saying.[155] She therefore applauded the Court when finally, in 1975, it struck from the books every state law that treated men and women differently without rational basis.[156]

When the Senate received news of the House victory, to Griffiths' chagrin, it immediately offered a counterproposal retaining sex distinctions. Because of this, ERA proponents were glad the Senate bill never got to the floor in 1971. Undaunted, Griffiths wrote to all who had congratulated her after the House vote urging them to keep at their Senators. "Go to them quietly," she counseled, and explain why the original bill was mandatory.[157] At the beginning of the 1972 Congressional session, she took the occasion of Susan B. Anthony's 152nd birthday to stress how sex discrimination "continued to poison this most free of nations." Surely, in the context of civil rights awareness there was irony in the fact that a woman's average earned income in 1968 was 58.2 percent of a man's, and 5.7 percent less than it was in 1955. Did it bother no one that only 8 percent of the country's law students were women, that 5 percent of the graduate students in business and commerce were women, or that there was but one woman in the Senate and eleven in the House? The women's liberation movement, she asserted, served a useful purpose in pointing out the obvious and "we may well wonder at our blindness and insensitivity to it."[158]

On the last day of February, the Senate Judiciary Committee, after having rejected several encumbering amendments, reported the original bill to the floor. That same day, Griffiths told the House how much she deplored Ervin's misrepresentation of the Roper poll that showed the apparent opposition of women to the ERA. That women affirmed the bill's substantive issues like equal pay and equal employment opportunities was evidence to her that they were behind the proposal and that it was needed.[159]

In the next month support mounted for passage, despite Ervin's persistent protest that the "Tonkin Gulf Resolution of the American social structure" would soon put women in foxholes, strike sodomy from criminal law, and leave helpless girls to the whims of rapacious employers.[160] At this critical juncture, Griffiths made sure the women did not let up. On the weekend before the final vote, President Nixon also broke his long silence and endorsed the ERA, a move that aided the bill immeasurably.

In the ensuing five-day debate, Ervin engaged in his final foray to exempt women from the draft and combat zones and to preserve state labor lesislation. That his colleagues thought it necessary to resort to an amendment to nullify a handful of disfavorable protective laws impressed him as being "about as wise as using an atomic bomb to exterminate a few mice."[161] On the last day of debate, Griffiths, New York Representative Bella Abzug, and Massachusetts Republican Margaret Heckler were on the Senate Floor. Eileen Shanahan of the New York Times reported that "Mrs. Griffiths sat at the back-row desk usually occupied by Senator Edmund S. Muskie . . . keeping her personal count of the rollcall."[162] The tally registered 84 in favor, 8 opposed. Demonstrations in the galleries, notwithstanding the Chair's remonstrations, told of history being made that March 22, 1972.

A month later, Griffiths reflected on her experiences of the next 36 hours:

> When the Equal Rights Amendment had finally gone through the Senate and I met with the press afterwards and the girls who had helped put the amendment through, I was ecstatic. It was the second amendment that women had asked for in the Constitution, but it was the first amendment that had ever been offered by a woman.
>
> That night I went to the University of Michigan dinner. While we were having cocktails, a member came up to me and told me that Hawaii had just ratified the Equal Rights Amendment. I could hardly believe it. . . .
>
> The next day, [?] Thompson of General Motors [lobbyist for the corporation] sent a lei of carnations and I was the first person to speak on the floor after Carl Albert, the Speaker, had signed the amendment. I pointed out that I wore the flowers because of the fact that Hawaii had ratified the amendment.
>
> At 3 o'clock that afternoon, I took a plane for Oklahoma City. I had to go to [i.e. via] Chicago. I stepped off from the plane and bought all the papers. There was mention in each and every paper of the fact that the amendment had been passed by the House and Senate.
>
> When I arrived in Oklahoma City, I was met by the Mayor in her lovely limousine and the press. I was speaking to the Theta Sigs in Oklahoma City. Many of them were for the amendment, but I could tell that there were those in the audience who questioned the desirability of

such an amendment. Women were afraid. They
were content in a way with their change.
They do not exactly understand what the amendment will do.163

If Sam Ervin was typical of anti-ERA zealots, the ERA was in for a bitter struggle in spite of Griffiths' contention that it would be easily ratified within the seven-year limit. Ervin sent an appeal to the state legislators in hopes that they would see the ERA as not being "in the best interests of women in America." He was also certain that the women who had battled for the amendment would fight as hard as he in the months ahead. "Sometimes I question the soundness of my convictions that women should not be converted into combat soldiers," he confessed the day the Senate turned the amendment over to the states. "If the militant women who demand that Congress submit the equal rights amendment to the states without changing a dot over an 'i' or cross over a 't' have the capacity to frighten the enemy like they frighten male politicians, the enemy might hoist the white flag without firing a shot."164

Before the end of 1972, 22 states had ratified the ERA. Eight others followed within a year to date of Senate passage. Rapid approval was predictable. But the equal speed by which anti-ERA forces, especially among women, began to gather momentum surprised Griffiths.165 The opposition was often virulent, if not vicious, and sufficiently influential to keep the states from voting the resolution into law.166 By the end of 1978, only 35 had ratified, 3 short of the requisite number.

ERA foes were many and varied. Fundamentalist groups like the John Birch Society, the Ku Klux Klan, and Billy Hargis' Christian Crusade opposed the amendment on principle. Hoping to preserve the status quo, the National Council of Catholic Women, Mormons, Orthodox Jews, and some union leaders among those affiliated with the AFL-CIO joined hands with the newest antagonists: Happiness of Womanhood (HOW), The League of Housewives, Citizens against the ERA, Humanitarians Opposed to Degrading our Girls (HOTDOG), and, most important of all, Phyllis Schlafly's Stop ERA.

Within a relatively short period, Stop ERA had active units in over half the states, had a vigorous system of communication, and was amply funded. As former Vice President of the National Federation of Republi-

can Women and founder of her own organization, "The
Eagles are Flying," Schlafly was no political neophyte
and she knew how to direct her appeals. Referring to
herself as a mother, author, and Radcliff graduate, she
portrayed the American woman as "the most privileged
. . . of all the classes of people who ever lived."
When the ERA, therefore, threatened to rob her of "the
greatest privileges of all: (1) NOT to take a job, (2)
to keep her baby, and (3) to be supported by her husband,"
Schlafly felt compelled to speak out for the
majority of her sex. "We do not want to trade our birthright
of the special privileges of American women—for
the mess of pottage called the Equal Rights Amendment,"
she wrote in one of her monthly newsletters.[167]

Under the slogan, "You Can't Fool Mother Nature,"
Stop ERA made its case.[168] ERA would hurt the family
by requiring a woman to carry half the support of husband
and children; by depriving an older woman of her
benefits as wife, even possibly forcing a husband to
pay extra Social Security for a non-working spouse; and
by mandating unnecessary child-care centers. The ERA
would also legalize homosexual marriages and give women
a constitutional right to abortion on demand.

In addition to its harmful effects on the family,
according to Schlafly the ERA worked other great damage.
It made women subject to military combat, deprived them
of advantageous working conditions, and excluded them
from special rates for life and automobile insurance.
As a federal power grab, it reached far and deep. It
prohibited single-sex facilities and events like motherdaughter
banquets; it compelled seminaries to admit
women up to and possibly including ordination, and it
forbade physical examinations of police applicants.
Moreover, there was no compensation for all this domestic
hurt and public mischief. ERA would not add to
rights already won, such as equal pay and better educational
opportunities, nor would it help women in athletics.
Neither would it protect privacy; instead, it
could prohibit it.

These anti-ERA efforts greatly vexed Griffiths.
The New York Times, which had earlier taken issue with
the ERA over the elimination of all protective laws,
wondered at the "combination of reaction and frivolity,
. . . propaganda largely intended to prove that women
either already enjoy or do not really want equal rights,"
propositions, the editor noted, that were "patently
untrue."[169] In her earliest phase of canvassing the

states, Griffiths had concentrated on a reasoned up-to-
date analysis of court decisions that either denied
women the equal protection of the law or created confusion about its application. After 1972, however, she
found herself increasingly obliged to answer her critics
and she counseled ERA supporters to do the same. Certain points had to be stressed. The ERA would not com-
pel married women to work, would not invalidate rape
laws or interfere with the constitutional right of privacy. Moreover, the elimination of the draft would remove military service as an issue; all the ERA would do
would guarantee the same rights to all military volun-
teers. The ERA would further invalidate the few remaining alimony laws which barred payment by women and would
leave the courts to decide the support provisions between former partners. Although the amendment would
nullify state protective laws, many had already been
dropped and all would be declared invalid under the 1964
Civil Rights Act. In January 1973 the Supreme Court
Ruled on the abortion question that of itself had nothing to do with the ERA.[170] From the outset Griffiths
had made it a cardinal principle never to take a stand
on abortion for fear of hurting her amendment. "It is
an issue," she once told an audience, "on which there
are only losers."[171]

When Griffiths retired from the Ninety-third Congress, 33 states had ratified the ERA. The question
was: Where were the other 18? Had Schlafly and her
allies proved so persuasive as to have slowed the process virtually to a halt? Why were some states that
had ratified now seeking to rescind their action? Was
the ERA fast becoming the sixth of the unratified amendments?

Although the story was far from being told, at the
beginning of 1975 assessments were already being made.
Griffiths had her own. She was distressed that the
media had not made ERA successes national news nor selected experts to present the facts to the public. She
understood the psychology of the scare tactic used during hard times on men who feared for their jobs. She
witnessed the debilitating effects wrought by strident
feminists who hung their abortion and lesbian demands
around the ERA like so many albatross. From years' experience she knew when the only argument was the out-
right payment, the the implied threat, or the assured
vote. She also perceived the power of language. The
concern she raised over "equal" in the Equal Pay Act
came back to haunt the movement. Those, like herself,

who best understood the ERA, were not suggesting that every person was the equal of every other; rather, they were forcing the legal issue that under the Constitution every person should be guaranteed the equal protection of the law. How Griffiths wished during these days that the ERA had been called by another name.[172]

Despite ERA setbacks, Griffiths continued to hammer at sex discrimination, hoping her agitation would keep the issue alive. Her persistence helped to open Little League Baseball to girls,[173] to further the movement for women on police forces,[174] and to insure a minimum wage for women domestics.[175] Moreover, to break down stereotypic roles, she introduced a bill to permit fathers in the delivery room during the birth of their children.[176] Of greatest concern, however, was the blatant and pervasive sexism embedded in credit institutions and higher education.

Because academe escaped the constraints of the Equal Pay Act and the 1964 Civil Rights Act, university women experienced the whole gamut of discrimination, from admission to graduate schools to appointment as high-level administrators. Where the 1968 federal contract compliance order might have helped, it proved a hindrance. For some time HEW did not require submission of affirmative action plans nor keep accurate files on complaints. There were instances where investigations were conducted in secrecy and cases handled with little sense of urgency, the findings often withheld from complainants, as revealed in the proceedings against Griffiths' alma mater, the University of Michigan.[177] Statistics seemed to indicate that contemporary women academics were less fortunate than their forebears. "The men . . . who run the universities," Griffiths concluded caustically," are the most bigoted, the most provincial group of people in the country."[178]

The attention focused on these abuses by the Edith Greens and the Martha Griffiths and by organizations like WEAL and the American Association of University Women began to bear fruit after 1970. Congress amended the Civil Rights statute to cover all colleges and universities and added a provision to the Equal Pay Act to include executive, administrative, and professional personnel. The Educational Amendments Act of 1972 prohibited sex discrimination in federally assisted programs. Extending the jurisdiction of the Civil Rights Commission over sex bias further strengthened the cause of women in higher education, as did passage of the ERA.

Satisfied with what had been achieved by the end of 1972, Griffiths moved to combat sexism in credit.

She well understood what equal access to credit meant for American women. It potentially increased their purchasing power on a day-to-day basis, enhanced the quality of housing for themselves and their families, broadened their educational opportunities, and opened up careers in business. Discrimination conversely promoted a second-class status and a closed system. Credit discrimination was also hard to fight since it was bias based on both sex and marital status. Lenders and insurance companies considered any woman as an inherently poor risk—a "clunker"—and a woman without a husband was the poorest investment of all.[179]

As the result of discriminatory practices, a single woman had great difficulty in establishing credit on her own. The credit of a married woman was basically reckoned on the earnings of her husband; she borrowed and bought in her spouse's name even though she was personally liable for her debts or was an independent earner. When a couple applied for a mortgage, the lender discounted the wife's income either totally or partially, and if the woman was in her childbearing years, she or her husband generally had to produce a "baby letter" verifying they were sterile or practicing birth control. Widows and divorcees, considered the most unstable of all women, correspondingly suffered the greatest indignities. A separated or divorced woman could expect to pay double security deposits for her rent or face increased automobile insurance premiums even if she was a faultless driver. A widow could be hounded by the bank and the Federal Housing Administration to pay off the mortgage with her insurance money and she might have to resort to her dead husband's credit cards for non-cash transactions.

Griffiths was incensed by these practices. While she believed they were not always motivated by conspiracy or vengeance, she maintained they were wholly benighted and had to be eliminated. That federal lending agencies did nothing to prevent these kinds of bias was reprehensible to her; that they actually fostered them was sheer mockery. She refused to tolerate "the smooth answer" that there was no discrimination. "This, of course, has been a complete lie," she told Congress. The situation, as Griffiths perceived it, was all the more "preposterous" because women controlled most of the consumer dollars, generally determined their pregnancies,

and at all times could decide whether or not to quit
their jobs. And, as far as she knew, there was no evidence that women defaulted on their debts more than
men; the opposite, in fact, appeared to be the case.[180]

To give direction to the movement on credit equity,
Griffiths told the National Commission on Consumer Finance that it was responsible both for raising public
awareness on sex bias among credit institutions and for
demanding proof that women were poorer credit risks than
men. She further urged the Commission to recommend corrective action to Congress. Though convinced of the
pervasiveness of prejudice against women, the Commission
advised close surveillance of discriminatory practices
by the Bureau of Consumer Credit.[181] Meanwhile, Griffiths joined Edith Green in advancing a federal standard
against sex discrimination in the insurance business.[182]

During 1973 Griffiths made sexism in credit a subject of her JEC inquiry on the economic problems of women. These hearings underscored the fact that the legal
emancipation of women was slow but irreversible.[183] In
1974 Congress passed the Equal Credit Opportunity Act
which outlawed discrimination in credit transactions
because of sex or marital status. By helping women
achieve creditworthiness, this law brought them one step
further into the economic mainstream—if women had both
the education and the will to make the law work on their
behalf.

Despite the Watergate distractions of 1973, Griffiths proceeded with hearings on the economic problems
of women—she often being the only member of JEC present.[184] The conclusion that emerged from six days'
testimony was that the federal government was not serious about affirmative action even in those programs
where it had been prescribed, to say nothing about current sex-based differences in Social Security, public
assistance, and the tax code.[185] Although the EEOC had
been empowered in 1972 to bring antidiscrimination
suits, it had filed only 122 cases and settled 3. Its
backlog numbered 65,000 cases which were expected to
rise to 90,000 in 1974. Former EEOC Commissioner Aileen
C. Hernandez told the JEC panel that during her tenure
the majority of commissioners and staff had "little or
no commitment to eliminating sex discrimination—we had,"
she said, "an Executive Director who traveled around
the country making poor jokes about Playboy Club bunnies."[186]

The Labor Department fared no better. The Assistant Secretary for Employment Standards could not tell the JEC why only 48 percent in back pay had been recovered from violations of the Equal Pay Act. And former Director Elizabeth Duncan Koontz found it "perfectly ridiculous" that the Women's Bureau, the only agency that could assist working women, was hamstrung by lack of funds and staff. The Department did not even have maternity guidelines for its own personnel.[187]

Nor did the Office of Federal Contract Compliance have anything to boast of. It had not terminated a single contract because of sex discrimination since its establishment, had not hired one woman professional in any of its field offices, and did not require contractors to disclose their affirmative action programs. Furthermore, HEW had yet to resolve one class complaint from the colleges and universities. Herbert Stein, chairperson of Nixon's Council of Economic Advisors, admitted to the obvious: the Executive branch exercised no surveillance over the enforcement of Title VII, the Equal Pay Act, or the contract compliance order,[188] a revelation the newspapers predicted was sure to unleash a flood of women's bills.[189] After hearing the testimony, Griffiths suggested that women join with minority groups everywhere to make their common disenchantment felt.[190]

When Griffiths left Congress in December 1974, the progress that had been made in securing justice for women gave her little reason for rejoicing. A few months crisscrossing the country, however, convinced her that women had taken up their cause for liberation. "There is no peace," she told an Emory University audience in the fall of 1975. Homemakers and working wives everywhere were awakening to their true status as they experienced early widowhood, separation, or divorce. As a result, they were demanding laws more reflective of modern life, a need that even the Supreme Court was beginning to recognize.

Government was also changing from within. Although few women held public office, especially at the national level, men being selected were increasingly the products of female-headed homes, an experience that was bound to affect their attitudes toward women. Griffiths thought it all to the good. "The world that is to come," she said, "will be infinitely better, with happier, better adjusted people." But it had to be a different world—where sex would no longer be a barrier to human dignity and full citizenship.191

[1] Quoted in Phineas Indritz and David L. Schurtz, "Sex-based Criteria Eliminated from the D.C. Code—A Guide," *District Lawyer* 2 (Winter 1977): 26-29.

[2] Interview with Don Edwards, Washington, D.C., January 27, 1978.

[3] Burns, "Excerpt from News Briefing by Dr. Arthur Burns, Counsellor to the President for a Group of Reporters on May 15, 1969," in Griffiths Papers, Bentley Library.

[4] Griffiths, "Statement of the Honorable Martha W. Griffiths for the First Quarterly Newsletter of Federally Employed Women," February 1969, in Griffiths Papers, Bentley Library; U.S., Congress, Joint Economic Committee, *Private Pension Plans, Hearings before the Subcommittee on Fiscal Policy*. 89th Cong., 2d sess., April 26-27, May 2-3, 9-11, and 16, 1966 (1966), 2: 395.

[5] The statistics are drawn from the following: Griffiths, "The Law Must Reflect the New Image of Women," *Hastings Law Journal* 23 (November 1981, reprint): 1-2; U.S., Congress, Joint Economic Committee, *Economic Problems of Women, Hearings before the Joint Economic Committee*. 93rd Cong., 1st sess., July 10-12, 24-26, and 30, 1973 (1973), 1:2-3.

[6] Griffiths, Milton Shober, and Charles F. Haywood, tape of panel, "Sex Discrimination in Credit Granting," Association of Credit Bureau Conference, Washington, D.C., May 1973, in Griffiths Papers, Bentley Library.

[7] Griffiths, "Queens College Commencement Address, 1972," Griffiths Library. Several of Griffiths' speeches during this period, especially to academic communities, highlighted the Supreme Court cases which in her mind created confusion and brought about legal inequities for women.

[8] *Weinberger v. Weisenfeld*, 420 U.S. 636 (1975).

[9] Griffiths, Speech to [ ], San Francisco, September 21, 1972, in Griffiths Library.

[10] Griffiths' equal pay bill differed from others in establishing a three-year ban on federal contracts to violators and in requiring all government contracts to write in antidiscrimination wage provisions.

[11] Arthur J. Goldberg, "Statement of Arthur J. Goldberg, Secretary of Labor, before the Select Subcommittee on Labor, House Committee on Education and Labor, on H. R. 8898 and H.R. 10226, 'Equal Pay Act of 1962,'" May 26, 1962, in Griffiths Papers, Bentley Library.

[12] U.S., Congress, House, 87th Cong., 2d sess., July 25, 1962, *Congressional Record* 108:14758; Griffiths, "Statement before the Select Committee on Labor," March 27, 1962, in Griffiths Papers, Bentley Library.

[13] U.S., Congress, House, 87th Cong., 2d sess., July 25, 1962, *Congressional Record* 108: 14767-71; Esther Van Wagoner Tufty, news release, July 27, 1962, in Griffiths Papers, Bentley Library.

[14] *Congressional Quarterly Almanac*, 1963, p. 513.

[15] In a real sense, Griffiths was the author of the amendment because of her effective influence on its passage. Most equal rights persons credit her as *the* person who made it possible. (Interviews with Marguerite Rawalt, Arlington, Virginia, January 25, 1978, and Phineas Indritz, Washington, D.C., January 23 and 27, 1978). Griffiths would have liked to have amended the amendment to cover all aspects of sex discrimination in the Civil Rights Act. She was convinced, however, she never would have succeeded in getting it through the House. (Interview with Griffiths, Romeo, August 31, 1978).

[16] Marguerite Rawalt, for example, believed in Smith's sincerity (Interview, January 25, 1978) and Griffiths said she welcomed his support (U.S., Congress, House, 89th Cong. 2d sess., June 20, 1966, *Congressional Record* 112:13054-60). Most, however, believed Smith really did not want the amendment and was anxious to defeat it. (Interviews with Charles C. Diggs Jr., Washington D.C., January 25, 1978; Don Edwards, January 27, 1978; Edith Green, Columbia, South Carolina, March 5, 1978; and Edna F. Kelly, Briarcliff, New York, March 5, 1978; also *Washington Star*, September 26, 1968, clipping in Griffiths Library.)

[17] Andrew J. Biemiller to Griffiths, February 3 and 5, 1964, in Griffiths Papers, Bentley Library.

[18] Interviews with Dorothy Haener, Detroit, Michigan, December 9, 1977, and Virginia Allan, Washington, D.C., January 31, 1978.

[19] Interview with Edith Green, March 5, 1978. Green admitted that black women perceived sex discrimination more hurtful than racial bias. "As a black person, I am no stranger to race prejudice," Representative Shirley Chisholm noted. "But the truth is that in the political world I have been far oftener discriminated against because I am a woman than because I am black." (U.S., Congress, House, 91st Cong., 1st sess., May 21 1969, <u>Congressional Record</u> 115:13380-81.

[20] Griffiths, "Women and the Legislators," article written for the Unitarian Universalist Women's Federation, accompanied by letter; Griffiths to Mary Lou Thompson, March 20, 1970, in Griffiths Library.

[21] Griffiths to Caroline Bird, February 6, 1968, in Griffiths Papers, Bentley Library.

[22] The following debate, including Griffiths' contribution is found in U.S., Congress, House, 88th Cong., 2d sess., February 8th, 1964, <u>Congressional Record</u> 110:2484-92. See, also, Griffiths, "Women and the Legislators."

[23] <u>Minor v. Happersett</u>, 21 Wall. 162, 168 (1874); <u>Bradwell v. State</u>, 16 Wall. 130 (1872); <u>Inn v. Lockwood</u>, 154 U.S. 116 (1894); <u>Goesaert v. Cleary</u>, 335 U.S. 464 (1948).

[24] Griffiths to Myra K. Wolfgang, February 17, 1964, in Griffiths Papers, Bentley Library.

[25] Griffiths, "Women and the Legislators"; and Interview with Rawalt, January 25, 1978.

[26] For a typical response, see Mildred A. Klafter to Griffiths, February 11, 1964, in Griffiths Papers, Bentley Library.

[27] Wolfgang to Griffiths, February 10, 1964, in Griffiths Papers, Bentley Library.

[28] Griffiths to Wolfgang, February 17, 1964, in Griffiths Papers, Bentley Library.

[29] Interview with Griffiths, Romeo, November 9, 1977.

[30] Interviews with Indritz, January 23 and 27, 1978.

[31] U.S., Congress, House, 89th Cong., 2d sess., June 20, 1966, <u>Congressional Record</u> 112:13054-60.

[32] John S. Warner to Griffiths, including Griffiths' nota-

tion, June 23, 1966, in Griffiths Library.

[33] Hernandez to Griffiths, June 22, 1966, in Griffiths Library. Several other letters in Griffiths Papers, Bentley Library; also *Chicago Tribune*, July 3, 1966, clipping in MWG Scrapbooks, Griffiths Library.

[34] "You will be interested to know that the organization NOW . . . was organized at a luncheon table the day you spoke to the State Commissions on the Status of Women," Yale Professor Pauli Murray informed Griffiths, August 9, 1966. (Letter in Griffiths Papers, Bentley Library).

[35] U.S., Congress, House, 89th Cong., 2d sess., June 20, 1966, *Congressional Record* 112:13055-9.

[36] Memorandum, William Kendrick to Griffiths, August 8, 1966, in Griffiths Library.

[37] Griffiths said the Executive Order ranked with "Lincoln's freeing of the slaves." U.S., Congress, House, 90th Cong., 1st sess., October 16, 1967, *Congressional Record* 113:13389.

[38] *Washington Star*, September 26, 1968; Griffiths to Editor, *Life Magazine*, December 11, 1968; William H. Brown III to Griffiths, July 28, 1969; and Arthur B. Hanson to Director of Federal Contract Compliance, February 27, 1969, in Griffiths Library.

[39] Griffiths to George Hay Brown, Director of the Bureau of the Census, January 26, 1973, in U.S., Congress, House, 93rd Cong., 1st sess., January 31, 1973, *Congressional Record* 119:2884-5.

[40] U.S., Congress, House, 89th Cong., 2d sess., June 20, 1966, *Congressional Record* 112:13059; Griffiths to Mrs. Richard B. Lansdale, January 28, 1969, in Griffiths Papers, Bentley Library.

[41] "Statement of United Air Lines, Inc. to Equal Employment Opportunity Commission, 'Sex as a Bona Fide Occupational Qualification for Stewardesses,' April 1966," copy in Griffiths Library.

[42] Arthur M. Wisehart to Equal Employment Opportunity Commission, September 21, 1966, copy in Griffiths Library.

⁴³The Griffiths-Mason correspondence running from October 4 to November 1, 1966, is found in Griffiths Library.

⁴⁴The Justice Department refused to bring suit until the EEOC heard the case. "It had been the Department's policy to withhold action where private individuals or private organizations are financially capable of bringing suit to vindicate their rights and where there is no climate of fear or intimidation standing in their way," wrote Assistant Attorney General John Doar to Griffiths, February 15, 1967 (Griffiths Library). Griffiths had this letter sent to Indritz and Betty Friedan, the head of NOW.

⁴⁵Interview with Griffiths, Romeo, August 31, 1978; and *Columbia Missourian*, November 14, 1966; *Detroit Free Press*, October 27, 1966; *Detroit News*, October 27, 1966, clippings in MWG Scrapbooks, Griffiths Library. Also in the Griffiths Library is a sheaf of laudatory as well as irate letters. For the latter, see Mrs. James Kindt to Governor George Romney, November 24, 1966.

⁴⁶Griffiths to Thomas Riney, October 29, 1966, and Griffiths to Cass S. Hough, January 16, 1967, in Griffiths Library.

⁴⁷Griffiths to Henry H. Wilson Jr., Administrative Assistant to the President, April 6, 1967; Griffiths to Mrs. Richard B. Lansdale, January 28, 1969, in Griffiths Papers, Bentley Library.

⁴⁸In 1973 a United States District Court established the "nexus" between the "no marriage" rule and employee resignations. (*Gerstle v. Contintntal Airlines*, Inc., 358 F. Supp. 545). Prohibition against the rule was reiterated even more forcefully in *Inda v. United Airlines Inc.*, 405 F. Supp. 426 (1975).

⁴⁹Interview with Margaret Heckler, Washington, D.C., January 24, 1978; Diane Robertson to Griffiths, January 13, 1969, in Griffiths Library.

⁵⁰U.S., Congress, House, 90th Cong., 1st sess., May 17, 1967, *Congressional Record* 113:13110; U.S., Congress, House, 91st Cong., 1st sess., August 4, 1969, *Congressional Record* 115:22164-6; Interview with Griffiths, Romeo, June 5, 1977; Griffiths, "Legislation Needed to Protect the Rights of Women," phone speech to BPW

of Grand Rapids, January 10, 1967, in Griffiths Library.

[51] United States v. Darby Lumber Co., 312 U.S. 100 (1944); Goesaert v. Cleary, 335 U.S. 464 (1948).

[52] Edwards v. North A. Rockwell Corp., 291 F. Supp. 199 (1968); Griffiths to J.W. Turley, September 30, 1968, in Griffiths Papers, Bentley Library.

[53] Cheatwood v. South Central Bell Tel. & Tel. Co., 303 F. Supp. 754 (1968).

[54] U.S., Congress, House, 91st Cong. 1st sess., September 11, 1969, Congressional Record 115:25183-5; U.S., Congress, Senate, Committee on the Judiciary, Equal Rights 1970, Hearings before the Committee on the Judiciary (S.J. Res. 61 and S.J. Res. 231). 91st Cong., 2d sess., September 9-11, and 15, 1970 (1970), p. 223.

[55] The Boyer-Griffiths correspondence found in the Griffiths Papers, Bentley Library, ran from March 31, 1968 to November 6, 1968.

[56] U.S., Congress, Senate, 90th Cong., 2d sess., September 20, 1968, Congressional Record 114:11176-83.

[57] Proxmire to Griffiths, September 27, 1968, in Griffiths Library.

[58] Griffiths, "Dear Colleague" letter, June 8, 1970, in Griffiths Library.

[59] Perkins to Griffiths, June 10, 1970, in Griffiths Library.

[60] H. Res. 344, March 24, 1971.

[61] Griffiths to Attorney General Ramsey Clark, December 12, 1967; Griffiths to Attorney General John N. Mitchell, June 27, 1969, in Griffiths Library.

[62] Griffiths, "What to do about Discrimination," AAUW Journal 64 (November 1970):12.

[63] Griffiths to Daniel M. Friedman, July 23, 1968, in Griffiths Library.

[64] In Ballard v. United States (329 U.S. 187 [1946], the Supreme Court had guaranteed equal treatment for women

in the selection of federal jurors.

[65] Hoyt v. Florida, 368 U.S. 57 (1961). In White v. Crook, 251 F. Supp. 401 (M.D. Ala. 1966), a federal district court struck down an Alabama statute excluding all women from jury duty. This case, however, was the exception rather than the rule.

[66] Griffiths, "Women and the Legislators"; U.S., Congress, House, 89th Cong., 2d sess., July 26, 1966, Congressional Record 112:17125-6; Griffiths, "The Rights of Modern Women," speech before the Detroit Public Library Centennial Program," January 10, 1966, in Griffiths Library.

[67] Griffiths, "Testimony before Senate Subcommittee on Constitutional Rights on Civil Rights Bill S. 3296," Friday, July 15, 1966, draft in Griffiths Library; Griffiths, speech to Columbian Women of George Washington University, Saturday, February 18, 1967, second draft in Griffiths Library; Griffiths to Ann H. Kerwin, August 2, 1966, in Griffiths Papers, Bentley Library.

[68] Griffiths, "Statement of Martha W. Griffiths before Subcommittee #5 of the House Committee on the Judiciary, H.R. 12652," February 24, 1972, in Griffiths Papers, Bentley Library; Griffiths to James Eastland, September 19, 1967, in Griffiths Library.

[69] Griffiths to Macy, May 25 and June 15, 1966; February 21, 1968, in Griffiths Papers, Bentley Library; U.S., Congress, Joint Economic Committee, Private Pensions, Hearings. . . , 2:408-10.

[70] John M. Morgan to John B. Ahern, March 5, 1965, copy in Griffiths Papers, Bentley Library.

[71] U.S., Congress, House, 89th Cong., 2d sess., June 21, 1966, Congressional Record 112:13706-7; Griffiths, speech to the Public Personnel Association, National Capitol Chapter, September 13, 1967, in Griffiths Library.

[72] Griffiths to Henry H. Wilson Jr., Administrative Assistant to the President, April 6, 1967, in Griffiths Library.

[73] Griffiths inveighed against such practices as requiring women enrollees in the Air Force to submit full

face and full body photographs. "What kind of nonsense is that?" she asked. Griffiths, "A Government View: Women and Legislation," in George Bugliarello et al., <u>Women in Engineering: Bridging the Gap between Society and Technology</u> (University of Illinois: Chicago, 1971), pp. 21-27.

[74] U.S., Congress, House, 91st Cong., 2d sess., December 7, 1970, <u>Congressional Record</u> 116:40136.

[75] U.S., Congress, House, 91st Cong., 2d sess., June 24, 1970, <u>Congressional Record</u> 116:21346-7; U.S., Congress, House, Committee on Post Office and Civil Service, <u>Survivor Annuities, Hearing before the Subcommittee on Retirement, Insurance, and Health Benefits</u>. 91st Cong., 2d sess., August 4, 1970 (1970) p. 65.

[76] U.S., Congress, House, 92d Cong., 1st sess., August 2, 1971, <u>Congressional Record</u> 117:7637-40.

[77] Griffiths, "Statement of Martha W. Griffiths before the Subcommittee on Education and Training of the Committee on Veterans' Affairs (H.R. 3965)," December 8, 1971, in Griffiths Library.

[78] U.S., Congress, House, 93rd Cong., 1st sess., May 16, 1973, <u>Congressional Record</u> 119:3703; <u>Frontiero v. Richardson,</u> 411 U.S. 677 (1973).

[79] Ruth Crothers to Griffiths, October 25, 1966, in Griffiths Papers, Bentley Library.

[80] Griffiths once said, "The inequities of the Social Security Act against the woman worker was my pet peeve." (Griffiths, "The Equal Rights Amendment and the Arguments Used Against It," speech [c. 1976], in Griffiths Library).

[81] Interview with Griffiths, Romeo, January 7, 1978.

[82] Griffiths, "Women and the Legislators"; U.S., Congress, House, Committee on Ways and Means, <u>Unemployment Compensation (H.R. 8282), Hearings before the Committee on Ways and Means</u>. 89th Cong., 1st sess., August 9-13, 16-20, 23-27, and 30, 1965, 3:1336.

[83] The plight of working women was conveyed to Griffiths by several correspondents. (See letters January through May 1967, Griffiths Papers, Bentley Library.)

[84] Griffiths contended that the dependency test was slipped into the bill enroute to the White House. The then HEW chief, Wilbur J. Cohen, denied such a charge. (Interviews with Griffiths, Romeo, June 4, 1977 and January 7, 1978; and Cohen, Ann Arbor, Michigan, December 14, 1977).

[85] Griffiths to Richard P. Edgar, January 25, 1967, in Griffiths Papers, Bentley Library; U.S., Congress, Senate, Special Committee on Aging, Future Directions in Social Security, Hearing before the Committee on Aging. 94th Cong., 1st sess., October 22, 1975 (1976), 18-1674.

[86] Weinberger v. Weisenfeld, 420 U.S. 636 (1975).

[87] Griffiths, notation on Artie E. Cullen to Griffiths, February 14, 1961, in Griffiths Papers, Bentley Library.

[88] U.S., Congress, Joint Economic Committee, Private Pension Plans Hearings . . . , 2:388-9; U.S., Congress, House, Committee on Ways and Means, President's Proposals for Revision in the Social Security System (H.R. 5710), Hearings before the Committee on Ways and Means. 90th Cong., 1st sess., March 1-3, 1967 (1967), 1:239-49; U.S., Congress, House, 93rd Cong., 1st sess., November 14, 1973, Congressional Record 119:9990-10001.

[89] U.S., Congress, Joint Economic Committee, Private Pension Plans Hearings . . . , 2:388-9; U.S., Congress, House, Committee on Ways and Means, Social Security and Welfare Proposals, Hearings before the Committee on Ways and Means. 91st Cong., 1st sess., October 15-16, 21-24, 27-28, 30-31; November 3-7, 10, and 12-13, 1969 (1970), 1:301.

[90] Interveiw with Griffiths, Romeo, January 7, 1978; Griffiths to Daniel H. Kruger, November 28, 1969, in Griffiths Papers, Bentley Library.

[91] Griffiths to Raymond W. Andress, April 24, 1967, in Griffiths Papers, Bentley Library. "In the strictest justice," she wrote, "working couples ought to be able to collect social security benefits four ways: the husband as worker, the wife as worker, the wife as wife, the husband as husband. . . . However, paying four benefits to every working couple in the country would clearly bankrupt the social security system."

[92] U.S., Congress, Senate, Special Committee on Aging, Future Directions in Social Security, Hearing . . . ., 18:1672.

[93] "Report of the HEW Task Force on the Treatment of Women under Social Security," February 1978. Also see, U.S., Congress, Senate, Special Committee on Aging, Women and Social Security: Adapting to a New Era, by the Task Force on Women and Social Security, Committee Print (Washington, D.C.: Government Printing Office, October 1975).

[94] The idea and substance of the bill was drafted by former HEW Secretary Wilbur Cohen. According to Jordan, the genesis of the bill was "Wilbur Cohen coming to Washington and talking to me and talking to Martha and then the two of us talking to each other." (Interviews with Jordan, Washington, D.C., January 24, 1978, and Cohen, December 14, 1977).

[95] Griffiths, speech to the managers of Michigan Consolidated Gas, Detroit, Michigan, January 19, 1978, in Griffiths Library.

[96] Barbara McDowell and Hans Umlauf (eds.), The Good Housekeeping Woman's Almanac (Newspaper Enterprise Association: New York, 1977) p. 473.

[97] U.S., Congress, Senate, Committee on the Judiciary, Equal Rights Amendment (S.J. Res. 61), S. Rept. 1013, 79th Cong., 2d sess., March 1946, p. 10: Billy James Hargis to a Riverton TV listener, [n.d.], in Griffiths Library.

[98] U.S., Congress, House, 91st Cong., 2d sess., August 10, 1970, Congressional Record 116:7963-4; Mary Russell, "Mother of the ERA," Washington Post, July 13, 1976, clipping in MWG Scrapbooks, Griffiths Library; Interview with Rawalt, January 25, 1978.

[99] Griffiths to Mary Stewart, March 17, 1969, in Griffiths Library; Griffiths, "The Equal Rights Amendment and the Arguments Used Against It."

[100] Griffiths to Wendell Lund, July 8, 1948; Griffiths re: "Equal Rights," October 7, 1954, in Griffiths Library. For one of her early ERA Congressional speeches, see U.S., Congress, House 86th Cong., 1st sess., February 16, 1959, Congressional Record 105:2416.

101 One of the most charming notes on Griffiths ERA crusade was from former Member of Congress Jeanette Rankin who had voted for the suffrage amendment. (To Griffiths, February 28, 1967, in Griffiths Papers, Bentley Library).

102 Miller to Griffiths, January 7, 1969, in Griffiths Library.

103 Interview with Griffiths, Romeo, September 12, 1977.

104 Interview with Allan, January 31, 1978; Griffiths, "The Equal Rights Amendment and the Arguments Used Against It."

105 <u>Hoyt v. Florida</u>, 368 U.S. 57 (1961); <u>White v. Crook</u>, 251 F. Supp. 401 (M.D. Ala., 1966).

106 In 1971 the Supreme Court upheld the decision of the Fifth Circuit Court of Appeals (<u>Phillips v. Martin Marietta Corp.</u>, 400 U.S. 542).

107 Griffiths, "Statement of the Honorable Martha W. Griffiths on the Outlook for Legislation Affecting Women in the 91st Congress, for publication in <u>The National Business Woman</u>," February 19, 1969, in Griffiths Papers, Bentley Library.

108 Interview with Rawalt, January 25, 1978.

109 <u>U.S., Congress, Senate, Committee on the Judiciary, The Equal Rights Amendment Hearings before the Subcommittee on Constitutional Amendments (S.J. Res. 61)</u>. 91st Cong., 2d sess., May 6-7, 1970 (1970), p. 24.

110 U.S., Congress, House, 91st Cong., 2d sess., June 11, 1970, <u>Congressional Record</u> 116:5437; Griffiths, "Dear Colleague" letter, June 17, 1970, in Griffiths Library.

111 William "Fishbait" Miller, <u>Fishbait</u> (Prentice-Hall: Englewood, New Jersey, 1977) p. 374; Interview with Griffiths, Romeo, September 10, 1977.

112 Griffiths recounted her petition episode in Griffiths, "The Equal Rights Amendment and the Arguments Used Against It."

113 Interview with James C. Corman, Washington, D.C.,

January 26, 1978. Edith Green said Griffiths literally took her male colleagues by the arm to the signing desk. (Interview, March 5, 1978).

[114] Interviews with Allan, January 31, 1978; and with Rawalt, January 25, 1978.

[115] Interview with Gerald R. Ford, Jr., Vail, Colorado, July 19, 1978.

[116] Interviews with Barber B. Conable, Washington, D.C., January 27, 1978; with Ford, July 19, 1978; Ford to Griffiths, August 3, 1970; and Griffiths, speech [?], in Griffiths Library.

[117] J.F. TerHorst, "A Victory for Woman Power," *Detroit News*, July 21, 1970.

[118] In his report to his constituents, Representative Richard Bolling stated that "very few indeed could honestly say that they foresaw the overwhelming passage in the House." ("Report from Washington," [n.d.], in Griffiths Library).

[119] Griffiths, "Dear Colleague" letter, August 5, 1970, in Griffiths Library.

[120] For the House debate, see U.S., Congress, House, 91st Cong., 2d sess., August 10, 1970, *Congressional Record* 116:7948-53.

[121] "Breakthrough for Women," *Evening Star* (Washington, D.C.), August 11, 1970; "Two for the People: Women and D.C.," *Washington Post*, August 13, 1970, clippings in Griffiths Library.

[122] Dingell to Emily George, R.S.M., March 6, 1978; Richard A. Ryan, "2 From State Dissent in Rights Vote," *Detroit News*, August 11, 1970, and John Askins, "Nedzi, Dingell Defend Women's Rights Vote," *Detroit Free Press*, August 13, 1970, clippings in MWG Scrapbooks, Griffiths Library.

[123] Interview with Rawalt, January 25, 1978.

[124] Andrew J. Biemiller to Griffiths, August 5, 1970; Elliot Carlson, "Proposal to Broaden the Rights of Women May Bring Surprises," *Wall Street Journal*, August 10, 1970; "The Henpecked House," *New York Times*, August 12, 1970, letter and clippings in Griffiths

Library. Ervin widely circulated Freund's article, "The Equal Rights Amendment is Not the Way," <u>Harvard Civil Rights-Civil Liberties Law Review</u> 6 (March 1971): 234-42.

[125] Ervin's "Dear Senator" letter, August 15, 1970, copy in Griffiths Library.

[126] Griffiths, "International Women's Year is Just the Beginning," <u>American Bar Association Journal</u> 60 (October 1974): 1238. Ervin published a number of strongly worded anti-ERA editorials in the Record. (U.S., Congress, Senate, 91st Cong., 2d sess., September 1, 1970, <u>Congressional Record</u> 116:14786-14813).

[127] U.S., Congress, Senate, 91st Cong., 2d sess., October 14, 1970, <u>Congressional Record</u> 116:18075; <u>Washington Post</u>, October 18, 1970, clipping in Griffiths Library.

[128] For samples of Griffiths' arguments, see U.S., Congress, Senate, Committee on the Judiciary, <u>Equal Rights 1970 . . .</u>, pp. 222-8; U.S., Congress, Senate, 92d Cong., 1st sess., January 28, 1971, <u>Congressional Record</u> 117:471.

[129] Griffiths, notes on equal rights legislation, October 22, 1971, in Griffiths Papers, Bentley Library.

[130] Griffiths to Ruth Church Gupta, October 30, 1967, in Griffiths Papers, Bentley Library; Ruth Dean, "Woman to Seek High Court Post?" <u>Evening Star</u> (Washington, D.C.) October 7, 1969; and Penny Girard, "Nation's Law Courts Loom as Barricades for Women's Rights," <u>Home Furnishings Daily</u>, September 30, 1970, clippings in MWG Scrapbooks, Griffiths Library.

[131] U.S., Congress, Senate, 91st Cong., 2d sess., August 19, 1970, <u>Congressional Record</u> 116:13706; October 7, 1970, 116:17336; October 12, 1970, 116:17751; and October 13, 1970, 116:17893.

[132] U.S., Congress, Senate, 91st Cong., 2d sess., October 14, 1970, <u>Congressional Record</u> 116:18075-8.

[133] Bernice Sandler to Bayh, October 25, 1970; Aileen C. Hernandez to Bayh, October 30, 1970; "Reasons for Opposing the Bayh Substitute to the Equal Rights Amendment: A Statement Prepared by Members of the Legal Committee, National Women's Party"; Gladys

O'Donnell to Marlow Cook, October 26, 1970; Citizen's Advisory Council on the Status of Women, "Statement on Bayh Substitute and Ervin Amendment to the Equal Rights Amendment," October 29, 1970; Thomas I. Emerson to Bayh, November 6, 1970, copies in Griffiths Library.

[134] Sharon Galm to Griffiths, Memorandum: "Evaluation of the Bayh Amendment," October 22, 1970, in Griffiths Library.

[135] Bayh to Sandler, October 29, 1970, copy in Griffiths Library. Bayh appended the following note to Griffiths: "I hope this will do the job. You are our expert and we need your thought and leadership!"

[136] U.S., Congress, Senate, 91st Cong., 2d sess., November 16, 1970, Congressional Record 116:18192-3.

[137] Interview with Rawalt, January 25, 1978; Rawalt, "On the Status of the Equal Rights Amendment," November 27, 1970, in Griffiths Library.

[138] Ibid.; Conroy, McCalls 98 (May 1971):37.

[139] Arlen J. Large, "Fallen Women: An Amendment Fails," Wall Street Journal, December 22, 1970, in MWG Scrapbooks, Griffiths Library.

[140] Griffiths, "Forward to Women and the Equal Rights Amendment," for R. Cary Bynum, February 24, 1972, in Griffiths Papers, Bentley Library.

[141] Griffiths, "Gridiron Speech," November 21, 1970, in Griffiths Library. Vice-President Agnew had been bandying about colorful labels for Administration foes and radical organizations.

[142] Griffiths, "Dear Colleague" letter, January 25, 1971.

[143] U.S., Congress, Senate, 92d Cong., 1st sess., January 28, 1971, Congressional Record 17:469-73.

[144] Bayh to Griffiths, September 14, 1971, in Griffiths Library.

[145] Reed v. Reed, 404 U.S. 71 (1971); Stanley v. Illinois, 405 U.S. 645 (1972).

[146] For example see Hoyt v. Florida, 368 U.S. 57 (1961)

and Allied v. Heaton 364 U.S. 517 (1960).

[147] U.S., Congress, House, Committee on the Judiciary, Subcommittee No. 4, Equal Rights for Men and Women 1971, Hearings before Subcommittee No. 4 on the Committee on the Judiciary (H.J. Res. 35, 208, and Related Bills and H.R. 916 and Related Bills). 92d Cong., 1st sess., March 24-25, 31; April 1-2, and 5, 1971 (1971), pp. 36-54.

[148] Interview with Don Edwards, January 27, 1978.

[149] U.S., Congress, House, Committee on the Judiciary, Subcommittee No. 4, Equal Rights for Men and Women 1971, Hearings . . ., pp. 71-72.

[150] Griffiths, letter to all women state legislators, July 17, 1971 in Griffiths Library; "Set Stage for New Equal Rights Battle," Right Now (McCalls' monthly newsletter for women), May 1971, clipping in MWG Scrapbooks, Griffiths Library.

[151] Don Edwards et al., "Dear Colleague" letter, September 16, 1971; U.S., Congress, House, Committee on the Judiciary, Equal Rights for Men and Women (H.J. Res. 208), H. Rept. 92-359, 92d Cong., 1st sess., July 14, 1971, p.8.

[152] Griffiths, "Dear Colleague" letter, September 20, 1971; Celler and McCulloch, "Dear Colleague" letter, October 9, 1971; U.S., Congress, House, Committee on the Judiciary, Equal Rights for Men and Women (H.J. Res. 208), H. Rept. 92-359, p. 11.

[153] Interview with Edwards, January 27, 1978.

[154] Reed v. Reed, 404 U.S. 71 (1971).

[155] Judy Flander, "Only a Women in Office Gets Action," Washington Post, December 7, 1971, clipping in MWG Scrapbooks, Griffiths Library.

[156] Stanton v. Stanton, 421 U.S. 7 (1975); Griffiths, "Justice through Law—America's Goal," presented at the University of Michigan Law Day Dinner, April 18, 1975, in Griffiths Library.

[157] Griffiths, response to congratulatory letters, [n.d.], in Griffiths Library.

[158] U.S., Congress, House, 92d Cong., 2d sess., February 9, 1972, <u>Congressional Record</u> 118:1025-6.

[159] U.S., Congress, House, 92d Cong., 2d sess., February 29, 1972, <u>Congressional Record</u> 118:6143.

[160] U.S., Congress, Senate, Committee on the Judiciary, <u>Equal Rights for Men and Women</u>, S. Rept. 92-689, 92d Cong., 2d sess., March 14, 1972, p. 36.

[161] U.S. Congress, Senate, 92d Cong., 2d sess., March 28, 1972, <u>Congressional Record</u> 118:4885.

[162] Eileen Shanahan, "Equal Rights Amendment is Approved by Congress," <u>New York Times</u>, March 23, 1972, in Griffiths Library.

[163] Griffiths, taped notes of Martha W. Griffiths, April 20, 1972, in Griffiths Library.

[164] Ervin, "Dear Friend," [n.d.], copy in Griffiths Library; U.S., Congress, Senate, 92d Cong., 2d sess., March 28, 1972, <u>Congressional Record</u> 118:4890.

[165] Betty J. Blair, "Women v. Women," <u>Detroit News</u>, September 18, 1977, in Griffiths Library.

[166] One woman wrote: "I wish you had given birth to at least one child, maybe this ERA, brainstorm of your frustrations, would never have materialized." (Halina M. Frizzelle to Griffiths, November 4, 1974 in Griffiths Library).

[167] "The Phyllis Schlafly Report," February, 1972.

[168] Stop ERA, "You Can't Fool Mother Nature." In another flyer, "The Abortion Connection," the organization noted that in almost every instance pro-abortionists also supported ERA.

[169] Griffiths, tape of BPW convention, Chicago, Illinois, 1974, July 22, 1974, in Griffiths Papers, Bentley Library; "The Price of Equality," <u>New York Times</u>, May 28, 1973, in Griffiths Library.

[170] <u>Roe v. Wade</u>, 410 U.S. 113 (1973).

[171] For a sample of her early statements, see her "Testimony before Michigan State Legislature," April 27, 1972, in Griffiths Papers, Bentley Library. For a

letter outlining areas for rebuttal, Griffiths, "Dear Friend," February 9, 1973, and Griffiths to Miriam Brown, February 15, 1973, in Griffiths Library; also Griffiths, edited transcript of "Women's Movement—What Next," conference for the Washington Journalism Center, December 1974, in Griffiths Library.

[172] Interviews with Griffiths, Romeo, September 10, 1977; Griffiths, "The Equal Rights Amendment and the Arguments Used Against It"; "Press 'Unfair' on ERA, Says Mrs. Griffiths," Detroit News, May 5, 1975; and "Mrs. Griffiths on ERA Aims and Its Foes," Washington Star, January 19, 1976, clippings in MWG Scrapbooks, Griffiths Library. For more recent views, see Betty J. Blair, "Support for Lesbians Splits Feminist Ranks," Detroit News, December 28, 1977; and Laura Berman, "ERA: From Simple Statement to Powerful Symbol," Detroit Free Press, August 3, 1978. Regarding the approach, Margaret Chase Smith wrote: "As I have said many times publicly and privately if those women desiring to see the ratification of the Equal Rights Amendment would follow Martha Griffith's [sic] example in pursuing the objective quietly, knowledgeably and thoroughly answering the questions and attacks with facts and seriousness there would be no question about the results." (Smith to Emily George, R.S.M., January 7, 1978).

[173] U.S., Congress, House, 93rd Cong., 1st sess., June 4 and 20, 1973, Congressional Record 119:17823-7 and 20552-3. "Let me assure you," she told Congress, "that if Billy Martin of the Detroit Tigers or Leo Durocher of the Houston Astros had a chance to sign a woman who hit home runs like Hank Aaron, fielded like Al Kaline, or pitched like Wilbur Woods, they would do their best to get that woman's name on a contract." Peter J. McGovern, chairperson of Little League Baseball, resented the "dangerous headlong impulse perpetrated by National Organization for Women" to get girls into Little League but admitted, "apparently we have no choice and must throw in the sponge." (McGovern to Herman Schneebeli, June 10, 1974, in Griffiths Papers, Bentley Library). Griffiths always thought the reason for keeping women out of "men's" sports was a matter of money. (Ann Wood, "Girls Baseball Foes Blasted for Profits," Philadelphia Inquirer, March 27, 1974, clipping in MWG Scrapbooks, Griffiths Library).

[174] Griffiths, "Remarks of Congresswoman Martha W. Grif-

fiths at Police Foundation Symposium on Women in Policing," May 29, 1974, in Griffiths Library. Griffiths' agitation helped to open the Capitol Hill Police force to women candidates. (Carl Albert to Griffiths, August 2, 1974, in Griffiths Library).

[175] U.S., Congress, House, 93d Cong., 1st sess., June 6, 1973, Congressional Record 119:18342. Representative Shirley Chisholm wrote Griffiths, "I feel that you and Edith [Green] really set the tone of the debate and insured the passage of the [minimum wage] provision." (June 22, 1973, in Griffiths Papers, Bentley Library).

[176] "A Family Affair," Ms. Magazine, April 1973, clipping in MWG Scrapbooks, Griffiths Library.

[177] U.S., Congress, Joint Economic Committee, Economic Problems of Women, Hearings before the Joint Economic Committee. 93d Cong., 1st sess., July 10-12, 24-26, and 30, 1973 (1973) 1:119 and 2:434-5; Griffiths, "Statement of Honorable Martha W. Griffiths, 17th District of Michigan, Concerning Section 895 (To Prohibit Discrimination) of H.R. 16098—The Omnibus Post Secondary Education Act of 1970," [n.d.], in Griffiths Library; U.S., Congress, House, 91st Cong., 2d sess., June 3 and September 22, 1970, Congressional Record 116:18197-18204 and 33256; U.S., Congress, House, 93d Cong., 1st sess., February 28, 1973, Congressional Record 119:6004-5; Griffiths to Marjorie C. Kirkland, July 25, 1973, in Griffiths Papers, Bentley Library.

[178] U.S., Congress, House, 90th Cong., 1st sess., February 28, 1967, Congressional Record 113:4813-4; 91st Cong., 2d sess., March 9, 1970, Congressional Record 116:6398-6400; 92d Cong., 1st sess., November 4, 1971, Congressional Record 117:39254.

[179] For a description of sexist credit practices, see Griffiths, "Testimony of Martha W. Griffiths before The National Commission on Consumer Finance on Sex Discrimination in Consumer Credit," May 22, 1972, in Griffiths Library; U.S., Congress, Joint Economic Committee, Economic Problems of Women, Hearings . . ., 1:213 and 3:546-58; Griffiths, speech to Automotive News World Congress, Dearborn, Michigan, July 26, 1976, in Griffiths Library; Griffiths to Eileen Shanahan, July 18, 1973, in Griffiths Papers, Bentley Library; Griffiths, Shober, Haywood, panel, "Sex Discrimination in Credit Granting." Griffiths told

of a beauty operator, widowed one week, who received a call from an FHA representative asking her to pay off the mortgage on which she alone had made payments several years. (U.S., Congress, House, Committee on Ways and Means, *Tax Reform, 1969, Hearings before the Committee on Ways and Means.* 91st Cong., 1st sess., February 18-21, 24-28; March 3, 10-12, 14, 17-18, 20-21, 24-28; April 1-3, 14, 22-24, 1969 [1969] 8:2780).

[180] U.S., Congress, House, 92d Cong., 2d sess., April 11, 1972, *Congressional Record* 118:12280; Griffiths to Anthony J. Vinci, September 11, 1973; Griffiths to Ted Mutch, December [ ], 1972, in Griffiths Papers, Bentley Library.

[181] Green to Griffiths, May 31, 1972, in Griffiths Library.

[182] Excerpt from the 1972 report of the National Commission on Consumer Finance, in Griffiths Library.

[183] U.S., Congress, Joint Economic Committee, *Economic Problems of Women, Hearings . . .*, 1:281-4.

[184] Eileen Shanahan, "All the Pigs are More Equal," *New York Times*, July 29, 1973; Vera Glaser, "Martha to Head Bias Hearings," *Detroit Free Press*, June 13, 1973; clippings in MWG Scrapbooks, Griffiths Library. JEC Chairperson Wright Patman asked Griffiths to chair the probe which was a departure from normal practice.

[185] U.S., Congress, House, 93d Cong., 1st sess., July 24, 1973, *Congressional Record* 119:25799-80.

[186] U.S., Congress, Joint Economic Committee, *Economic Problems of Women, Hearings . . .*, 1:97 and 130-1.

[187] Ibid., 1:99-108, and 117-8.

[188] Ibid., 1:38-50.

[189] "Sex Bias Fight Moving Too Slowly, Says Probe," *Tampa (Florida) Tribune-Times*, July 15, 1973; Mary Russell, "Low Pay for Women Blamed on Inexperience," *Washington Post*, July 11, 1972; "Hearings May Unleash Flood of Women's Bills," *St. Louis Globe-Democrat*, [n.d.], clippings in MWG Scrapbooks, Griffiths Library.

190U.S., Congress, Joint Economic Committee, <u>Economic Problems of Women, Hearings</u> . . ., 1:73-74.

191Griffiths, "The Context of Change (The Legal Rights of Women)," speech to Emory University, October 9, 1975, in Griffiths Library. The self-liberation of women and the emergence of a new economic order were constant themes of Griffiths' speeches after 1974. (For example, Griffiths' remarks at Michigan State University Commencement, December 4, 1976, in Griffiths Library).

CHAPTER V

A great idea takes form when a person of influence "recognizes when the stars are in the right conjuncture," Nelson D. McClung told an enquirer in discussing the genesis of Martha Griffiths' three-year welfare study. Then the former JEC staffer reiterated his point more pragmatically. It takes a person, he said, who "knows the world and moves effectively and appropriately when the times are right."[1] There is hardly a policy maker in Washington who has not heard of Martha Griffiths' study and who does not list it among her top personal achievements. More significantly, <u>Studies in Public Welfare</u> is a matter of public import. As the first comprehensive analysis of the federal welfare system by <u>any</u> branch of Government, it set the pattern for all future welfare reform because of its fundamental validity.[2]

According to McClung, the germ of the study was buried in a series of income-maintenance hearings held by Griffiths' Fiscal Policy Subcommittee in June 1968. By that time it had become evident to Americans that Johnson's War on Poverty had not succeeded despite such costly endeavors as the job-training programs. What was even more disturbing was that poverty was not only continuing—but deepening—in the Great Society. Griffiths ascribed this intolerable contradiction to the welfare system and offered the services of her Subcommittee to study income options. The 1968 hearings were accordingly held as an attempt "to initiate a public review of the objectives and operation of the welfare system. . . [and] to demonstrate that it is possible to conduct a rational discussion of welfare design." Once into the hearings, Griffiths further admitted that the Subcommittee was about its work because "the States have broken down" as administrative agents.[3]

The result of nine days' testimony was support for some form of maintenance scheme like a negative income tax or family allowance, either to alter, or, more significantly, replace current public assistance that participants across the board described as demeaning, inefficient, inadequate and incentive-destroying.[4] Scores of economists throughout the country affirmed the need for radical reform along the lines suggested by the hearings, but the Chairperson of JEC, Senator William Proxmire of Wisconsin, felt no one else would go along and so at the time made no attempt to move the dialogue ahead.

A year later, however, the issue could no longer be ignored. Nixon proposed his Family Assistance Plan (FAP) which represented a radical departure from welfare programming: in the place of Aid to Families with Dependent Children (AFDC), the Administration recommended $1,600 for a family of four. FAP passed the House but foundered in the Senate over work incentives. At this critical phase, knowledgeable persons on the Hill concluded that if any headway was to be made on welfare, an entirely new strategy had to be devised. They further agreed that if anyone could recognize the conjuncture of the stars, it would be Martha Griffiths.

Griffiths perforce was already steeped in the welfare debate as a member of Ways and Means where FAP had originated. There she had faced with her colleagues the unpleasant AFDC facts of 1970: 6.7 million recipients as compared to 2.4 million in 1960, tripled costs in ten years, three-fourths of all AFDC families abandoned by the fathers or headed by unmarried mothers. She understood the Nixon approach as reform and therefore appreciated it and its capacity to generate strong opposition. "The less said about the bill, the better," she counseled. "It's a step toward a nationalized welfare system, and I'm for it." She predicted that in one or two years after the bill took effect, the states would be able to cut taxes sharply because of substantially reduced welfare burdens. This particularly pleased her because she looked upon welfare as a national responsibility. Her experience had led her to conclude that the current system of taxing city and state property was destroying the cities. In a speech to the House in April 1970, she likewise expressed her desire that FAP eventually be amended to eliminate female dependency by requiring mandatory work for all AFDC women and mandatory schooling or job-training for pregnant high-school girls. And she believed that welfare benefits should be equitably distributed: "I think that the poor, the single poor and the married childless poor should be paid also," she told her colleagues.[5]

In reporting FAP out of committee, Ways and Means underscored how badly AFDC needed structural readjustment. The Committee was confident that on three major counts FAP proposed to be that kind of reform. First, it recognized the needs of the working poor. Second, it reduced the variation in payment levels among the states through the introduction of a federal floor. And, third, it encouraged AFDC recipients to get off welfare by requiring them to register for employment or training. The Committee itself had strengthened the Administration bill by building in guarantees for child support and by mandating work-training for all, including the working poor.[6] The House accepted the Committee version only to have it later rejected by the Senate.

During the next Congress, the Administration returned with a modified FAP that Ways and Means folded into an omnibus welfare measure. The Nixon provisions were nearly killed in the House by a liberal-conservative coalition, but the Senate struck the blow by its inaction. In the context of these abortive attempts toward welfare revision, Griffiths was especially anxious to launch her path-breaking study.

Although she had supported FAP through both the Ninety-first and Ninety-second Congresses, she was the first to admit that the absence of data partially excused her colleagues from enacting the reform. In her mind, the lack of reliable and coordinated information on so serious a matter as federal welfare was a tragic flaw in the entire legislative process since so much hinged on the welfare dollar. The FAP debates had proved this beyond doubt. Moreover, no one was talking about AFDC in relation to Social Security, to housing, to health, or to food. This lack of data left unanswered other questions which were critical to the passage of the President's proposal. How adequate were the benefit levels and how valid the claims that FAP would improve work incentives? Was there wisdom in extending FAP benefits to male-headed families with children and to families already participating in other forms of assistance? Was FAP another administrative level, and could reform be achieved better through the coordination or substitution of other welfare programs besides AFDC?[7] Daniel Patrick Moynihan, presidential counselor during the FAP controversy, told Griffiths some time later that if the Administration had had the answers found in her study, the Nixon bill would have passed.[8]

The absence of data convinced Griffiths of what had to be done. As one of her later aides put it, "She wanted to get a handle on the whole thing."[9] For some time she had been thinking about a comprehensive study out of her Fiscal Policy Subcommittee. Writing former presidential adviser Walter Heller as early as February 1971, she said she was going to put her "puritan ethics" to use and investigate welfare. "There has been altogether too much revenue sharing in this program," she commented on the topic of controversy between herself and the economist, "and no facts whatsoever are available in the entire federal establishment. I think we will have an interesting time and I hope we don't get lost in the quagmire."[10]

As project formulation began in the summer of 1971, Griffiths worked closely with James W. Knowles, research director for JEC. Knowles estimated the cost of a two-year study and helped Griffiths identify her staff. It was Griffiths' business, however, to get the funds, a matter she pursued with adroitness and alacrity. First, she approached Mills because of Ways and Means' ultimate jurisdiction over welfare legislation. Mills not only approved the project but promised to give his support should she need it with the chairperson of House Appropriations, George H. Mahon. Griffiths also secured the backing of John W. Byrnes, ranking Republican on Ways and Means, and Wright Patman, JEC chairperson. Only Proxmire, the vice-chairperson of JEC, reserved judgment, and in the meeting to determine whether or not approval would be given, he attempted to derail Griffiths' plan and place the study under the aegis of the full committee—over which he would soon preside. Senators Javits and Ribicoff objected, however, and Griffiths got her vote of confidence. Having secured the endorsement of both Ways and Means and JEC, she approached Mahon and Frank T. Bow, the ranking Republican on Appropriations. Mahon agreed to her request, as did the Ohioan who insisted that Griffiths, not the chairperson of JEC, approve every expenditure, a suggestion representing a notable departure from normal practice.[11] To Knowles' utter amazement, Griffiths had her money in a very short time.

The next order of business was to find a project director. The care with which Griffiths, aided by Knowles, made this choice attested to the importance she placed on the undertaking as well as on her own active participation in it. After interviewing several candidates, she selected Alair A. Townsend, whose husband, Robert Harris, had also been a candidate and was well known to the JEC staff as the former director of the President's income-maintenance commission. The youthful Townsend, a postgraduate sociologist, was "enthralled" over doing something that promised to be extraordinarily exciting. She was fascinated further by the prospect of working with a member of Congress she thought of as "remarkable" and as having direct legislative input to and responsibility over many of the program areas that would be studied. Townsend perceived the project as "action-oriented" and that delighted her. She also knew from the start that she was being asked to direct a study which Griffiths herself intended to shape. "She just knew too much and had too many good ideas" to permit it to be otherwise, Townsend recalled. What she also came to appreciate was Griffiths' willingness to trust her staff and to remain open to the results of the study or as Townsend put it, "to, in a sense, let the chips fall as they may, [despite] some preconceived notions. . . ."12

That Griffiths had "some preconceived notions" was to be expected from her years on Joint Economic and on Ways and Means. At the conclusion of the study—and the end of her Congressional career—she ascribed her interest in welfare reform to her experience, especially on Ways and Means. Her recollection bears recording.

> When I became a member of the Ways and Means Committee in 1962, I was first struck by the incredible inequities of social security, which returned on the same tax payments a greater sum to a man-supported family than to a woman-supported family and more to many families where the woman remained at home than to families where both husband and wife worked, although the latter families might in fact have paid more tax than the one-worker families.
>
> Years ago I held hearings on private pensions, and retirees drilled into my head the fact through quirks in the labor contract or outright dishonesty in the pension setup, they had been deprived of the tax money that should have been paid on these pensions, and now the Nation maintained these people on welfare.
>
> I watched for whatever else I could find on the law's strange workings.
>
> Some years ago, I received a letter from a woman in my district who earned $5,300 gross per year. She outlined her taxes, her take-home pay and her problems. The next day I received a call from a woman living in a far better area of my district whose home had been purchased under section 235 [of HUD's subsidized rental program] and who was drawing, she said,

$750 per month, untaxed, in AFDC money, including $200 per month for a housekeeper. My "tired lady," earning $5,300, was paying taxes to help support a woman at a $750 rate per month. I seethed. There are no jobs of which I am aware that increase your pay because you have children.

Shortly after that day I began to investigate the possibility of making a complete survey of all income maintenance programs.[13]

Griffiths' abiding concern over the American welfare system intrigued her colleagues on Ways and Means. One noted how "she'd look into it in her home district and spoke usually from personal experience about 'What they are doing in my district.' And she abhorred waste," he said, ". . . and brooded a lot about how to improve it."[14]

With the opening of each new Congress, Ways and Means was handed a spate of Social Security amendments, many of them directly related to the care of the needy. What became particularly noticeable and disturbing after 1965, however, was that one Social Security program, AFDC, grew faster in participants and funds than any other federally aided plan. While all persons receiving federal assistance from June 1966 to June 1967 increased 7.4 percent, AFDC recipients soared 11.3 percent. That same year, AFDC expenses shot 8 percent above the costs of all other programs combined.[15] It was no wonder that Congress began to focus its attention on what seemed to be a wayward progeny.

Griffiths was fundamentally at odds with the welfare system.[16] She believed that the Social Security Act intended that welfare wither and eventually disappear as needy persons qualified for pensions under the old-age and survivors insurance. Instead, since 1935, AFDC had developed into a compensatory scheme for the nation's fiscal and monetary ills, thousands of persons being added each year to the welfare rolls. As Griffiths saw it, the Mills Committee had fostered racism through the Social Security system: as each revision bestowed new assistance-type benefits on whites, more poor blacks, especially black women, went on AFDC.[17] Indeed, all was not well.

Griffiths had discovered several other major deficiencies. The system was an administrative jungle:

costly, inefficient, and bureaucratic. More seriously, it was grossly inequitable. Because each state determined its own requirements and appropriations, beneficiaries and benefits varied significantly throughout the nation. In some states, large numbers of poor received no aid at all, forcing migration to states, such as Michigan, where aid was more munificent and qualifications less stringent. There were, in effect, no state boundaries where welfare was concerned. "It cannot be questioned any longer," Griffiths said in 1967, "that welfare is a national program. Let the Federal Government run it."[18] She further observed that large industrial states disproportionately bore the system's financial costs with money needed so sorely by the cities. Moreover, because of the taxing structure—no taxes for the very poor, loopholes for the very affluent —middle-class dwellers, like her own constituents, were paying almost totally for poor relief that the suburbanites avoided in their escape to society's outer fringe. It was high time, she told her colleagues on Ways and Means, to equalize burdens among the rich, the poor, and middle-class Americans.

Besides these basic inequities on the more populous states and on the middle-class, welfare was structured on the age-old prejudice that women were economic dependents. More than any other factor, this attitude perpetrated welfare cruelties, a fact Griffiths had come to believe HEW could never comprehend and, therefore, would never address. Year after year as bevies of HEW secretaries and commissioners appeared before Ways and Means to discuss their projects, the branch was confused with the root because these administrators were men who, according to Griffiths, lived in a "gingerbread world."[19] While her criticism seemed harsh, the welfare situation disturbed her so profoundly that even without all the facts she could not sit idly by and watch in silence what was being done to the poor, expecially to poor women and their children.

Her quarrel with HEW was that the system it administered and defended kept welfare mothers in the bondage of dependency. The system was to her blatantly sexist. By not making employment and job-training available— even mandatory—these women could never "break the iron case of welfare."[20] She told Congress in 1968 that its job was "to get these women into the mainstream of American life" and to do this would mean making work and training more profitable than the welfare check.[21] It would be necessary as well to change the law so that a woman might work, draw supplemental benefits without penalty, and live with her lawful husband. The current system, so ardently defended by the men on Capitol Hill, destroyed all incentive to work and laid the ax to family life, thereby intensifying the dependency cycle. "I have often said," she told an audience of family counselors in 1973, "that the Ways and Means Committee . . . should be called The Committee Against Marriage."[22] Her arguments likewise pointed to another deep wound on the body politic: as long as women were permitted only the lowest paying jobs, any welfare reform to relieve poor women of their economic dependency was doomed to failure. Reform required a workplace to which all women had equal access, where they were paid comparably to men, and where promotion was available to all irrespective of race or sex.

Not all agreed with Griffiths' deduction that welfare dependency would be mitigated once AFDC mothers were given the chance for gainful employment. Some noted that there were just not that many jobs; others, that this solution automatically indicted AFDC recipients as lazy, a view Griffiths would not have wished ascribed to her. Most of her opponents opposed compulsory employment for mothers of children under six. A typical reaction was voiced by two of her colleagues on Ways and Means. One said that it went against nature. The other: "We are just not going to do that, Mrs. Griffiths. And, bless your soul, why don't you come up and help these women get into the business of being mothers?"[23]

Griffiths would not be put off by the "natural law" or by "forced labor" arguments which she believed had more to do with prejudice and self-interest than with humanitarianism. She opposed the notion that only women could be the caretakers of their children. She had come to regard some mothers as "the creators of other welfare recipients" and, in these instances, thought it more advisable that others, including the fathers, nurture their offspring. "Do you really feel," she bristled, "that it is a good idea for a woman with a 400 word vocabulary to remain home with 13 illegitimate children, or have a little 14-year old girl saddled with an illegitimate child never to have the opportunity to be trained, never to have the opportunity to get out of the house, and never have day care for that child? How silly."[24] To maintain otherwise was what she meant by living in a "gingerbread world."

As for the "forced labor" argument, she responded that mandatory work or training was the only way to get local welfare administrators to move into the twentieth century. It was likewise her observation that most AFDC mothers really wanted to get into the labor force.[25] No one would ask the women if their children were born in or out of wedlock, only that they support them; it was the business of government to see that jobs and/or job-training were available. Griffiths believed firmly that to bar mothers with pre-schoolers from employment was to reinforce the myth that mothers of young children did not work; to assume that mothers were the ideal persons to raise children; and to perpetuate inequity for working women, especially poor working women who supported welfare mothers by their labor. It wearied her to listen to the jaded arguments of the last thirty years repeated over and over. Griffiths also had some firm convictions about the deleterious effects welfare had on the children of the poor. Because the system fed on itself, children born in poverty were its real victims as nothing was being done to insert them into the mainstream of American social and economic life. Malnourished, ill-housed, and isolated, these innocents promised to be the indigents of the future. She, therefore, looked for ways, even partial solutions, to address this crime against humanity. She proposed to allocate portions of public assistance to children in their prenatal and early childhood years. "I am for beginning at the bottom," she told her colleagues on Ways and Means in 1969.[26] That year she introduced a bill for a three-meal-a-day plan for poor children as an alternate to the current school-lunch program that fed the rich as well as the indigent. In presenting her proposal she said it was "a new approach. . . to guarantee to every child that he will eat. . . . Then," she said, "let us check the effects."[27] She likewise advocated decreased child allowances as pregnancies increased. To do less was "actually to subsidize bastardy."[28] She also favored the idea that poor children be taken from their deprived environments and placed in day-care centers as provided by the Social Security amendments of 1967.[29] Finally, to prevent children from being used for fraudulant claims she strongly recommended Social Security numbers at birth, a suggestion that met with strong negative reaction when she formally introduced it in 1972.

The years had also given Griffiths a few thoughts about fathers implicated in the poverty cycle. She was patently disturbed that a two-parent family in which the father was employed did not qualify for AFDC assistance. In the Ways and Means debate on FAP she had argued against the prevailing notion that women and children of poor families deserved larger grants than the men. In Griffiths' mind, her colleagues had yet to admit to changed reality: men no longer were the sole supporters of their families; in fact, many were as poor as their wives and children. She observed how yesterday shaped supposedly contemporary reform. Of two Ways and Means members who had been reared by widows and who were drafting FAP she noted: "You could watch them go back in memory and take care of that widowed mother and help that little boy they used to be."[30] As deeply as Griffiths sympathized with poor men, just as strongly did she condemn those child-support delinquents who lived well and beyond the reach of law. In 1967, 75,000 runaway fathers averaging two years of college and earning $6,000 paid nothing for the children they had abandoned. This behavior Griffiths classified as immoral; and, when added to the other welfare inequities and inadequacies, made her angry.

In the summer of 1971 then, as she readied to begin her study, Griffiths had come to hold the American welfare system as practically bankrupt. Since her income-maintenance-hearing days, she pressed hard for comprehensive reform, convinced that the annual process of amending Social Security piece by piece was like the blind identifying the parts of an elephant. Since no one ever had a grasp of the total system, no one knew what it looked like. Any attempt, then, to deal with the nation's poor in a rational way was out of the question.[31] Griffiths' study proposed to tackle the whole beast, and everyone agreed that it was as impenetrable as the hide of a pachyderm.

The welfare probe was planned along two major lines: first, a series of hearings, held March through June 1972, to assess the quality of welfare administration, particularly at the local level; and, second, twenty studies on the practical and theoretical aspects of public-assistance programs compiled over the two-and-a-half year period from April 1972 to January 1975. As the project progressed, hearings on revenue sharing in the fall of 1972 were integrated into the data along with a June 1974 survey by the General Accounting Office (GAO) on delinquent fathers. Useful, though less directly related, were Griffiths' JEC hearings on the economic problems of women held in the summer of 1973.

Not to be overlooked during the nearly three-and-a-half years devoted to the welfare scrutiny was Griffiths' involvement in the Equal Rights Amendment and the Health Security Act, both related to the search for a just income-support system. "The people who are poor are women," Griffiths often pointed out. "If you had ERA, if you began to look at women as human beings and as under the Constitution, you'd cut a lot of that welfare."[32] Equality before the law and equity before the public till were not dissociated. Griffiths further argued that welfare and her health bill were "absolutely related." Because one dollar of assistance qualified a welfare recipient for health services under Medicaid, national health coverage promised to reduce the welfare load and redistribute medical care among the general population.[33]

In September 1971, Alair Townsend presented Griffiths and Knowles with a rationale for the study. Quite simply it was to "<u>uncover</u>" the critical welfare issues, focus research and analytical work on them, and arrive at some workable solutions for Congressional and Executive consideration. The perplexing aspect facing a new welfare design, as Townsend saw it at the time, was that welfare advocates of the past had attempted to build a system on conflicting goals, the most troublesome being poor relief versus programs to effect systemic change.[34]

Griffiths left her technical director free to select her own staff—mostly young scholars eager to translate their knowledge into social reform. In their manner of approach, they decided to seek their information independent of HEW, which was precisely the way Griffiths would have proceeded. Their method of study was also shaped by Griffiths' comprehension of how best to engage her colleagues on Capitol Hill. "She knew what was important to members in policy terms," Townsend recalled. "It was a unique combination of blending ideas and ways of reporting it. She introduced into the income-maintenance language. . . both several ways of analysis, methods and concepts—and new words." Of the latter, the most distinctive was "benefit reduction rate" for "tax rate." By describing in this way the decrease of assistance that accompanied the increase of a recipient's earned income, Griffiths conceptually isolated the factor which she believed did more than anything else to discourage work among welfare recipients.[35]

Although Townsend was not terribly enthusiastic about the hearings on welfare administration, Griffiths considered them mandatory if the project was to be spared the criticism of being solely academic.[36] She accordingly scheduled four sessions for the spring and summer of 1972: the first to focus on the Washington administrative bureaucracy; the latter three to be on-site reviews of local operations in New York, Detroit, and Atlanta.[37] As chairperson of the Fiscal Policy Subcommittee, Griffiths planned to preside at these hearings; and, as it turned out was often the only member of the Subcommittee present.

To inaugurate her study, Griffiths called on Elmer B. Staats, U.S. Comptroller General. Fortuitously, she scheduled his testimony following his report to Congress on the problems of welfare administration in the HEW Social and Rehabilitation Service. In that presentation Staats had told Congress that the GAO had investigated the Service because its costs had tripled in ten years. In reviewing the eight states that expended 50 percent of their budgets on welfare—California, Colorado, Louisiana, Maryland, Michigan, New York, Ohio, and Texas—the GAO discovered that HEW's 1964 and 1970 quality controls had been implemented partially by six of the states and totally disregarded by the other two. Even more disconcerting, HEW did not seem equipped to deal with the problems because of chronic understaffing, nor had it been able to persuade the states that there were any problems at all. Equally disturbing to the GAO was the absence of trained personnel at the regional level. That 90 percent of all cases involving eligibility requirements and payments could not be verified was adequate proof of chaotic management.[38]

In his testimony before Griffiths' Subcommittee, Staats again blamed local inefficiency on staffing problems: the paucity of numbers and the lack of preparation in dealing with volumes of conflicting welfare regulations. He admitted that HEW might not have had a "tough enough attitude" in taking the situation in hand and making it work, but he was more concerned about the apparent absence of a real system. The problems were profound: complexity and lack of uniformity; difficulties in providing relief without creating dependencies and disincentives, particularly the disincentive to stabilize the family unit. The prolongation and deepening of these problems had led Staats to consider American welfare as it stood as incapable of cure. He even conceded that a FAP-type reform could probably not go far enough in justifying the annual expenditure of 45 percent of the total federal budget on welfare programs.

Staats' conclusion was bleak: "We don't really have an overall Government rationale today," he told the Subcommittee.[39]

The second witness, HEW Under-Secretary John J. Veneman, was no more optimistic than the Comptroller General. He pointed out that the present structure, true to the original intent of having welfare administered at the local level, cast the federal government in the role of "a beneficient and distant uncle." "Charles deGaulle once remarked," he said, "that it was impossible to govern a nation that had 246 kinds of cheese. He should have tried governing a welfare empire that has 1,152 autonomous units. Every welfare agency is an island unto itself." Lack of computerization, except in 20 percent of the regional units, spawned inefficiency and abuse. A recent HEW survey had revealed that 5 percent of those getting aid were ineligible and that an additional 25 percent received incorrect amounts. "It is a chaotic do-it-yourself system that is cheating the whole Nation," lamented Veneman.

Griffiths asked what plans HEW had for collecting adequate welfare data, Veneman replying that his department had to depend on the states. She further wondered if the system ought to be nationalized. Veneman answered affirmatively on the basis that the states had the best of two worlds. The federal government paid while the states continued to "call the shots," he said. Griffiths wanted to know whether or not HEW intended to force the states into improving their administrative procedures? It would penalize innocent people the Under-Secretary responded. "So what it all boils down to is this: under existing law we can make rules, plead for compliance, document the chaos, and pay the bills—that's it."[40] Griffiths appreciated the candor but felt little comfort. No one could tell her who was getting $85 billion! "It's incredible," echoed the Chicago Tribune.[41]

Following the first hearing, Griffiths symbolized the need for Social Security reform by introducing an amendment which would have required a Social Security number for every resident of the United States. By this means she felt fraudulent claims could be checked expeditiously and effectively. Both Staats and Veneman agreed that this rather elementary procedure would result in significant savings in information gathering and record keeping and would do much to simplify the entire system.[42] Several editors and civil libertarians, however, expressed outrage. "A type of cradle-to-grave surveillance the country can well do without," declared the New York Times. "Zero wrong," protested the Baltimore News American. The New York Post objected that the amendment did not address the substantive issues of poverty.[43] Griffiths responded pointedly to her critics. What justification, she asked, was there in requiring a Social Security number for a baby with a bank deposit but none for a baby receiving welfare? "If you do not want the long arm of the Federal Government butting into you affairs on the day you are born," she concluded, "be a bastard."[44]

The day after Griffiths introduced her number-at-birth bill, she released the first of the Studies in Public Welfare. Typical of Griffiths, these grew out of root questions. Who got what? Or more specifically, who and how many were eligible for welfare? How did welfare recipients differ from non-recipients? Why had the welfare rolls increased so rapidly? How were assistance programs integrated with regard to benefit levels, administration, and work incentives? What was the relationship between welfare employability and the structure of the labor market? What was the equivalency of welfare benefits to earned net income? How did the welfare system affect the family and poverty? Finally, and central to Griffiths' approach, how many recipients participated in multiple benefits and what issues were raised by this overlap? Overlap was the central focus of the first study, Public Income Transfer Programs, prepared by James R. Storey of the Townsend staff.

One of the myths Griffiths had attempted to debunk over the years was that only cash assistance was welfare. She believed otherwise. Because all forms of aid had monetary value, she insisted that all unearned benefits be counted as income in establishing true welfare. Storey reviewed the $142 billion outlay in public assistance, social insurance, and veterans programs, as well as in food, housing, and health benefits. He found that 60 million individuals received 119 benefits, and that programs explicitly designed for the needy had 64 million participants, but actually served no more than 25 to 30 million persons—while 23.5 million Americans still fell below the 1970 poverty level.

As shocking as these facts were, the issues raised by program overlap were even more overwhelming. The unsystematic development of independent benefit packages resulted in confusion and counterproductivity within the system. Moveover, benefits were inequitable, welfare recipients often faring better in income equivalents than wage earners. Women received more than men; southern households more than northern; and the aged lived at the mercy of mercurial eligibility standards. Further, a combination of benefits often drastically reduced the financial gain from working. Not only did welfare serve as a work deterrent, it was a positive disincentive to retaining the family unit since benefits were more easily procured by female-headed households. Additionally, the system of multiple benefits spawned inefficiency, complexity, and error, while the plethora of administrating agencies created massive chaos.[45] In presenting these data to Congress, Griffiths told her colleagues that it was time both they and the Executive agencies "take off the blinders imposed by jurisdictional responsibilities" and together examine how they could change the congeries of programs.[46]

In the midst of digesting the Storey analysis, Griffiths took her Subcommittee to New York City to see how the most munificent of welfare states administered its programs. These and the Detroit and Atlanta hearings, held April through June 1972, provided the substance for the fifth staff paper, subtitled, <u>Welfare—An Administrative Nightmare</u>.[47] Except in Detroit where she encountered pickets,[48] Griffiths was received enthusiastically by caseworkers, welfare directors, and staff personnel eager to recount the impossible circumstances of their employment. The core issue seemed to be that the system had metastasized beyond control. There were simply too many sources of aid, categories of beneficiaries, and policy makers. Local agencies could neither set welfare rules nor implement them without interference by state and federal agencies. For example, HEW and the states concurrently oversaw the assistance provisions of the Social Security Act, including AFDC, but the Department of Labor was responsible for enforcing the AFDC work requirement and for monitoring food stamps. Food programs, however, were under the Agriculture Department and state welfare agencies. As every benefit had its many agents, so too did it have countless regulations for eligibility, payments, recertification, and termination. In Atlanta the regulations required welfare applicants to fill out twenty-seven forms; food-stamp workers in Detroit were responsible for forty. Nothing encouraged staff turnover more than this red tape; hence, the chronic understaffing and the resultant victimization of welfare recipients. A New York social service director painted for the Subcommittee the classic portrait of rule by "regs":

. . . because you can't handle clients, the problem gets worse and worse and it keeps piling on, one problem keeps piling on another. Because when a client can't get a service by mail and a client can't get service by a telephone and a client can't get a check because of the breakdown of the EDP (electronic data processing) system, or something like that, she has no recourse but to come in. And if she comes in, and it happens in many centers, and there is such a crush of clients there, she can't even get in because the doors are closed. So by the time she does get to see a worker she can be so frustrated and so full of hostility that a spark will set her off.[49]

That there was error, fraud, and deceit was easy enough to explain in light of administrative confusion. "Some of us learn to be more devious than others," a program director told the Subcommittee.[50] Arthur Spiegel, executive director of the New York Department of Social Services, reported that New York had spent $5.5 million in 1970 for fraud control and that there still was a backlog of 30,000 cases of recipients who had received at least two checks.[51] As dismal as this appeared, it could not even approximate, as far as Griffiths was concerned, the harm that was being done to persons in the name of the law. In the following exchange, she outlined for Spiegel the progressive depravity of AFDC:

> Griffiths: Aren't we saying in the law on welfare, 'You select the place where you want to live and the rest of us will support you there?' Isn't that what we are saying?. . .
>
> Spiegel: Yes, I think we are.
>
> Griffiths: Of course, we are saying that. 'If you want to live in New York, go to New York, we will be glad to take care of you there. Or you can live in Atlanta, and we will support you there.' Aren't we saying that?
>
> Spiegel: I would agree. . . .
>
> Griffiths: Now, isn't the next thing that we are saying now, to any woman, any young

	girls, 'If you want to have a baby, you have it, and if you want to marry the father, why, it's all right with us; but if you don't want to, why, don't marry him and the rest of us will take care of you.' Aren't we saying that? Doesn't the law really say that? Don't you think so, Mr. Spiegel?
Spiegal:	Yes.
Griffiths:	Of course, it says that.
Spiegal:	I think a lot of very fundamental work has to be done to build into the law the kind of incentive that can reintegrate family life.
Griffiths:	Aren't we also saying to a wife and a mother of several children, 'If you want to live with this man, your husband and the father of these children, why, do so: but if you would rather leave, why, leave him; the rest of us will take care of you?' We are saying that, aren't we? The law says that in so many words, really: 'You don't have to put up with anything; the rest of us are going to take care of you.'

Now we have gone a step further. When you have no investigation and no authority to investigate and you cannot compel the woman to admit where the father is, or that he is the father, we are then saying, 'Why, you can continue to have the father live right in the house, just don't marry him, and we will support you. And he can have a job that pays $25,000 a year.' Aren't we saying that? This is in reality what this welfare law is; is it not? I haven't heard your answer. |
| Spiegal: | No, I think it's a very chaotic law. It does have the one advantage of providing some money to people who don't have it. But when one begins to look at the incentives it creates in life, in society, and in people, it is abso- |

lutely crazy.[52]

Sympathizing with caseworkers and local administrators, Griffiths returned to Washington armed with data from her three visitations. "They have an impossible job," she said. The New York hearings in particular had convinced her that public assistance in large and medium-sized cities was unadministrable, the regulations unenforceable, and the inequites and disincentives too severe to admit of a piecemeal cure.[53] "The whole mess should be junked and we should start over," she told Congress in June.[54] In September the Fiscal Policy Subcommittee rounded out its hearings by a three-day review of revenue sharing. The vast increase of federal matching payments—127 percent in FY 1972 and 177 percent in FY 1973—suggested to Griffiths that state-aid programs were being refinanced upwards 75 percent. She argued that this was not the intent of Ways and Means in legislating welfare. Refinancing current programs vitiated the ultimate goal of public assistance which was to put people on their feet and off the dole. It likewise created new money to spend on questionable projects. "Does it make any sense to you," she asked Under-Secretary Veneman, "that we are picking up, for instance, 75 percent of a state's expenditure to teach grooming to parolees and yet withholding federal funds to which public housing authorities are legally entitled? What kind of nonsense is that?" Further testimony of welfare directors from every sector of the nation underlined what had now become to the Subcommittee a jaded catalogue of welfare sins: inequities and disincentives, mismanagement and disorganization, and unjustifiable costs. The system was also discriminatory and sexist, factors that Griffiths understood more clearly than most. Because the system provided welfare instead of work, women were degraded and the nation robbed of their talents, while men were given an unfair advantage in the economic and labor markets.[55]

While Griffiths went about her hearings, Townsend and her staff were working toward the publication of four other papers before the end of 1972, including a handbook of comparative data on the income-transfer programs earlier treated by Storey.[56] In a second study, <u>Income Transfer Programs: How They Tax the Poor</u>, three economists described what happened when welfare benefits were reduced as the result of earned income: recipients found ways, such as purchasing non-essentials, to decrease their incomes rather than lose their assistance for housing, food, and other necessities. Because of the benefit reduction rate, the welfare system was confiscatory in practice: it penalized the more frugal, and discouraged people from engaging in gainful employment. As Griffiths told Washington correspondent Edmund LeBreton, it was easier for people to argue that the poor were shifty and that jobs were few than to ask how much the available jobs were worth to the beneficiaries of public relief.57 The study advised that there be a clean break from any welfare solution that advocated a stiff reduction of benefits such as FAP and a negative income tax. Work _and_ welfare was central to a new system.58

Of the four analyses, Jon H. Goldstein's The Effectiveness of Manpower Training Programs: A Review of Research on the Impact on the Poor and Sharon Galm's Welfare—An Administrative Nightmare elicited the most immediate reaction. The press termed the system Galm described in her research as a "mess." While new welfare policy was in the making, the Detroit News counseled interim measures towards streamlining the present system, especially in eliminating duplication. "That way, we may still have a welfare mess but a slightly neater and more equitable one." James J. Kilpatrick of the Washington Sunday Star and Daily News said that Hercules' task of cleansing the Augean stables was nothing compared to "cleaning up the welfare mess." But, he concluded dismally, nothing probably could be done—or would be, as "neither Congress nor the White House has mastered the Herculean touch."59

The Goldstein work on manpower training was of particular interest because of the program's claims to eliminate unemployment, to make the poor self-sufficient, and to provide for occupational mobility of low-income groups. From the outset, Griffiths took the position that these goals were basically illusory for, in and of themselves, they could not effect the massive economic and social changes intended. Program effectiveness could be measured, however, by ascertaining whether or not the $6.8 billion spent over ten years for 6.1 million trainees paid for itself in participants' increased earnings. Isolating six programs for analysis—the Manpower Development and Training Act program (MDTA), Neighborhood Youth Corps (NYC), Job Corps, Job Opportunities in the Business Sector (JOBS), and the Work Incentive Program (WIN)—Goldstein undertook an intensive review of all evaluative literature for which the government had spent $179.4 million. In his research he discovered that the "robust expenditures" had produced only an "anemic set of conclusive and reliable findings." Goldstein ascribed the reasons to ill-conceived or badly executed research designs and to the use of erroneous criteria such as placement rates and business sales in judging success. The lack of creditable information on the Job Corps, WIN, and JOBS Goldstein thought particularly unfortunate as these programs had been specifically set up for welfare recipients and the disadvantaged.

From the data he compiled, Goldstein drew three tentative conclusions: first, with the exception of MDTA and NYC, the expenditures could not be justified in strict cost-accounting terms; second; job-training did not decrease the need for income supplements for the poor; and third, the state of the economy and the inclinations of individual trainees had as much to do with increased earnings as did program design.[60] As a result of these findings, newspapers across the country railed against the government's manpower efforts. The <u>Los Angeles Times</u> spoke for many when it recommended that less money be spent on job training and more on job creation. "The biggest boondoggle since Croesus stashed gold," chided the <u>Memphis Commercial Appeal</u>, and the <u>Detroit News</u> harshly called WIN for mothers on welfare "a program with a fat problem—bloated with layers of bureaucracy, overweight with regulations and slowed down by flabby performance."[61] If the press thought they had an issue here despite the paucity of evidence provided, the GAO investigation of benefit distribution was sure to be cause for alarm.

This study was Griffiths' idea. Townsend recalled that when Griffiths conceived the project she wanted "to get some fix on who was getting what" and thought an objective survey of welfare records was the way to do it. "At the staff level we mulled that around quite a bit," Townsend remembered. "We checked out all the alternatives and we concluded she was absolutely right."[62] Toward the end of the study, Griffiths confessed that her goal in approaching Comptroller General Staats had been "to demonstrate to my colleagues beyond any doubt that the public welfare system was in fact no system at all."[63] But what she did not perceive at the time was the extent to which vast sums of money sustained a horribly inequitable gaggle of programs.

The GAO review was built on two of Griffiths' welfare convictions. First, program overlap deepened rather than broke the poverty cycle. Second, it was use-

less to define poverty—the result was always subjective
and arbitrary when based on some technician's notion of
how people ought to live and what was minimally required
to sustain them.[64] She believed it more important to
calculate the monetary value of all welfare benefits to
ascertain "who got what," how this value measured against
what people were earning, and whether or not it represented a fair distribution of the taxpayers' money.

The GAO study was designed to provide raw data on
100 welfare benefits distributed on a monthly or annual
basis to 1,700 households in 6 nationally representative
low-income areas. Because the sites, comprising 5 cities
and a multi-county rural location, were profoundly depressed, the number of beneficiaries was expected to be
atypical. Staats, however, assured Griffiths that the
degree of program overlap would be the same as for any
other sector of the country. He further assured her
that the data would suggest what welfare patterns were
operating among the poor. Central to the analysis was
agreement among Griffiths' co-workers that traditional
sources of information like the census did not yield
the kind of detail on a broad range of welfare benefits
necessary to evaluate the system as a matter of social
policy. All major benefits in cash, goods, and services
would have to be checked. Included would be AFDC, Social Security, unemployment insurance, workmen's compensation, agricultural subsidies, subsidized food,
health and housing programs, manpower training, scholarships, day care, public employment, and legal aid. As
the first study to document the flow of all these benefits to specific households, the GAO review would be a
landmark.[65] Precedent setting, too, would be the use of
the House computer to analyze federal budgetary items.
That welfare expenditures amounted to $142 billion pointed to a project of notable achievement.

The data published by the staff were not comforting.[66]
Fifty to 75 percent of the households in the designated
sites received public aid, with 10 to 25 percent benefiting from 5 or more programs. Of the latter, 20 percent had income equivalents beyond the poverty level and
were, therefore, better off financially than a sizable
number of taxpaying wage earners.[67] In fact, at two
sites, the annual income averaged $6,500 which was $4,100
more than proposed by FAP. Contrary to popular
belief, the data also showed that in themselves multiple
benefits did not always eliminate poverty; hence, the
doubtful value of program overlap. Verified, too, was
the fact that while it was legally possible to "milk"

the system for as many as eleven benefits, that same system bypassed numbers of indigents who did not know how to play the welfare game. If the primary purpose of public assistance was to provide a reasonable amount of aid to those who needed it, this information had to arouse concern.

The data likewise refuted the popular image of the welfare family as the non-working woman with several illegitimate children. The survey revealed that many <u>need-based</u> benefits were received by households headed by employable males, by childless families, and by single, non-aged individuals, and that a large percentage of these households had working members. From this information, Griffiths and her staff concluded that categories as "employable" and "unemployable" based on sex and other such characteristics were false classifications in awarding assistance, and needed to be abolished.

These categories, especially when added to geographical benefit variation, led to the worst of inequities. For example, at the eastern site, the GAO found a woman raising her three children on $714 a month: $355 from earnings and $359 from benefits of which $281 was AFDC. In the same location a man and his family of three lived on a total of $371, comprising twenty-five dollars in unemployment insurance and $346 in salary, nine dollars less than that earned by the welfare mother. Because this family had a working father in residence, it was automatically ineligible for AFDC. At the rural counties site, two neighboring aged couples were discovered with significant income disparities. One couple qualified for surplus food and Medicaid (this was before Supplemental Security Income) because of their $184 Social Security check. The other couple, who received seventy-five more Social Security dollars, could not get free food commodities or the basic health services of Medicaid but only physician coverage under Medicare if they paid the premium. The difference between the two benefit packages was $220.[68] Assistance variants on account of sex, age, residence, employment, and marital status were astounding.

The GAO facts also highlighted two reasons why welfare recipients did not want to work. First, under the tax-free, multiple-program system, it was far easier to amass benefits than to work in low-paying jobs or in low-paying sectors of the country. Second, the benefit reduction rate, notably in AFDC, food stamps and rent subsidies, made sweating through the uncertainties of unemployment appear rather unreasonable when a check was guaranteed each month. In simple arithmetic, it did not pay to work.

For those who could read between the lines, the GAO study pointed to four policy directions. First, Congress and the Executive branch needed better and more regular information about all assistance programs. Second, Congress needed a data clearing house to deal with major welfare bills. Third, policy makers had to reeducate themselves to look at how welfare programs were related to one another and to all other sources of income accruing to recipient households. Finally, Congress needed to exercise its imagination and foresight in developing a contemporary response to assist needy persons as simply and as directly as possible.[69]

Secretary of HEW, Casper W. Weinberger, called the study "a most significant contribution to the public dialogue on the current problem of our welfare 'non-system,'" and he assured Griffiths that it would be "an invaluable source of information" to his Department in examining welfare options.[70] Griffiths was concerned that Weinberger would not attend to these data soon enough. "Before the President declares an end to the war on poverty," she warned, "maybe he really needs to know how many prisoners of war are left behind." Griffiths had also heard unofficially that because of the study Weinberger had instructed his staff to read everything her office put out. Pleased though she was with these accolades and with the positive response of her colleagues, she looked upon the survey as merely academic unless it prompted action. She sympathized with poor people who were not part of the system, or who were a very small part of it, like those with only Social Security. She sympathized with local administrators who were confused by a system over which they had no effective control. She even understood those who took advantage of every legal loophole to get as many benefits as they could. But, she said, "if you're going to have the programs, everyone should have a fair shot at them." The problem was the programs: 21 major benefits—the jurisdiction of 10 House committees and 9 Senate committees and the administrative responsibility of 11 federal agencies. Lacking any semblance of coordination, it was not surprising to Griffiths that welfare was not more dysfunctional than it was. What was mandated was a streamlined, accessible system. "If people are in need," she told Congress, "perhaps we should help all of them uniformly and fairly." In March 1973 she was already thinking of some form of guaranteed annual income to relieve the situation but, until her study was completed, she was not ready with the specifics. These would be forthcoming by the end of the year.[71]

When the GAO report got out, newspapers took it up to indict welfare as a "national disgrace." "[Welfare] works bizarrely, erratically, unfairly, lucratively, degradingly," stated James J. Kilpatrick in the Norfolk (VA) Ledger-Star. The St. Louis Globe-Democrat insisted that the study had factually proved that Griffiths was an advocate of the poor because it identified who they really were. Moreover, the press agreed with her that something immediate had to be done. To stall, wrote the Flint (Michigan) Journal, would be to invite "further demoralization of both givers and receivers of assistance." The Chicago-Sun Times, however, was less than sanguine that might happen. "Gamesmanship will continue to triumph over common sense," it said, but urged Congress to use the report as the basis for reform.[72]

A year after this major GAO study, Griffiths approached Comptroller General Staats for a lesser investigation on runaway fathers.[73] By June 1974 her staff had produced eight additional papers, many touching the child-support issue; HEW was also busy about a new welfare design. Despite the national distraction of Watergate by midyear 1974, Griffiths thought it important to continue addressing the problem so that when reform was approached in earnest, the matter would have already been considered. Because of the obvious connection between male default in child-support payments and female dependency on welfare, Staats also perceived that Griffiths' interest in the woman's question had prompted her request.[74] Nor had she ever rested easy with the demands made on harrassed taxpayers. "Whose responsibility is the support of a child—the parents' or the taxpayers'?" she asked.[75]

Griffiths proposed that in tracking down cases of nonsupport the survey focus on relatively affluent areas. The GAO staff was so dubious about this approach that Staats asked Griffiths to share a pilot study of 49 fathers under court order in Alameda County, California. This particular document revealed that more than half of the fathers earned over $8,000 a year; 13 between $10,000 and $14,000; and 5 over $15,000—and most were in arrears in their support payments. One $50,000-a-year executive paid nothing to support his five children. That all welfare fathers were winos, idlers, or off hunting low-wage pickup jobs was a myth as far as Griffiths was concerned. Some were, she said, but some were not—and she meant to find the latter. She was looking for answers to the following questions: What were the income characteristics of these middle- or upper-class non-supporters? How much had the court ordered them to pay and why did they not pay? The object of gathering this information was to convict Congress for having done practically nothing to collect a just debt and thereby decrease welfare expenditures. "Issuing vague commands" she believed was not enough. The key to action was data, and HEW had none on the incomes and responsibilities of financially able fathers. What spotty records there were had never been analyzed with other relevant material on a case-by-case basis.

Griffiths thought that for Congress to nod at willful payment neglect was to be party to the crime. It was also a refusal to confront societal change. As Griffiths reasoned, no law required fathers to remain with their families, but to demand nothing by way of supporting the children they had sired was to provide them the best of two worlds. Moreover, to subject these children to welfare when their fathers earned sizable incomes was unmerited injury. Finally, for Congress not to act was to place unjust burdens on mothers and taxpayers. The GAO study, Griffiths said, would help Congress face up to the facts—and its own responsibilities.[76]

Specifically, Griffiths asked Staats to focus his survey on AFDC homes for two reasons: first, to establish the potential for child-support payments; and, second, to learn how the child-support program operated under Social Security. The survey, made at 10 localities in 7 states, drew from 2 samples of AFDC families: one comprising 500 families with fathers under court order or agreement; the second comprising 1,000 families without any stipulated child-support payments. The staff first searched every available court, welfare, and support-collection record for the Social Security numbers of the absent fathers. Using this information, it then combed state employment records, the primary resource at its disposal. From this investigation the staff was able to isolate only 149 parents from the first sample and a lesser number from the second. The paucity of vital statistics made it clear why child-support payments were hard to collect.

Of the 149 subset, 26 percent of the fathers earned $6,000 to $9,000 annually; 24 percent, $9,000 to $12,000; 13 percent $12,000 to $15,000; and 5 percent, $15,000 or more. Median monthly earnings were $712 and median support, $95 or $50 per child. On the other side of the ledger, the former spouses, almost half employed outside the home, received a median monthly cash income of $288, including $211 in welfare. The GAO review also revealed disturbing features about the payments which tended to be pitifully meager—as small as 27¢ a day per child. Support was unrelated to income and payment inconsistencies prevailed in every county. A parent earning $6,000 was as likely to have the same stipulated support as one earning twice that amount and living in the same area. Payments were erratic. Only one-fourth of the 149 fathers paid 90 percent or more for child support. Of the rest, half made partial payments; the other half, almost nothing at all. Staats estimated that $3.1 million could be collected annually once support criteria were regularized and payments collected. The question was: Why did HEW allow these fathers to default? The answers were much the same as for all welfare programs: no single organization had total responsibility (six HEW agencies had some relationship to child support); there was lack of coordination; and basic program information was unavailable.[77]

In one of her last speeches before the House, Griffiths urged the Judiciary Committee to "stop dragging its feet" on enforcement legislation. "Until we clamp down on fathers who can contribute to their children's support but do not while their children live on welfare," she said, "we shall have difficulty helping needy fathers who cannot contribute and needy fathers who do contribute."[78] In 1975 Congress amended the Social Security Act to provide for the Office of Child Support Enforcement. Implementation, however, proved slow for want of money and because of the ensuing controversy of whether or not divulging Social Security numbers in tracking down recalcitrant fathers violated the 1974 Privacy Act.[79] Griffiths often remarked that it would take years to effect a workable child-support program, particularly in the absence of total welfare reform.[80]

To complement these two in-depth but restricted GAO surveys, Griffiths' staff gathered an equally unique set of facts to describe how the public-benefit system functioned nationally. Choosing for its review a scientifically selected sample of 100 counties, the staff asked state and local administrators for information on several hypothetical cases representing ten family types of various personal and income characteristics. The data were to include the benefits available for the specific family types; the cash value of the benefits provided; the amount of net earnings equal to the benefit value; the comparison of benefits with wages; the net gain or loss from work; and the differences in benefits for a couple, an unmarried mother, and a couple who had separated. Because of what this investigation revealed about their constituents, members of Congress "grabbed for those [studies] like hotcakes."[81] The survey confirmed much of what the GAO had discovered sixteen months before in its study of the six low-income areas: one, while welfare benefits tended to be low, a combination of them mounted to more than the net income of low-wage earners; two, work incentives were minimal; three, the inducement to break up families, or not form them in the first place, was compelling; and, four, there was a large financial bonus for women to have their first child, but there were lesser economic rewards for additional children. The "shocker" was the administrative morass at the state and local levels. Supposedly responsible agents did not know the regulations or how to apply them. In two states, they could not even respond to the survey; some took six months to do so; and a large number of the reports were riddled with errors.[82] Across the nation, welfare administration was a shabby enterprise.

In addition to collecting current facts, Townsend asked her staff to focus on a number of policy issues that needed to be addressed should a new structure emerge. These issues included the integration of major welfare programs; the relationship of pensions to public assistance; the balance between welfare payments and work incentives; and the effects of welfare, notably AFDC, on family stability. Also to be scrutinized were the effects of the haphazard development of welfare since 1935. The study of program integration revealed two disturbing facts: first, many low- and moderate-income workers gained little or nothing from their own or their employers' contributions to Social Security and unemployment insurance because of the peculiar relationship of these programs to cash-welfare assistance; and, second, within programs as diverse as day care, health, and housing, a two-tier benefit system had developed which penalized the middle-class by providing direct subsidies to the poor and income-tax deductions for the rich. No less distressing to the staff were the following: Social Security had grown beyond its original insurance function into a welfare program; increased Social Security taxes mortgaged the incomes of young workers; and most of the primary benefits, especially unemployment insurance and day care, discouraged economic independence. At base, the study pointed to a profound lack of integrity among programs.[83]

This lack was also demonstrated in the interaction of Social Security with the private pension system, the object of two staff analyses. To increase Social Security benefits on the basis of old formulas was seen by the reviewers as inequitably endowing retired pensioners with benefits they had really not earned. At the same time, since nearly half of all private workers were in jobs with no pension plans, the Social Security-pension function clearly discriminated to the benefit of pensioners. Just as arbitrary was the retirement test which penalized non-pensioned retirees for working to supplement their meager Social Security incomes, but which guaranteed the full Social Security grant to nonworking persons with lucrative pensions.[84] Since her initial study in the 60s on private pensions, inequities such as these had deeply troubled Griffiths.

Family stability and welfare was another issue for policy consideration to which the Townsend staff gave a great deal of attention. Its analysis indicated that public assistance had fostered a considerably high percentage of female-headed families where out-of-wedlock births ran as high as 30 to 35 percent. The gravity of the situation could be deduced from the fact that nationally the birth rate was declining and more and more women were entering the labor force. The reasons for the growth of one-parent families among low-income groups were manifold and complex. Included among contributing factors were the relatively high welfare benefits that encouraged already broken families to set up their own households, rather than live in the households of parents or other adult relatives. Welfare assistance rose sharply because of the extension of eligibility to higher income levels and improved health conditions heightened fertility. But according to staff findings, the primary reason for the rapid growth of one-parent households was that it paid off. It was supreme irony that a family was ineligible for AFDC as long as the working father was in residence but that it qualified once he had deserted or had feigned desertion.[85] "It is not equal rights that is destroying the American family," Griffiths told a human resources council in 1975. "It's the welfare system."[86] Illegitimacy, especially among higher socio-economic families, complicated the already capricious system. Not only did it increase short-range costs, but ultimately deprived children of their long-term rights to life and health insurance—all which contributed to the perpetuation of welfare, dependency, and high taxes.

That three-fourths of all female-headed families depended almost totally on welfare was proof to Griffiths that the system was self-defeating. Not to be given the opportunity to contribute to the nation's growth by personal labor, to be always on the receiving line, was to her a kind of economic servitude. Not to enable persons to be responsible for their own lives was one of the worst kinds of tyranny, whether the benefactors knew it or not. A renewed welfare system clearly had to be based on policies designed to reverse the status quo. As the result of her staff's analyses and her many years' experience, Griffiths suggested several welfare policy considerations related to family stability. First, welfare needed to be treated as income supplement so that able-bodied adults could find other sources of support without being penalized. Second, assistance needed to be given equitably to all low-income persons irrespective of marital status, family size, or sex. Third, in two-parent families larger benefits needed to be given to the adults. Fourth, the choice of family size belonged to parents as those primarily responsible for their children. Government needed to provide family planning services, but could not be expected to subsidize large families. Fifth, mothers in one-parent families should be required to work, which meant that sex discrimination in employment, in training, and in education had to be attacked systematically. Finally, fathers of one-parent families should be compelled to pay just alimony and child support, the latter requiring that paternity be determined vigorously and evenhandedly. Griffiths sympathized with the many poor who were faced with the trauma of changing family structures and perhaps were ill-prepared to do so. Nonetheless, she firmly believed that there were basic family responsibilities no government could fulfill.[87] The sooner policy makers came to terms with this fact, she believed the more equitable and just welfare would become.

Welfare's disincentive factor had by now become glaringly obvious to all serious students of the system. The question as Griffiths put it to her colleagues was not whether or not assistance should be given—she believed it should—but how to revamp the system so that recipients would be encouraged to work. In two papers, Townsend's staff set forth the policy dilemma: the more ample the benefits, the less they seemed to inspire employment; fewer benefits, however, had a lesser impact on the indigent. That generosity inherently stifled the will to work was further amplified by a study of New York welfare. All the evidence pointed to a new design that would strike a balance between work and welfare, or, as Griffiths put it: "mak[e] reasonable and rational compromises to achieve the best results overall."[88]

In the summer of 1973, while still in the midst of the welfare considerations, Griffiths conducted her JEC hearings on the economic problems of women demonstrating how societal issues were inextricably linked. In the fall she led the debate against the Supplemental Security Income (SSI), a Social Security cash-income guarantee for the aged, blind, and disabled. For Griffiths and her staff, who had reviewed SSI from the viewpoint of impact and unresolved questions,[89] the income-maintenance dialogue had advanced far beyond the Nixon FAP proposal, of which SSI was a by-product.

SSI's exclusion of other needy groups was for Griffiths a prime example of the haphazard approach to welfare that had plagued the system from the beginning. That it conflicted with other welfare goals exhibited what happened to a good idea when Congress and the Executive branch functioned independently in devising welfare schemes. During the SSI debates, Ways and Means member, Barber B. Conable Jr., pointed this out in a rhetorical exchange with Griffiths:

> Conable: Is it not true there is a major problem in the welfare system because of multiple programs?
>
> Griffiths: Of course.
>
> Conable: And duplicating phaseout?
>
> Griffiths: Of course.
>
> Conable: And overlapping administration?
>
> Griffiths: Of course.[90]

Griffiths was particularly alarmed that SSI proposed to boost benefits for the disadvantaged in states where awards were already above the national average but not in jurisdictions where the need was greater. She predicted that at most only ten of the wealthiest states would participate in the program, which in the main would not protect the really poor, that is, those persons getting minimum Social Security benefits or having some small asset which disqualified them for additional welfare. Unable to stay the passage of the bill, she nonetheless successfully fought against a "hold harmless" provision which would have permitted the rich states to grant larger SSI supplementation than the less affluent. Griffiths told the members of Congress that there was "at least one principle that we can all agree to: . . . as far as the Federal Government is concerned, a poor, aged, blind, or disabled person has the same claim on the Federal Treasury, no matter where he lives. Someone's health and comfort should not be worth more in one State and less in another in terms of Federal dollars."[91]

In addition to its limited scope and its capacity to propagate welfare inequities, SSI raised other doubts in Griffiths' mind because of its very complicated eligibility norms for food stamps. Even more disturbing was that the measure embedded Social Security more deeply in the welfare syndrome. By shifting payments from income tax revenues to Social Security-payroll taxes, contemporary wage earners would be required to support a program from which they would never profit because SSI grants tended to outstrip Social Security. This feature badly blurred the distinction between earned and unearned benefits and, for all practical purposes, rendered it meaningless to insure oneself against the future.[92] Testifying before the Senate Select Committee on the Aging in July 1974, Griffiths emphasized her strong opposition to adding SSI to the already welfare-impacted Social Security programs. "Social Security's quasi-welfare features," she protested, "have proved to be a careless way to help the needy which, at the expense of workers, give windfalls to the nonpoor." She offered three recommendations. First, Congressional actions should be based on cold facts and not merely on warm feelings. Second, assistance to the aged should be separated from Social Security and provided on a need-related basis. (She was particularly concerned about the many aged poor who, because they were neither indigent nor rich, "[fell] between the cracks.") And, third, once removed from Social Security and distributed according to need, SSI payments should be increased and the asset test liberalized. On a concluding note, Griffiths pleaded with the Senate Committee to attend to the acute needs of nonaged persons, especially those needing health insurance. Within a limited budget, hard choices would have to be made, she said, and she urged her Congressional colleagues to approach welfare options with the fullest possible information about the consequences of their actions.[93]

Within the year, Griffiths was again inveighing against incremental benefits—this time food stamps and fuel and housing subsidies. Because they were costly and disincentives to work, she opposed all stamp programs, a matter then under survey for her staff by the Agriculture Department.[94] She likewise opposed HUD rent subsidies as confusing the maintenance of the poor with their need for decent housing.[95] In addition to her resistance against a non-comprehensive welfare plan, she disagreed with in-kind benefits which she believed fostered an endless piecemeal list of needs and which tended toward increasing complexity. They involved administrative red tape, seldom realized their cash value, and limited choice for the recipient. Moreover, they were costly—often twice the value of the program—and created serious difficulties in accounting. As a substitute, Griffiths suggested that the needy be given cash which they could determine how to spend. It was patronizing for the government both to decide for the poor what their needs were and then to deprive them of the responsibility of budgeting for themselves and their families. From these arguments Congress could infer that the proposal to emerge from Griffiths' welfare study would be a cash design.

The press and the public took kindly to the policy considerations Griffiths and her staff had worked through during the many months of fact-finding and analysis.[96] It was increasingly difficult not to agree with Griffiths that the present system was "'impossible'" and that the government could expect a citizens' revolt unless suitable remedies could be found to enable the largest segment of the population to pay their bills, retain an adequate purchasing power, and avoid excessive indebtedness. If lawmakers continued to ignore "the backbone American"—middle-class workers and professionals—while at the same time allowing the rich to escape through tax loopholes, they could not press for justice for minorities. The tax structure burdened the average citizen, especially working wives, who, with their middle-class sisters, experienced a kind of economic discrimination ironically spared the poor. Through welfare taxes, the middle-class provided better health care for the poor than for themselves, subsidized day-care facilities for welfare mothers, and financed college education for ghetto blacks. Many middle-income workers gained little or nothing from their Social Security contributions; and their pensions, if they had them, were not guaranteed. It appeared more profitable to remain poor and unemployed than to be middle-class.[97] "I suppose this situation can be viewed as both the essence and weakness of our democratic system," Griffiths told the Urban Institute shortly after the SSI fight.[98]

In February 1974, Nixon announced that HEW Secretary Weinberger would soon present a direct cash proposal to replace all major assistance programs, including AFDC and the recently enacted SSI. Since his unsuccessful FAP days, the President had increasingly come to oppose welfare tinkering by both the Executive and Legislative branches. He was anxious, therefore, that Congress mount an all-out offensive against a system he termed a "monstrous, consuming outrage."[99] By this time, the Griffiths' staff, now in its last year of research, was also in the process of developing a cash-payments plan. That persons as politically diverse as Casper Weinberger, Governor Ronald Reagan's former finance director, and Martha Griffiths should agree to the same basic direction in welfare reform was indeed newsworthy.[100] Unfortunately, more newsworthy as 1974 progressed was the Watergate scandal. When HEW was finally ready to release the promised Income Supplement Program in late 1974, a new President was at the helm determined to steer the Ship of State into welfare waters other than those charted by his predecessor.

Bringing her study to term in 1974 was particularly urgent to Griffiths once she announced she would not seek re-election in November. In 1975 approximately 34 million persons would be on the $142 billion welfare system. The question was: How long could Congress morally tolerate this system? In recommending a simplified, coordinated, and rationalized plan, Griffiths hoped to give her colleagues something to do when she was gone. Through her study, she and her staff had identified four clusters of problems.[101] First, by having placed recipients in categories great disparities had resulted as to who got what. Only one federal program, food stamps, was open to all on the basis of family size and income. Cash grants were limited to two major groups: first, the aged, the blind, the disabled (SSI); and, second, one-parent families with dependent children or children whose fathers worked no more than 100 hours monthly (AFDC). There were no cash benefits for other needy such as childless couples or for that vast array of persons who were neither aged, blind, nor disabled but disadvantaged in some other way such as by early widowhood. Moreover, cash aid, having nearly quadrupled in eight years, had placed an extraordinary strain on Social Security-insurance programs thereby subverting the original purpose of the 1935 statute.

The second group of problems centered on benefit levels. AFDC, which the staff labeled an unambiguous failure, was classic because of its dependence on state standards. Maximum awards for a family of four ranged from $60 to $400 monthly and, despite the government's professed goal to assist poorer states the Treasury paid four or five times more for a destitute family in New York than it did for a similar family in Mississippi. The multibenefit system had likewise engendered the third probelm of work incentives. In all but thirteen states, the combined value of AFDC and food stamps exceeded the net pay from a fulltime job at the minimum wage. Additionally, the benefit-loss rate of a number of programs made it simply unprofitable to work. These three problems understandably resulted in a fourth: management inefficiency and confusion. The waste of time, energy, and taxpayers' dollars, to say nothing of profound administrative frustration and a high incidence of error, especially in overpayments, had become too severe to be tolerated and too complex to be cured from within. Particularly appalled by the system's devastating effects on the family and the gross income inequities fostered within and without the system, Griffiths was for "wip[ing] out the whole thing."[102] Even those members of the Fiscal Policy Subcommittee who did not totally subscribe to the final design did not argue with the staff's analysis of welfare's major deficiencies. The study's attraction, as Representative Richard Bolling saw it, was that Griffiths had steered the middle course in demonstrating to "liberals" that there were "rip-offs," and to "conservatives" that there were a great many needy people who did not benefit from the system. "That's a fundamental problem that we had to face," he said about his colleagues, "and I think her study helped us face it."[103]

In bringing her welfare study to its conclusion, Griffiths sought a plan that would assist all low- and moderate-income persons with federal funding while at the same time enable them to exert personal responsibility for at least a portion of their income. The translation of this concept into the Tax Credits and Allowances Act was the fruit of a lengthy and thorough sifting of options begun in 1972. The fact that two of the Townsend papers dealt specifically with the issue of welfare design indicate how seriously various reform strategies were evaluated.[104] Griffiths initially favored a flat payment to everyone—the demogrant—subsequently popularized by George McGovern in his 1972 presidential bid.[105] Operating as a refundable tax credit the demogrant assumed no reduction in work effort, promised to do away with all major welfare programs, and offered a more progressive income tax by taxing the credit back with rising income. Not only did the demogrant recommend itself toward the amelioration of the four problem areas inherent in the multibenefit system but, since everyone received the same grant, it removed the social stigma between those who could support themselves fully by their own efforts and those who could not. The rub, unfortunately, was the price: it would have required more than a 50 percent rate on personal taxable income, a fact that precluded further consideration of the option.

A work-conditioned supplement was also scrutinized. But outweighing its strong appeal of regular employment were its costliness and the prospect of subsidizing the program participants above the subsistence levels of many working Americans. Griffiths also saw as disadvantageous to women the administrative interpretation of who was employable and who was not. "The man gets the job," she predicted, "the woman gets welfare."[106] At her request, Robert L. Lerman, Townsend's staff economist, looked at a public employment and wage-subsidy proposal, the JOIN plan. Lerman concluded rather quickly that a public work program was one of the least desirable income plans for the following reasons: a relatively small number of persons would be reached; it would not address the question of need differences without possibly violating the equal pay for equal work principle; and the federal government had little experience in managing this kind of effort. Moreover, that the government would be the ultimate guarantor of work and that the program would introduce an endless controversy over what was public employment and what was private were added reasons for Griffiths and her staff not to endorse a public work plan.[107] Other lesser options were also reviewed, but like the major ones were found wanting. Only the Tax Credits and Allowances Act, which combined welfare reform with tax reform, seemed to Griffiths to be a rational approach to the very complex problem.[108] What this proposal could not do, however, in its efforts to redistribute personal income was to protect current welfare recipients from large benefit losses, which perforce would make it politically controversial.

Any reform which would bear the Griffiths' name would have to eradicate what Griffiths considered welfare's twin evils: one, benefit inequities; and two, eligibility norms which led to the destruction of the family. Of the latter, she wrote: "The public policy of the country must be to encourage marriage."[109] The Tax Credits and Allowances Act addressed both shortcomings through a universal rebatable per capita tax credit designed principally to assist low- and moderate-income workers. Unlike the personal exemption which it replaced in the income-tax structure, the tax credit stood to achieve an equitable income-distribution system intended by the Sixteenth Amendment. The tax credit further recommended itself for a relatively easy adjustment to the rise in the cost of living and, even more importantly, for its potential in directing a basic income system toward the eventual elimination of all explicit aid. There would no longer be state variations in awarding federal assistance, although state and local governments could dispense their own aid. To remove income distribution "completely from the sociologists," Griffiths provided that the Tax Credits and Allowances Act be administered by the Internal Revenue Service.[110] It was her hope that by melding income maintenance with income distribution the meaning of welfare would change altogether. "We wouldn't even call it welfare anymore. We would do away with that word forever," she told a Maryland audience.[111] HEW, stripped of all its welfare activities, would be forced to face the original intent of Social Security as income replacement, a prospect which Griffiths strongly favored. The Tax Credits and Allowances Act held the promise of revolutionizing the system.

Although the bill's first concern was for the largest number of less affluent Americans, it also attended to the very poor through the Allowances for Basic Living Expenses. As a monthly supplement, ABLE, in conjunction with the tax credits, provided a federal income floor. A penniless two-adult family of four could qualify for $3,600; a one-adult family, $3,000. In its formulation, ABLE represented a fusion of several key principles. By providing uniform payments to all the destitute, it hoped to prevent family splitting under AFDC. It further assumed that even the nation's lowest economic groups had other sources of income such as child support and private earnings, and it discouraged large families by tailoring the aid downward with additional children. Additionally, benefit-loss rates were orchestrated with net earnings so as to encourage work and yet allow support for real needs. As a case in point, two-earner families and working heads of households would be given special consideration because of their work expenses.

The proposed bill wiped out AFDC and food stamps and merged the other welfare benefits, such as subsidized housing and day care, into a coordinated system. (SSI—without food stamps—was retained because it had just gone into effect.) The goal was the eventual elimination of all cash and in-kind supplements through the reformed tax structure. Griffiths and her staff estimated that initially half of the $15.4 billion in net federal cost would go for tax relief and thereby reduce the number of poor by some 2.5 million. Phasing the plan over three or four years proposed to minimize start-up costs to avoid disrupting local labor markets and to allow for changes as the program developed. The act seemed administratively feasible since the government had successfully managed six pilot projects similar to the tax-credits bill and the Treasury Department had declared itself capable of running such a system nationwide. Congress, too, looked like it might favor the act as it had recently dealt with other tax-credit proposals[112] as well as had considered universal coverage of food and fuel stamps and housing subsidies. While Griffiths said she was not wedded to the particulars of her plan, she pleaded with her colleagues not to write themselves off as "partner[s] in change."[113]

With an aura of both farewell and legacy, Griffiths introduced the Tax Credits and Allowances Act on December 5, 1974. She was extremely proud of what she and her staff had done and admitted later that had she remained in Congress she would have reorganized the rest of the welfare system.[114] Through her study she had presented the facts for which numerous welfare watchers accorded her a vote of thanks.[115] She likewise gave her critics something worth talking about. Even if some thought that a federally controlled system was unacceptable and too costly or that handing it over to the Internal Revenue System was "crazy,"[116] she had entered welfare into the public debate. Or had she?

An argument could be made that since nothing substantial has been done since Griffiths left Congress, notwithstanding the cosponsorship of her bill in 1976 by Senator Javits and Representative Robert J. Cornell of Wisconsin,[117] the nearly three-and-one-half years' research was, in the estimate of former HEW chief Wilbur J. Cohen, the preserve of academicians "like Dr. Eliot's five-foot bookshelf, which has a lot of information."[118] On more than one occasion Griffiths herself admitted that as she toured the country she found universities and non-legislative persons more conversant with her findings than the nation's lawmakers.[119] In view of Congress' apparent disinterest in promoting welfare reform, has the Griffiths' study really been effective? How reconcile Congressional inaction with Washington appraisals of her work as "a basic pattern for welfare reform," "a landmark effort," and "a starting point for a serious and thorough consideration . . . of the solution of this acute national and urban and moral problem"?[120] Its impact very possibly lies in the future. Former Social Security Commissioner Robert Ball said that the study got people thinking. And Comptroller General Staats, whose own work was significant in bringing the study forward, saw it as an essential piece in a yet-unfinished story.[121] What Griffiths wrote in 1974 as preface to her final report remains a sharp challenge to her legislative successors—and the hope of all Americans. "This work began because of the inequity in the law," she noted with a sense of purpose. "It is dedicated to equality in justice."[122]

[1] Interview with McClung, Washington, D.C., January 27, 1978. Much of the description for the genesis of the welfare study was taken from this interview.

[2] Almost everyone interviewed in Washington spontaneously mentioned the study. Griffiths' colleagues and associates on Ways and Means and Joint Economic were particularly impressed by it. Representative Richard Bolling of Missouri called it a "landmark effort" and said it was "fundamentally valid" (Interview with Richard Bolling, Washington, D.C., January 26, 1978).

[3] U.S., Congress, Joint Economic Committee, Income-Maintenance Programs, Hearings before the Subcommittee on Fiscal Policy, 2 vols., 90th Cong., 2d sess., June 11-13, 18-20, and 25-27, 1968 (1968), 1:1 and 368; Washington Post, June 3, 1968, clipping in MWG Scrapbooks, Griffiths Library.

[4] For example, see the testimony of Lisle C. Carter Jr., Commissioner of New York State Department of Social Services and former Assistant Secretary of HEW for Individual Family Services, JEC, Income Maintenance Programs, 1:4; of Joseph E. Pechman of the Brookings Institution, Ibid., 1:98; and of Robert A. Levine, Assistant Director for Research, Plans, Programs and Evaluation of the Office of Economic Opportunity, Ibid., 1:162.

[5] "Nixon's Proposals for Welfare Reform Win Tentative Approval from Key House Panel," Wall Street Journal, February 27, 1970, clipping in MWG Scrapbooks, Griffiths Library; U.S., Congress, House, 91st Cong., 2d sess., April 16, 1970, Congressional Record 116:12028-29.

[6] U.S., Congress, House, Committee on Ways and Means, Family Assistance Act of 1970 (H.R. 16311), H. Rept. 91-904, 91st Cong., 2d sess., 1970, pp. 9-11.

[7] Griffiths, "Welfare Research and Welfare Policy," speech delivered by a surrogate to the 14th Annual Conference on Welfare Research and Statistics, Boston, Massachusetts, August 6, 1974, in Griffiths Library.

[8] Griffiths, speech to the Annual Meeting of Health and Welfare Council of Central Maryland, March 19, 1975, in Griffiths Library.

[9] Interview with Alair A. Townsend, Washginton, D.C.,

January 24, 1978.

[10] Griffiths to Heller, February 1, 1971, in Griffiths Papers, Bentley Library.

[11] Interview with Martha Griffiths, Romeo, Michigan, February 22, 1978.

[12] Interview with Townsend, Washington, D.C., January 24, 1978.

[13] U.S., Congress, Joint Economic Committee, Income Security for Americans: Recommendations of the Public Welfare Study, by Subcommittee on Fiscal Policy, Joint Committee Print (Washington, D.C.: Government Printing Office, 1974), pp. vi-vii.

[14] Interview with Barber B. Conable Jr., Washington, D.C., January 27, 1978.

[15] Education and Public Welfare Division, Legislative Reference Service, the Library of Congress, to Griffiths, January 17, 1968, in Griffiths Library.

[16] The material on Griffiths' views on welfare before 1971 is drawn from the following sources (only direct quotations on interviews will be specifically identified in the text itself): U.S., Congress, Joint Economic Committee, Revenue Sharing and its Alternatives: What Future for Fiscal Federalism, by Harley H. Hinrichs (ed.), Joint Economic Print Washington, D.C., Government Printing Office, 1967; U.S., Congress, House, Committee on Ways and Means, President's Proposals for Revision in the Social Security System, Hearings before the Committee on Ways and Means on H. R. 5710. 90th Cong., 1st sess., March 1-3, 1967 (1967); Griffiths, "Testimony before the Senate Finance Committee on Welfare Provisions of H.R. 12080," September 22, 1967, in Griffiths Library; U.S., Congress, Joint Economic Committee, Income Maintenance Programs, Hearings. . .; U.S., Congress, House, Committee on Ways and Means, Social Security and Welfare Proposals, Hearings before the Committee on Ways and Means. 91st Cong., 1st sess., October 15-16, 21-24, 27-28, 30-31, November 3-7, 10, and 12-13, 1969 (1970); U.S., Congress, House, 90th Cong., 1st sess., August 17, 1967, Congressional Record 114:23081; U.S., Congress, House, 90th Cong. 2d sess., October 4, 1968, Congressional Record, clipping in MWG Scrapbooks, Griffiths Library; and U.S., Congress, House, 91st

Cong., 1st sess., June 11, 1969, <u>Congressional Record</u> 115:15498.

[17] Interviews with Griffiths, Romeo, Michigan, June 3, 1977, and January 7, 1978.

[18] U.S., Congress, Joint Economic Committee, <u>Revenue Sharing and its Alternatives. . .</u>, 2:308.

[19] U.S., Congress, House, 90th Cong., 1st sess., August 17, 1967, <u>Congressional Record</u> 113:23081.

[20] U.S., Congress, House, Committee on Ways and Means, <u>Social Security and Welfare Proposals, Hearings. . .</u>, 4:1100-6.

[21] U.S., Congress, House, 90th Cong., 2d sess., July 17, 1968, <u>Congressional Record</u>, clipping in MWG Scrapbooks, Griffiths Library.

[22] Griffiths, "The Family, Poverty, and Welfare Programs," speech prepared for the Michigan Inter-Professional Association on Marriage, Divorce and the Family [ ], 1973, in Griffiths Library.

[23] U.S., Congress, House, Committee on Ways and Means, <u>Social Security and Welfare Proposals, Hearings. . .</u>, 4:1103-5. Members of the National Welfare Rights Organization were particularly upset by Griffiths' insistence that AFDC women work. <u>Ibid.</u>, 3:1023-34. A Nader group later used Griffiths' arguments to show that she was not attentive to the poor. "How Nader sees 3 Congressmen," (Farmington, Mich.) <u>Observer Newspapers</u>, October 25, 1972, in MWG Scrapbooks, Griffiths Library. UAW leadership likewise took the position that it was not possible to coerce welfare mothers to work because there were no available jobs. Interview with Dorothy Haener, Detroit, Michigan, December 19, 1977.

[24] U.S., Congress, Joint Economic Committee, <u>Income Maintenance Programs, Hearings. . .</u>, 1:179; U.S., Congress, House, 90th Cong., 1st sess., August 17, 1967, <u>Congressional Record</u> 113:23081.

[25] U.S., Department of HEW, "Materials on Employability of AFDC Recipients," [January 1970], in Griffiths Library. Griffiths told how Secretary of HEW, Wilbur J. Cohen, was surprised on learning that 70 percent of the AFDC women in New York City wanted to work. "And

I said to him, well, Mr. Cohen, the other 30 percent did not understand the question or they would have wanted to work, too. Who would not prefer to have a job?" U.S., Congress, Joint Economic Committee, Income Maintenance Programs, Hearings . . ., 1:77.

26U.S., Congress, House, Committee on Ways and Means, Social Security and Welfare Proposals, Hearings. . ., 4:1139.

27U.S., Congress, House, 91st Cong., 1st sess., March 11 and 20, 1969, Congressional Record 115:5922-3 and 7046. Judd Arnett, Detroit Free Press columnist, said this proposal showed that Griffiths was "given to compassion—and absolutely formidable." March [ ], 1969, clipping in Griffiths Library.

28U.S., Congress, Joint Economic Committee, Income Maintenance Programs, Hearings . . ., 1:178-79.

29This attitude represented a change from what Griffiths thought in 1962 when she argued that day-care centers subsidized employers and not working women. She would rather have had better wages so that AFDC mothers could have provided the child care of their choice. U.S., Congress, Joint Economic Committee, January 1962 Economic Report of the President, Hearings before the Joint Economic Committee. 87th Cong., 2d sess., January 25-26, 30-31, and 5-8, 1962 (1962), p. 793.

30Griffiths, "Women and Legislation," [ ], in Griffiths Library.

31Griffiths, "Of Government and Welfare," Human Ecology Forum (New York State College of Human Ecology, Ithaca, New York) 6 (Summer 1975): 1.

32Interview with Griffiths, Romeo, Michigan, February 22, 1978.

33Ibid.

34Alair A. Townsend, "Memorandum: To Martha Griffiths and James W. Knowles, 'Rationale for Study,'" September 8, 1971, in Griffiths Library.

35Interviews with Griffiths, Romeo, Michigan, January 6, 1978, and February 22, 1978; Interview with Townsend, Washington, D.C., January 24, 1978.

[36] Interview with Townsend, Washington D.C., January 24, 1978.

[37] U.S., Congress, Joint Economic Committee, Problems in Administration of Public Welfare Programs, Hearings before the Subcommittee on Fiscal Policy 3 vols. 92nd Cong., 2d sess., March 20, April 11-13, 1972; May 3-5, 1972; and June 6-8, 1972.

[38] U.S. General Accounting Office, Elmer B. Staats, Report to the Congress: "Problems in Attaining Integrity in Welfare Programs: Social and Rehabilitation Service, DHEW," March 16, 1972, pp. 1-2.

[39] U.S., Congress, Joint Economic Committee, Problems in Administration of Public Welfare Programs, Hearings . . ., 1:10, and 60-65.

[40] Ibid., 1:68-69, 78, and 84-85.

[41] Willard Edwards, "Who Gets Welfare? Nobody Knows," Chicago Tribune, March 23, 1972, clipping in MWG Scrapbooks, Griffiths Library.

[42] U.S., Congress, Joint Economic Committee, Problems in Administration of Public Welfare Programs, Hearings . . ., 1:56.

[43] New York Times, March 22, 1972; (Baltimore) News American, March 23, 1972; and New York Post, [n.d.], clipping in MWG Scrapbooks, Griffiths Library.

[44] U.S., Congress, House, 92d Cong., 2d sess., June 28, 1972, Congressional Record 118:22957. For further tongue-in-cheek remarks, see the Record for July 26, 1972, 118:25523.

[45] U.S., Congress, Joint Economic Committee, Public Income Transfer Programs: the Incidence of Multiple Benefits and the Issues Raised by Their Receipt, by James R. Storey, Joint Committee Print, Study Paper 1 (Washington, D.C.: Government Printing Office, 1973), pp. 1-3.

[46] U.S., Congress, House, 92d Cong., 2d sess., April 24, 1972, Congressional Record 118:14007-08.

[47] U.S., Congress, Joint Economic Committee, Issues in Welfare Administration: Welfare—An Administrative Nightmare, by James R. Storey et al., comps., Joint

Committee Print, Study Paper 5, pt. 1 (Washington, D.C.,: Government Printing Office, 1972).

[48] Interview with Griffiths, Romeo, Michigan, February 22, 1978; Norman P. Thomas to editor, Detroit News, April 17, 1972, clipping in MWG Scrapbooks, Griffiths Library. Thomas pointed out that while Griffiths spoke "sincerely," her facts were "often incorrect and distorted."

[49] U.S., Congress, Joint Economic Committee, Problems in Administration of Public Welfare Programs, Hearings . . . , 1:169.

[50] Ibid., 1:163; and 3:1275.

[51] Ibid., 1:209.

[52] Ibid., 1:202-3.

[53] Griffiths, "What's Wrong with Welfare," speech to the Urban Institute [?], [n.d.], in Griffiths Library; U.S., Congress, House, 92d Cong., 2d sess., April 24, 1972, Congressional Record 118:14008.

[54] U.S., Congress, House, 92d Cong., 2d sess., June 21, 1972, Congressional Record 118:21691.

[55] U.S., Congress, Joint Economic Committee, Open-Ended Federal Matching of State Social Service Expenditures Authorized under the Public Assistance Titles of the Social Security Act, Hearings before the Subcommittee on Fiscal Policy. 92d Cong., 2d sess., September 12-14, 1972 (1972) pp. 2, 6, 12, 23, and 227-29.

[56] U.S., Congress, Joint Economic Committee, Handbook of Public Income Transfer Programs, by Irene Cox, comp., Joint Committee Print, Study Paper 2 (Washington, D.C.: Government Printing Office, 1973). A revised edition was published in 1975 as Study Paper 20.

[57] Edmund LeBreton, "Welfare Rules Discourage Job Seeker, Hill Study Says," Washington Post, December 23, 1972, clipping in MWG Scrapbooks, Griffiths Library.

[58] U.S., Congress, Joint Economic Committee, Income Transfer Programs: How They Tax the Poor, by Robert I. Lerman, comp., Joint Committee Print. Study Paper 4 (Washington, D.C.: Government Printing Office, 1974), pp. vi-vii.

[59] Detroit News, [n.d.]; (Washington, D.C.) Sunday Star and Daily News, January 21, 1973, clippings in MWG Scrapbooks, Griffiths Library.

[60] U.S., Congress, Joint Economic Committee, The Effectiveness of Manpower Training Programs: A Review of Research on the Impact on the Poor, by Jon H. Goldstein, Joint Committee Print, Study Paper 3 (Washington, D.C.: Government Printing Office, 1972) pp. iii-iv, and 14.

[61] Los Angeles Times, November 28, 1972; Memphis (Tenn.) Commercial Appeal, February 1, 1973; and Detroit News, October 22, 1972, clippings in MWG Scrapbooks, Griffiths Library.

[62] Interview with Townsend, Washington, D.C., January 24, 1978.

[63] Griffiths, "Welfare Research and Welfare Policy."

[64] Griffiths to editor, Washington Post, April 19, 1973, clipping in Griffiths Library.

[65] Elmer B. Staats to Emily George, R.S.M., February 25, 1978. Comptroller General Staats wished that its uniqueness as the first full-fledged study of its kind be emphasized.

[66] U.S., Congress, Joint Economic Committee, How Public Welfare Benefits Are Distributed in Low-Income Areas, by James R. Storey et al., Joint Committee Print, Study Paper 6 (Washington, D.C.: Government Printing Office, 1973), pp. 1-10; U.S., Congress, Joint Economic Committee, Additional Material for Paper No. 6: How Public Welfare Benefits are Distributed in Low-Income Areas, by Alair A. Townsend, comp., Joint Committee Print (Washington, D.C.: Government Printing Office, 1973).

[67] The fluidity of the composition of households accounted for the range in percentages. By using the benefit approach in calculating income, the GAO estimated that from 8 to 35 percent of the households were poor; whereas, the Census Bureau, basing its figures on the sole criterion of cash assistance, established the percentages from 14 to 67.

[68] These examples were drawn from U.S., Congress, Joint Economic Committee, How Public Welfare Benefits Are

Distributed . . ., pp. 7 and 92.

[69] "Question for Paper No. 6 Press Conference," [n.d.], in Griffiths Library.

[70] Weinberger to Griffiths, May 11, 1973, in Griffiths Papers, Bentley Library. In a letter to Emily George, R.S.M., January 9, 1978, Weinberger said: "Her work and recommendations had considerable influence on the subject of welfare reform, and some of her recommendations were closely parallel to one which our Department made when we sent a formal, comprehensive program to the President. I think her committee's study also constituted a very valuable piece of work, and was a study that was essential at that time."

[71] U.S., Congress, House, 93rd Cong., 1st sess., March 27, 1973, Congressional Record 119:9527-30; Griffiths, Craig Palmer, and Arch Booth, "What's the Issue?" Chamber of Commerce radio recording, April 12, 1973, in Griffiths Papers, Bentley Library.

[72] St. Louis Globe-Democrat, March 31-April 1, 1973, and April 6, 1973; (Norfolk, Va.) Ledger-Star, August 25, 1973; Flint (Mich.) Journal, April 4, 1973; Chicago-Sun Times, March 28, 1973, clippings in MWG Scrapbooks, Griffiths Library.

[73] Compiled in U.S., Comptroller General of the United States, New Child Support Legislation—Its Potential Impact and How to Improve It; Office of Child Support Enforcement, Department of HEW, Report to the Congress, April 5, 1976.

[74] Interview with Elmer B. Staats, Washington D.C., February 23, 1978.

[75] U.S. Congress, House, 93d Cong., 2d sess., December 4, 1974, Congressional Record 120:38196-98.

[76] Griffiths, "Remarks of Congresswomen Martha W. Griffiths before Members of the General Accounting Office Staff," June 18, 1974, in Griffiths Library; Interview with Griffiths, Romeo, Michigan, February 22, 1978.

[77] The GAO report was not published for some time. Griffiths, however, used the data, as in Griffiths, "Child Support Collection Among Welfare Families," rough draft of an address to the House, November 1974, in

Griffiths Library.

[78] U.S., Congress, House, 93d Cong., 2d sess., December 4, 1974, Congressional Record 120:38196-98.

[79] U.S., Comptroller General of the United States, New Child Support Legislation. . . .

[80] Interview with Griffiths, Romeo, Michigan, February 22, 1978.

[81] Interview of Townsend, Washington, D.C., January 24, 1978.

[82] U.S., Congress, Joint Economic Committee, Welfare in the 70's: A National Study of Benefits Available in 100 Local Areas, by James R. Storey, Joint Committee Print, Study Paper 15 (Washington, D.C.: Government Printing Office, 1974), pp. iii-iv; Interview with Griffiths, Romeo, Michigan, February 22, 1978; Griffiths, "Welfare Research and Welfare Policy," . . . .

[83] U.S., Congress, Joint Economic Committee, Issues in the Coordination of Public Welfare Programs, by Alair A. Townsend et al., comps., Joint Committee Print, Study Paper 7 (Washington, D.C.: Government Printing Office, 1973) p.iii.

[84] U.S., Congress, Joint Economic Committee, The Labor Market of the Private Retirement System, by Robert Taggart, Joint Committee Print, Study Paper 11 (Washington, D.C.: Government Printing Office, 1973), pp. vi and 9-10; U.S., Congress, Joint Economic Committee, Issues in Financing Retirement Income, by Alexander Korns, Joint Committee Print, Study Paper 18 (Washington, D.C.: Government Printing Office, 1974), p. 187.

[85] U.S., Congress, Joint Economic Committee, The Family, Poverty, and Welfare Programs: Factors Influencing Family Instability, by Robert I. Lerman, ed., Joint Committee Print, Study Paper 12, pt. 1 (Washington, D.C.: Government Printing Office, 1973); and U.S., Congress, Joint Economic Committee, The Family, Poverty, and Welfare Programs: Household Patterns and Government Policies, by Robert I. Lerman, ed., Joint Committee Print, Study Paper 12, pt. 2 (Washington, D.C.: Government Printing Office, 1973). A good summary of both parts is welfare study releases, "Congressional Subcommittee Releases Studies on the Growth of Illegitimacy, Fatherless Families, and the Welfare

Rolls," November 4, 1973; and, "Representative Martha W. Griffiths Releases Studies on Household Patterns and Governmental Policies," December 3, 1973, in Griffiths Library.

[86]Griffiths speech to the Annual Meeting of Health and Welfare Council of Central Maryland. . . .

[87]Griffiths, "The Family, Poverty, and Welfare Programs," remarks prepared for the Michigan Inter-Professional Association on Marriage, Divorce, and the Family.

[88]U.S., Congress, Joint Economic Committee, How Income Supplements Can Affect Work Behavior, by Robert I. Lerman, comp., Joint Committee Print, Study Paper 13 (Washington, D.C.: Government Printing Office, 1974), pp. 59-60; U.S., Congress, Joint Economic Committee, Public Welfare and Work Incentives: Theory and Practice, by Vee Burke et al., Joint Economic Print, Study Paper 14 (Washington, D.C.: Government Printing Office, 1974) p. 43; U.S., Congress, Joint Economic Committee, Income-Tested Social Benefits in New York: Adequacy, Incentives, and Equity, by Blanche Bernstein et al., Joint Committee Print, Study Paper 8 (Washington, D.C.: Government Printing Office, 1973), pp. iii-iv; U.S., Congress, House, 93d Cong., 2d sess., May 1, 1974, Congressional Record 120:12540-41, and Griffiths, "The Family, Poverty, and Welfare Programs," remarks prepared for the Michigan Inter-Professional Association on Marriage, Divorce, and the Family.

[89]U.S., Congress, Joint Economic Committee, The New Supplemental Security Income Program-Impact on Current Benefits and Unresolved Issues, by James R. Storey et al., Joint Committee Print, Study Paper 10 (Washington D.C.: Government Printing Office, 1973), pp. iii-iv, and 2.

[90]U.S., Congress, House, 93d Cong., 1st sess., July 19, 1973, Congressional Record 119:24926-27.

[91]U.S., Congress, House, 93d Cong., 1st sess., November 14, 1973, Congressional Record 119:36958-60; Richard L. Madden, "House Approves a 2-Step 11% Rise in Social Security," New York Times, November 16, 1973, in MWG Scrapbooks, Griffiths Library.

[92]U.S., Congress, House, 93d Cong., 1st sess., October 10, 1973, Congressional Record 119:33704-05; Griffiths to editor, New York Times, April 24, 1974; Ron Cordray,

"Welfare Reform Needs Reform," <u>Flint (Mich.) Journal</u>, October 17, 1973, clippings in MWG Scrapbooks Griffiths Library; and, "Representative Martha W. Griffiths to Lead Floor Fight on Adult Welfare Provision," press release in MWG Scrapbooks, Griffiths Library. "As one examines the records of the various food programs," Griffiths told Congress, "a pattern emerges. It is a pattern of beginning programs, offering them as solutions, and then when they begin to catch hold, increasing the limitations, limiting accessibility, developing more restrictive requirements, and withholding money." U.S., Congress, House, 92d Cong., 2d sess., May 22, 1972, <u>Congressional Record</u> 118:18302.

[93]U.S., Congress, House, 93d Cong. 1st sess., March 13, 1973, <u>Congressional Record</u> 119:7519. U.S., Congress, Senate, <u>Future Directions in Social Security Hearings before the Special Committee on the Aging</u>. 93d Cong., 2d sess., July 16, 1974 (1974) 8:693-709. The committee staff told Griffiths that they had learned more about Social Security and SSI from her testimony than from any other source. Interview with Griffiths, Romeo, Michigan, June 3, 1977. Once SSI was passed, Griffiths was additionally upset with Secretary Weinberger for cancelling HEW's general information program on the new benefit, thereby leaving this task to local welfare agencies. Griffiths to Weinberger, June 6, 1973, in Griffiths Papers, Bentley Library.

[94]U.S., Congress, Joint Economic Committee, <u>National Survey of Food Stamp and Food Distribution Program Recipients: A Summary of Findings on Income Sources and Amounts and Incidence of Multiple Benefits</u>, by U.S. Department of Agriculture, Joint Committee Print, Study Paper 17 (Washington, D.C.: Government Printing Office, 1974), pp iii, and 1-3; Griffiths to the editor, <u>Washington, (D.C.) Star-News</u>, July 24, 1974, in Griffiths Papers, Bentley Library; John E. Peterson, "Food Stamp Cost May Triple, Rep. Griffiths Warns," <u>Detroit News</u>, April 15, 1974, and, Griffiths to editor, <u>(Washington, D.C.) Evening-Star</u>, August 20, 1974, clippings in MWG Scrapbooks, Griffiths Library.

[95]U.S., Congress, House, 93d Cong., 2d sess., June 20, 1974, <u>Congressional Record</u> 120:20255-56. A year before, Griffiths had severely castigated HUD for allowing repossessed houses to contribute to neighborhood decay. It was a "continued misallocation of our vital housing resources." U.S., Congress, House, 93d Cong., 1st sess., March 21 and June 27, 1973, <u>Congres-</u>

sional Record 119:8957 and 21877.

[96] Chamber of Commerce of the United States, "Statement Transmitted to Radio Stations," March 26, 1973; Timothy B. Clark, "A Second Look at the Incomes Strategy," National Journal Reports, December 15, 1973; Anthony Dolan, "What Ever Happened to the Welfare Crisis?" National Review, January 1, 1974, pp. 138 ff; "A Major Legacy from Martha," Detroit News, August 3, 1974; and "Unravelling the Welfare Mess," Detroit Free Press, August 5, 1974, clippings in MWG Scrapbooks, Griffiths Library.

[97] Griffiths to Jule M. Sugarman, December 19, 1973, in Griffiths Papers, Bentley Library; and, Alan Haas, "The Man in the Middle(Class)," Memphis (Tenn.) [ ], November 4, 1973, clipping in MWG Scrapbooks, Griffiths Library.

[98] Griffiths, "Remarks of Congresswoman Martha W. Griffiths to Urban Institute Public Welfare Seminar," October 11, 1973, in Griffiths Library.

[99] Quoted in Congressional Quarterly, February 2, 1974, p. 241; and Paul Delaney, "Nixon Legislation on Cash for Poor Expected to Go to Congress by Spring," New York Times, February 4, 1974, in MWG Scrapbooks, Griffiths Library.

[100] John K. Inglehart, "Welfare Report/HEW Wants Welfare Programs Replaced by Negative Income Tax," National Journal Reports, October 19, 1974, pp. 1559-66, clipping in MWG Scrapbooks, Griffiths Library.

[101] U.S., Congress, Joint Economic Committee, Income Security for Americans: Recommendations of the Public Welfare Study, by the Subcommittee on Fiscal Policy, Joint Committee Print (Washington, D.C.: Government Printing Office, 1974), pp. 4, 11, 47-49, 119, and 152-4.

[102] Griffiths, speech to Annual Meeting of Health and Welfare Council of Central Maryland.

[103] Interview with Richard Bolling, Washington, D.C., January 26, 1978; and, Bolling to Griffiths, October 15, 1974, in Griffiths Papers, Bentley Library.

[104] The first volume dealt with the demogrant, work-conditioned subsidy, and categorical public employment

guarantees. U.S., Congress, Joint Economic Committee, Concepts in Welfare Program Design, by Benjamin A. Okner et al., Joint Committee Print, Study Paper 9, pt. 1 (Washington, D.C.: Government Printing Office, 1973).

[105] Interview with Griffiths, Romeo, Michigan, February 22, 1978. Griffiths tried to reach McGovern before he announced his support for the demogrant. Unsuccessful, she managed to contact Thomas Eagleton who invited her to speak with his staff. By the time the staff meeting was set, Eagleton was off the Democratic ticket.

[106] Ibid.; Griffiths, "Welfare Reform," remarks to the Businessmen's Committee for the Federalization of Welfare, New York City, August 12, 1976, in Griffiths Library.

[107] U.S., Congress, Joint Economic Committee, Public Employment and Wage Subsidies, by Robert L. Lerman, Joint Committee Print, Study Paper 19 (Washington, D.C.: Government Printing Office, 1974), p. iii.

[108] U.S., Congress, Joint Economic Committee, A Model Income Supplement Bill, by James R. Storey, Joint Committee Print, Study Paper 16 (Washington D.C.: Government Printing Office, 1974), pp. 1-10.

[109] Interview with Griffiths, Romeo, Michigan, February 22, 1978; and "Summary [of Recommendations of Study Committee]," [n.d.], in Griffiths Library.

[110] Interview with Griffiths, Romeo, Michigan, February 22, 1978.

[111] Griffiths, speech to the Annual Meeting of Health and Welfare Council of Central Maryland. She also told her listeners: "I was down in Texas at the Lyndon B. Johnson School of Social Services and they said, 'You have changed the meaning of the word poverty. You have changed the definition. You have changed the definition of welfare.' So that as academia begins to send back these messages, there is some hope that the welfare structure will be changed."

[112] In March 1974, Griffiths introduced a bill providing the option of the standard $750 deduction or a $200 credit for parents and each dependent. Senator Walter F. Mondale, in sponsoring a similar bill in the

Senate, wrote Griffiths: "Your leadership in the
House dramatically increases the early action on the
bill." (March 7, 1974, in Griffiths Papers, Bentley
Library). Griffiths had also cosponsored in 1972 a
tax credit bill against tuition paid for elementary
and secondary education.

113 Griffiths, ["Tax Credits and Allowances Act"], a
fact sheet to be used within Congress, in Griffiths
Library.

114 Interviews with Griffiths, Romeo, Michigan, June 5,
1977; and, Townsend, Washington, D.C., January 24,
1978.

115 "Plans for Welfare Reform Could Aid Troubled System,"
Detroit Free Press, December 7, 1974; and, J. Philip
Wogamon, "A Second Chance for Guaranteed Income?"
Christianity and Crisis [ ] (April 14, 1975): 85-88.
Vincent J. Burke of the Washington Bureau, Los Angeles Times, wrote Proxmire, Chairperson of
JEC, January 10, 1973, that the welfare probe was
one of the most significant Congressional studies he
had seen in his twenty-five years as a Washington
correspondent. Griffiths replied to Burke on January
18 that she would have enjoyed seeing Proxmire's
face when he read Burke's letter (Letters in Griffiths Papers, Bentley Library).

116 "Hardley Seems the Way to Improve on Welfare," Asheville (N.C.) Citizen, December 6, 1974, in MWG Scrapbooks, Griffiths Library.

117 The Javits-Cornell Bill made two major alterations
in Griffiths' bill: first, it provided ABLE benefits
for all children; and, second, it eliminated the
dollar for dollar offset against an ABLE grant for
rent and education subsidies. U.S., Congress, Senate, 94th Cong., 2d sess., February 19, 1976, Congressional Record 122:1940. In presenting the Tax
Credits and Allowances Act, Representative Robert J.
Cornell lamented Congress' seeming lack of concern
in promoting welfare reform. U.S., Congress, Senate,
94th Cong., 2d sess., February 25, 1976, Congressional Record 122:E834.

118 Interview with Cohen, Ann Arbor, Michigan, December
14, 1977.

119 Griffiths, "Reforming Welfare: Is There an Easy Way

Out?" remarks prepared for the University of Michigan, Ann Arbor, February 1, 1974, in Griffiths Library.

[120] Ibid.; also interviews with Bolling, Washington, D.C., January 26, 1978, and John Stark Jr., Washington, D.C., January 30, 1978.

[121] Interviews with Ball, Washington, D.C., January 30, 1978; and, Staats, Washington, D.C., February 24, 1978. Senator Edward W. Brooke on the Housing and Urban Affairs Subcommittee believed the study of great assistance in determining legislation for low-income families. He also pointed out that HUD found the work extremely valuable in developing housing policy. Brooke to Ernest F. Hollings, April 29, 1974, in Griffiths Papers, Bentley Library.

[122] U.S., Congress, Joint Economic Committee, Income Security for Americans: Recommendations, p. vii. In a letter dated January 7, 1975, to the New York Times (in Griffiths Library), Griffiths asked the most recently elected members of Congress to center their attention on welfare reform and on the data and recomendations of her Subcommittee.

CHAPTER VI

Griffiths' announcement in February 1974 that she would leave Washington at the end of the year was made on no sudden impulse. In 1972 she and Hicks had planned her retirement with the goal of bringing all projects to a conclusion during the Ninety-third Congress.[1] The Tax Credits and Allowances Act introduced in December 1974, therefore, both capped the three-year welfare study and symbolized a house in order.

It was time for remembering. The personal cost in time and energy during those twenty years, to say nothing of the separation from Hicks, was incalculable. Legislating, however, had been Griffiths' trade. She found it "exhilarating" and fulfilling. "Politics is like poker," she once told a correspondent, "you can't quit a winner." Above all, she found great satisfaction in knowing that her influence had brought about more equitable laws.[2] She had left her mark on the tax code as well as on equal rights, Social Security, and pension legislation. Moreover, her contribution towards welfare reform and national health insurance had brought those issues into public awareness.

As a member of Congress, Griffiths had tried to be true to her trust. She had not only espoused issues important to the broadest base of Americans, but she had attempted to be as responsive as she could to her local constituents. And they, experiencing her concern, reciprocated. Three years after her retirement they still spoke of her as having been an intelligent, forceful, honest Representative who promptly met their demands with compassion. Even those who disagreed with her, admired her. "[She] took the hack out of 'politician,'" observed one self-styled Independent male who could not fathom how Social Security discriminated against women.[3]

This voter attachment did not just happen. Griffiths had worked at it. She put out a monthly newsletter and for several years held frequent radio and television conversations on pending legislation. Key to her open system of communication were her Detroit and Washington offices where she impressed on her hard-working staffs their responsibility to the public for money spent and service rendered. Friendly and caring toward her assistants, she was nevertheless firm in her expectation that her consitutents be treated professionally and expeditiously. The news got around—so much so that voters from other districts often came to her for help. She intervened in constituent crises and regularly read district mail in search of legislative ideas and case studies. That she insisted on signing every personal letter attested to the importance she placed on this link with the people back home.

Her most direct contact with the district was her local office, one of the few Congressional posts in Wayne County open five-and-a-half days a week. When possible, Griffiths was in on Friday and Saturday, her constant complaint being that unimaginative scheduling on Capitol Hill precluded more time for talking with constituents. Her local staff, a few faithful women who had been with her from her days in the Michigan Legislature, logged every call and recorded each constituent benefit on a precinct-by-precinct file which the Griffiths had set up when she first went to Congress. From this latter catalogue they kept an updated mailing list on which Griffiths could depend when she needed to call up support. The local staff also communicated daily with the Washington office where Griffiths had attracted capable college graduates to carry out routine matters. Despite the heavy demands made on her, she considered the direction of her offices as extremely important. As a consequence, the work of her staffs was perceived by constituents as the extension of her personal service to them, which was precisely what she hoped for.[4]

Success not only attended the operation of her offices but seemed to mark her career. By 1972 she was fourth on Ways and Means and, given a few years, could conceivably have become its powerful chairperson. She had often said in defense of the seniority system that the woman's way to the top was to get elected to a prestigious committee and after that outlive all the men.[5] Why then would she and Hicks settle on twenty years and no more?

A simple answer might be advanced that there was nothing left for Griffiths to do—that the time had come for moving on. She once told an audience that the observation of Ecclesiastes on time's leveling effect was worth considering. "The race is not to the swift," she quoted, "nor the battle to the strong, neither yet bread for the wise, nor yet riches to persons of understanding, nor yet favor to persons of skill, but time and chance happens to them all."[6] Past performance, however, suggests that in her political conclusions, particularly when her future was at stake, Griffiths was more complex than simple, more pragmatic than biblical.

Three interrelated factors seemed to have played a predominant role in directing her choice to leave Washington at the end of 1974. First, in January 1975, Griffiths would be sixty-three. She had no desire to die in the House nor to have her husband die while she was serving there.[7] She wanted to spend time with Hicks, close two residences, and move to a farm north of Detroit where she could enjoy her gardening, her books, and Uki, the magnificent family poodle.[8] Moreover, she had long advocated that members of Congress should relinquish their accumulated seniority rights at sixty-five in favor of junior members.[9] In fairness, therefore, what was good for the ganders was also good for the goose.

Second, Griffiths was tired—tired from the hard work and hassle of Congress, especially Ways and Means. The pressures of biennial campaigning likewise were not lessening. Having to appeal to new and large concentrations of Republicans, who had been incorporated into the 1972 redistricting, added to the physical strain of canvassing the District. While Griffiths had confidence in her ability to carry the electorate, her 1970 voting margin of 80 percent had dropped to 66 percent in 1972, an indication of the growing differences among her mixed constituency about who a Representative should be in a rapidly changing metropolis. During the 1972 campaign, grass-roots urban groups criticized her as unresponsive to consumer interests,[10] while the propertied middle-class made her out as unsympathetic because of her abstention on a series of antibusing votes.[11]

Finally—and most importantly, Griffiths had come to believe that she could never be chairperson of Ways and Means. The closer she came to the top, the more entrenched the three men ahead of her seemed to be.[12] These factors, together with the tumultuous internal affairs of Ways and Means after 1972, confirmed her resolve to retire at the end of 1974. Mills' drinking problem left the Committee virtually leaderless. While Al Ullman chaired the group during Mills' frequent absences, whatever he did was open to reversal as long as Mills held sway. Presuming that Mills would hold on for years, Griffiths concluded that the struggle could only worsen. Even should he retire, Griffiths reasoned that the attempt to recover his former power within the

Committee would usher in "a real donnybrook for quite a long time," a prospect she did not look forward to.[13]

There is indication, however, that Griffiths might have considered another term had she known earlier both that Mills would leave at the end of the Ninety-third Congress and that Ways and Means would be reorganized into subcommittees.[14] As it was, in February 1974, Ways and Means was in deep trouble with no sign of improvement. "Really, it's a shame," she confided to Henry Ford II about both the Committee and her personal future. "I had great ideas for reforming the tax code, including one chapter headed 'Loopholes.'"[15]

Griffiths' announcement to retire stunned many. Daniel Ryan from the food-stamp days reminded her that poor people would be the losers, and women from numerous sectors wondered what would become of the ERA. Her colleagues objected, as did President Nixon, who said she was one of few women who could legislatively compete with men. The media also lamented her loss, the Wall Street Journal specifically listing her with Senators J. William Fulbright and Sam Ervin among the most-to-be-missed legislators.[16] The UAW and the Michigan Democrats, however, were silent. Later when the Wayne County Democrats planned a fund-raising dinner to honor her, she made it clear that she wanted none of their belated recognition. She was a debtor to no one, to them least of all.[17]

But Griffiths' work was not over. Within a month after retirement, she was named to four corporate boards: Chrysler, Consumers Power, Burroughs, and National Bank of Detroit—appointments Griffiths viewed as unique opportunities for blending the interests of business with her experiences as a lawmaker and a woman. Other directorships followed, Griffiths serving on nearly forty non-for-profit organizations and committees, including a consultants panel to the Comptroller General, the Michigan Efficiency Task Force, and the Economic Growth Council of Detroit. She also joined the boards of several colleges and universities and a host of woman's groups—NOW, WEAL, the Women's Lobby, and the Center for Women Policy Studies—to name a few. Because of her enduring concern that Congress be in control of its own data, she helped found the Institute for Congress designed specifically to research critical policy issues that spanned the jurisdiction of several committees. Unfortunately, the Institute did not survive beyond its initial phase relying too much, in Griffiths' opinion, on the support of too few private donors.[18] During the early years of retirement she also kept attuned to party happenings, and in 1976 she was called upon to chair the Rules Committee for the Democratic National Convention.

By intent equal rights continued to play a part in her life.[19] She canvassed the states for the ERA and was in constant demand as a speaker, particularly on college and university campuses, where she accumulated some twenty honorary degrees within a relatively short span of time. She assumed key leadership of the Homemakers Committee of the Congress-designated International Women's Year Commission, and as such was a delegate to the 1975 IWY assembly in Mexico City. And it was under her prodding that a state-by-state analysis of laws pertaining to homemakers was achieved.[20]

Such involvement spoke volumes of Griffiths' incapacity to slow down. Her workweek was as busy as ever, with only a few more evenings on the farm to compensate for the 150-mile round trip to and from the Detroit airport. The public, seeing that she had lost none of her vigor, talked about renewed involvement with government. She was suggested for the Senate, HEW, HUD, the Supreme Court, and the vice presidency.[21] She was likewise sought out as a possible Michigan gubernatorial candidate for 1978.[22]

Of all these prospects, the Supreme Court especially appealed to Griffiths, as did HEW. Her chances for both looked good when her friend and former colleague Gerald Ford became President.[23] Griffiths considered herself particularly suited for HEW because of her welfare study and her sponsorship of national health insurance. Several of her bipartisan colleagues felt the same. Ford, however, sensitive to the unusual circumstances of his presidency, deemed it politically wise to name only Republicans to his Cabinet.[24] And his successor, intent on a bureaucratic shake down, was looking for a manager, rather than an ideologue, to head the massive social service department.

Since the mid-60s Griffiths had been suggested several times for the Supreme Court.[25] She particularly regretted not having prevailed on Associate Justice Abe Fortas to make his seat available while Johnson was President. When Fortas finally resigned in 1969, she knew Nixon would never appoint a Democrat to this post.[26] Another court possibility emerged in 1975 with the vacancy created by William O. Douglas. Unfortunately for

Griffiths, the memory of the Senate's successful fight against Nixon-nominees Clement F. Haynsworth and G. Harold Carswell influenced Ford to look for "a relatively non-controversial legal scholar" whom his stalwart partisans would confirm in haste.[27] Griffiths obviously did not fit the description.

Despite these unfulfilled aspirations. Griffiths could take pleasure from her twenty years in Washington. The lasting impact of her achievements will, of course, be judged by history. She may be reckoned, as one critic believes, an inconsequential player on the stage of history.[28] Or she may, in the estimation of an admirer, be among the most notable Americans of her day.[29] A balanced reading of her service will have to take into account both her legislative successes and the potential for systemic change embedded in the issues she espoused.[30] When the Constitution finally recognizes the legal equality of every person, then Griffiths will have achieved the goal of all her striving.

[1] Interview with Griffiths, Romeo, February 22, 1978; Marlene Cimons, "Griffiths' Retiring Shocks Colleagues," Los Angeles Times, March 1, 1974, clipping in Griffiths Papers, Bentley Library.

[2] Interview with Griffiths, Romeo, July 23, 1977; Griffiths to John S. Canterbury, April 17, 1959, in Griffiths Papers, Bentley Library; Griffiths, transcript of speech to General Accounting Office, "Federal Women's Day," November 7, 1973, in Griffiths Papers, Bentley Library; Griffiths, remarks of M.W. Griffiths, "Women in Politics," St. Mary College, Notre Dame, Indiana, October 13, 1975, in Griffiths Library; Barbara Seaman, "An Interview with Congresswoman Martha Griffiths," Family Circle, February 1972, clipping in MWG Scrapbooks, Griffiths Library.

[3] A survey of 250 former constituents was conducted by the author in October 1977. Twenty-five percent responded to inquiries including agreement or disagreement with Griffiths' positions and the impressions she left as a legislator. Several letters in the Griffiths Papers, Bentley Library, acknowledged the care with which she treated constituents, especially her promptness in attending to their requests.

[4] Interviews with Griffiths' former staffs: Detroit: Stephanie Stobierski, Detroit, Michigan, January 11, 1978; and Rose Stephen, Detroit, Michigan, August 14, 1978. The Washington staff: Mary Bernhard, Marilyn Mikulich, and Thomas Van Coverden, Washington, D.C., January 29, 1978; and Alair Townsend, Washington, D.C., January 24, 1978. Also interviews with Griffiths, Romeo, May 10 and July 21, 1977. The Newsletters, 1956-1974, are in Griffiths Library, and the radio scripts and videotapes in Griffiths Papers, Bentley Library. Griffiths' complaint against Congressional scheduling is found in her letter to the Editor, Chicago Tribune, March 8, 1974, in Griffiths Papers, Bentley Library. See, likewise, "Rep. M. Griffiths Really Serves Voters," Northwest Detroiter, September 12, 1963, clipping in MWG Scrapbooks, Griffiths Library.

[5] Griffiths, "What Politics and Politicians Have Taught Me," speech to Theta Sigma Phi, Detroit Press Club, October 16, 1962, in Griffiths Library. See also Marjorie Hunter, "House Democrats Given Vote on Committee Heads," New York Times, January 23, 1973, clipping in MWG Scrapbooks, Griffiths Library.

[6] Griffiths, "What Politics and Politicians Have Taught Me."

[7] Marlene Cimons, "Griffiths' Retiring Shocks Colleagues," Los Angeles Times, March 1, 1974, clipping in Griffiths Papers, Bentley Library. Former President Ford emphasized that Griffiths' love for Hicks was unusual and exemplary. (Interview with Ford, Vail, Colorado, July 19, 1978.)

[8] Griffiths particularly enjoyed a reporter's recognition that the family dog played a part in her retirement. (Richard L. Milliman, "Move Over, Jerry Ford," Portland Almanack, March 27, 1974, clipping in Griffiths Papers, Bentley Library.)

[9] Henry Clay Gold, "Parting Shots Aimed at Congress," Kansas City (Missouri) Star, May 26, 1974, in MWG Scrapbooks, Griffiths Library.

[10] Marsha Abramson for Ralph Nader Congress Project Citizens Look at Congress, "Martha W. Griffiths, Democratic Representative from Michigan," release October 22, 1972, copy in Griffiths Library. In a television interview with Nancy Dickerson for "Inside Washington," Griffiths accused Nader of shoddy investigative techniques. (Script based on conversation with Dickerson, October 5, 1972 in Griffiths Papers, Bentley Library.)

[11] "Why We Like Nixon; Griffin Over Kelley, Too," Southfield (Michigan) Sun, November 1, 1972, and "Bussing is the Key but not Only Issue," Detroit News, November 3, 1972, clippings in MWG Scrapbooks, Griffiths Library. On the day of the antibusing votes, Griffiths said she was not present in the House. (Griffiths to Mrs. H. C. Heller, August 29, 1972, in Griffiths Papers, Bentley Library.) Busing became an issue in Detroit in 1972 when District Court Judge Stephen Roth ordered cross-district busing for the Metropolitan area. While not an absolute opponent on all busing, as evidenced by her support of the Equal Educational Opportunities Act of 1972, Griffiths did not believe busing could achieve quality education. Rather, she and several Michigan delegates co-sponsored the Quality School Assistance Act which would have pumped $12 billion into local school districts with special assistance to depressed areas. Among her other antibusing activities, Griffiths signed a discharge petition for a constitutional amendment outlawing court-ordered busing.

¹²Griffiths to Henry Ford II, March 14, 1974, in Griffiths Papers, Bentley Library.

¹³Interview with Griffiths, Romeo, April 15, 1978; Griffiths, "Remarks at Michigan Foundation Conference," transcript sent from Patrick W. Kennedy, Foundation News, April 9, 1974, in Griffiths Papers, Bentley Library.

¹⁴Interview with Townsend, January 24, 1978. After the attempted so-called Bolling reform which Griffiths opposed because it separated Ways and Means' jurisdiction over program content from its taxing power, Congress adopted a series of mild changes such as enlarging the membership and prescribing subcommittees.

¹⁵Griffiths to Ford, March 14, 1974, in Griffiths Papers, Bentley Library.

¹⁶Several letters from her colleagues, women's groups, constituents, etc., in Griffiths Papers, Bentley Library, including Ryan's, February 25, 1974; and Nixon's, March 4, 1974; Judd Arnett, "If It's to be a Woman, How about Martha?" Detroit Free Press, February 18, 1975; and Alan L. Otten, "Politics and People," Wall Street Journal, June 27, 1974, clippings in MWG Scrapbooks, Griffiths Library; and James F. Clark to Griffiths, March 20, 1974, in Griffiths Papers, Bentley Library. In her 7-sentence announcement, Griffiths thanked all who had assisted her in career, especially Hicks, and said she hoped she had "pulled . . . [her] fair share of the load." (U.S., Congress, House, 93d Cong., 2d sess., February 21, 1974, Congressional Record 120:3854.)

¹⁷The silence of labor and the organized Democrats was noted by the press. (See Eileen Foley, "Quitting While She's Ahead," Detroit Free Press, March 20, 1974, clipping in MWG Scrapbooks, Griffiths Library.) When the thirty dollar fund-raising dinner was planned without her consultation she sent a letter to the Wayne County Chairman (Griffiths to Bruce A. Miller, May 30, 1974, in Griffiths Library) and "Dear Friend" and "Dear Democratic Official" letters (May 25, 1974, in Griffiths Papers, Bentley Library) denouncing the move as "exploitation of my name." The Michigan press praised her for her stand. (Detroit News, June 6, 1974; Macomb Daily, June 7, 1974; and Flint Journal, June 7, 1974, clippings in MWG Scrapbooks, Griffiths Library.)

[18] The idea for the Institute for Congress was originally conceived by five persons, including Cyrus R. Vance, president of the New York City bar association. Griffiths and William D. Ruckelshaus, former head of the Environmental Protection Agency and deputy attorney general under Nixon, were asked to serve as chairperson and vice-chairperson, respectively. (Interview with Griffiths, Romeo, August 31, 1978; and J.F. TerHorst, "Institute for Congress' Time is Here," Detroit News, December 14, 1978; Richard D. Lyons, "Institute Set Up to Provide Specialists to Aid Congress," New York Times, December 28, 1975; Griffiths and Rickelshaus, "Why Congress Needs Even More Help," Washington [D.C.] Star, October 12, 1975, clippings in MWG Scrapbooks, Griffiths Library.)

[19] Griffiths to Phineas Indritz, May 9, 1974, in Griffiths Papers, Bentley Library.

[20] See for example Sylvia Roberts, The Legal Status of Homemakers in Louisiana, National Commission on the Observance of International Women's Year: Committee on Homemakers, June 1976.

[21] The Senate speculation, one that Griffiths considered herself as early as 1954, was made by Judd Arnett, Detroit Free Press, September 25, 1975. HEW and the Supreme Court will be treated below. HUD was raised by Newsweek, November 15, 1976, p. 6, and the vice presidency, by Rosemary Beales, "Ex-Congresswoman Would Run for Veep," American Statesman (Austin, Texas), November 12, 1975, all clippings in MWG Scrapbooks, Griffiths Library.

[22] Bobby D. Crim, Speaker of the Michigan House of Representatives, confirmed in a letter to Emily George, R.S.M., December 14, 1977, that Griffiths had been asked by various individuals to run for governor.

[23] A discernible friendship existed between Ford and Griffiths. He helped her with ERA and she testified on his behalf when he was nominated for Vice-President. Griffiths believed everyone had a friend in the White House the day Ford succeeded Nixon. (Interviews with Griffiths, Romeo, June 4, 1977; Ford, Vail, Colorado, July 19, 1978; Robert P. Griffin, Detroit, Michigan, December 5, 1977; and Barber B. Conable Jr., Washington, D.C., January 27, 1978.) Ford once wrote about Griffiths: "She was a truly fine Member of Congress and I value her friendship." (Ford to Franklin B.

Lincoln Jr., June 13, 1975, copy in MWG Scrapbooks, Griffiths Library.)

[24] Interviews with Griffiths, Romeo, May 11, 1977; Gerald R. Ford, July 19, 1978. Wilbur J. Cohen, a former HEW head, thought the idea of Griffiths being appointed to HEW "poppycock" (interview with Cohen, Ann Arbor, Michigan, December 14, 1978), while Representative Barbara Jordan, who had also been mentioned for the post, wondered why Griffiths was bypassed (interview with Jordan, Washington, D.C., January 24, 1978). The Michigan press supported Griffiths for the job. (Detroit News, August 14 and 15, 1974; Flint Journal, December 11, 1974, clippings in Griffiths Library.)

[25] She was suggested in 1965 to fill Arthur Goldberg's seat (Detroit Free Press, July 7, 1965) and in 1968-69 for the vacancy created by Abe Fortas' possible accession as Chief Justice (Monette [Missouri] Times, August 31, 1968; Detroit News, May 12 and December 5, 1969; Detroit Free Press, May 21, June 29, July 11, July 13, and December 2-3, 1969, all clippings in MWG Scrapbooks, Griffiths Library). Edith Green also wrote Griffiths (August 14, 1968, in Griffiths Library) that she would like to get "a 'bandwagon' rolling" for her (Griffiths') appointment. Speculations were especially strong in 1971 when two associate judgeships were vacated by the retirement of Hugo Black and John M. Harlan. (Letters to President Nixon from Robert P. Griffin, September 21, 1971; from NOW, September 29, 1971; from Julia Hansen, October 4, 1971, and Dan Rostenkowski, September 24, 1971, in Griffiths Papers, Bentley Library; Beverly Craig, "2 Detroit Women Are Mentioned for Supreme Court," Detroit News, September 30, 1971; and Robert Lewis, "Nixon Court List No Longer includes Michigan Candidates," Grand Rapids [Michigan] Press, October 15, 1971, clippings in MWG Scrapbooks, Griffiths Library.) When asked in 1971 how she felt about the Supreme Court Griffiths said, "I am a lawyer. Yes, I would be interested in a seat on the Supreme Court." (Lloyd Schwartz, "Martha Griffith[s]: A Force in Congress," Pontiac [Michigan] Press, September 16, 1971, clipping in MWG Scrapbooks, Griffiths Library.)

[26] Interview with Griffiths, Romeo, May 11, 1977.

[27] Interview with Ford, July 19, 1978. For the press' viewpoint regarding the prospect, see Richard A. Ryan, "3 Michigan Women in Running to Fill Douglas' High

Court Seat," <u>Detroit News</u>, November 13, 1975; and "Ford, ABA Launch Search for a Successor to Douglas," <u>Detroit Free Press</u>, November 14, 1975, clippings in MWG Scrapbooks, Griffiths Library.

[28] Interview with Cohen, December 14, 1977.

[29] Carl Albert to Emily George, R.S.M., November 7, 1977. Former Speaker John W. McCormack (interview, Boston, Massachusetts, January 5, 1978) considered Griffiths as one of the most valuable members of Congress whom he knew.

[30] Women in particular recognized the fundamental contribution Griffiths had made in advancing legal equity for everyone and they were inspired to carry on her work. Mary Brown Parlee to Griffiths, February 22, 1974; Marguerite Rawalt to Griffiths, February 22, 1974; and Sue Barratt to Griffiths, June 27, 1974, in Griffiths Papers, Bentley Library.

BIBLIOGRAPHIC ESSAY

Perusal of the footnotes indicates the wealth of primary sources available to this study. This essay is an attempt to identify the most significant.

Currently, there are two main depositories of Griffiths papers: the Michigan Historical Collections in the Bentley Historical Library at the University of Michigan, Ann Arbor, and Hicks and Martha's personal library in Romeo, Michigan. The Bentley Library houses Griffiths' 1955-74 office files, an indispensable resource for official Congressional business during the period under consideration. Constituent letters from which Griffiths culled several legislative ideas and case studies comprise a sizable segment of this massive —and uncatalogued—acquisition. There are also a scattering of speeches, some video-tapes and recordings. Bentley's ancillary collections, especially the papers of G. Mennen Williams and Lawrence L. Farrell, provide additional data for the years when both Griffiths were active in state and local politics. (So does the Walter P. Reuther Library of Wayne State University, Detroit, Michigan.)

The Griffiths library with its family memorabilia and political momentos, is more personal. Hicks' papers are a plus; so, too, are Martha's ERA correspondence, her major speeches—many of them unpublished, and two series of scrapbooks. One series chronicles Martha Griffiths' terms in the Michigan Legislature and on Detroit Recorders Court; the other is a chronological catalogue of national and local newspaper articles— impressive for its completeness and convenient because of its arrangement. Also of value are Griffiths' books and journal articles, her constituent newsletters, and her file of legislative bills and voting records. The only major work done on Griffiths to date, Mary Pinola's 1976 masters thesis, is also available in Romeo. Entitled "A Burkeian Analysis of Selected Speeches on Equal Rights by Representative Martha Wright Griffiths," it was written for the speech communication department of California State University, Long Beach. Pertinent government documents, notably the <u>Congressional Record</u> and the <u>Hearings and Reports</u> of the Ways and Means and the Joint Economic Committees, make the Griffiths library an accessible storehouse of information.

Another principal source of data used in this study

are interviews with 42 persons specifically chosen for the different types of input they could contribute. Of singular importance was Martha Griffiths herself, interviewed several times between October 27, 1976 and February 24, 1980. Others with whom the author spoke were her husband, her pre-Congressional associates, and past and current members of Congress with whom Griffiths worked. Among the latter category were House leaders, members of the Michigan delegation, the women Representatives, and members and staffs of Ways and Means and the Joint Economic Committee. Also interviewed were Griffiths' former office staffs, her collaborators in the equal rights movement, and the heads of administrative departments who testified before the committees on which Griffiths served.

Those interviewed besides Martha and Hicks were as follows: Virginia Allan, J.P. Baker, Robert Ball, Mary Bernhard, Richard Bolling, James A. Burke, Wilber J. Cohen, Barber B. Conable Jr., James C. Corman, Charles C. Diggs Jr., Don Edwards, Lawrence Filson, Gerald R. Ford Jr., Edith Green, Robert P. Griffin, Dorothy Haener, Adelaide Hart, Margaret Heckler, Phineas Indritz, Mildred Jeffrey, and Barbara Jordan.

Likewise contacted were: Edith Kelly, Nelson McClung, John W. McCormack, John M. Martin Jr., Dorothy Meehan, Marilyn Mikulich, Wilbur Mills, Marguerite Rawalt, Henry Reuss, Dan Rostenkowski, Elmer B. Staats, John Stark Jr., Rose Stephen, Stephanie Stobierski, Alair Townsend, Thomas Van Coverden, G. Mennen Williams, and Nancy Williams. One interviewee wished to remain anonymous. Where information could not be obtained in person or by telephone, it was requested by letter. Reached in this way were Carl Albert, Bobby Crim, John D. Dingell Jr., Margaret Chase Smith, and Casper Weinberger. To ascertain how constituents viewed their former Representative, a 250-person random survey of the Seventeenth District was conducted in the fall of 1977.

Essential to the study were the Hearings and Reports of the committees on which Griffiths served, especially those of the Joint Economic and Ways and Means. Among the most useful JEC documents were:

<u>Economic Policies and Programs in Middle America: A Report to the Subcommittee on Inter-American Economic Relationships of the Joint Economic Committee,</u> by Martha W. Griffiths. Joint Committee Print. Wash-

ington, D.C.: Government Printing Office, 1963.

Fiscal Policy Issues of the Coming Decade, Hearings before the Subcommittee on Fiscal Policy of the Joint Economic Committee, 89th Cong., 1st sess., 1965.

Private Pension Plans. Hearings before the Subcommittee on Fiscal Policy of the Joint Economic Committee, 89th Cong., 2d sess., 1966.

Revenue Sharing and Its Alternatives: What Future for Federalism, by Harley H. Hinrichs, ed. 3 vols. Joint Committee Print. Washington, D.C.: Government Printing Office, 1967.

Revenue Sharing and Its Alternatives: What Future for Fiscal Federalism. Hearings before the Subcommittee on Fiscal Policy of the Joint Economic Committee, 90th Cong., 1st sess., 1968.

Income-Maintenance Programs. Hearings before the Subcommittee on Fiscal Policy of the Joint Economic Committee, 2 vols., 90th Cong., 2d sess., 1968.

Problems in Administration of Public Welfare Programs. Hearings before the Subcommittee on Fiscal Policy of the Joint Economic Committee, 3 vols., 92d Cong., 2d sess., 1972.

Studies in Public Welfare, including Income Security for Americans: Recommendations of the Public Welfare Study, by the Subcommittee on Fiscal Policy of the Joint Economic Committee. 20 study papers. Joint Committee Prints. Washington, D.C.: Government Printing Office, 1973-74.

Economic Problems of Women. Hearings before the Joint Economic Committee, 93rd Cong., 1st sess., 1973.

Almost all the Hearings and Reports of Ways and Means aided the study. Indicative of the quality of debate were:

Social Security and Welfare Proposals. Hearings before the Committee on Ways and Means, 91st Cong., 1st sess., 1970.

General Revenue Sharing. Hearings before the Committee on Ways and Means, 92d Cong., 1st sess., 1971.

Tax Treatment of Single Persons and Married Persons where Both Spouses are Working. Hearings before the Committee on Ways and Means, 92d Cong., 2d sess., 1972.

National Health Insurance Proposals. Hearings before the Committee on Ways and Means, 92d Cong., 1st sess., 1972.

National Health Insurance Proposals. Hearings before the Committee on Ways and Means, 93rd Cong., 2d sess., 1974.

Vital for the history of the ERA and the debate were:

Equal Rights 1970. Hearings before the [Senate] Committee on the Judiciary on S.J. Res. 61 and S.J. Res. 231, 91st Cong., 2d sess., 1970.

The Equal Rights Amendment. Hearings before the Subcommittee on Constitutional Amendments of the [Senate] Judiciary Committee on S.J. Res. 61, 91st Cong., 2d sess., 1970.

Equal Rights for Men and Women 1971. Hearings before Subcommittee No. 4 of the [House] Committee on the Judiciary on H.J. Res. 35, 208, and Related Bills and H.R. 916 and Related Bills, 92d Cong., 1st sess., 1971.

Of special interest were:

Hearings and Reports of the [House] Committee on Government Operations, 84th Cong., 1955-56.

Civil Defense for National Survival. Hearings and Report of the [House] Committee on Government Operations, 2 vols., 84th Cong., 1955-56.

Hearings for the Select [House] Committee on

Crime, 3 vols. 91st Cong., 1969-70.

Finally, the Congressional Quarterly Almanac and CQ Weekly Reports helped the author trace the circuitous routes characteristic of most legislative developments.

INDEX

Abzug, Bella, 181
Advisory Committee on Intergovernment Relations, 73
Agnew, Spiro, 177
Agriculture Committee (House), 40, 51
Agriculture Department, 39-40, 51, 225, 242
Aid to Families with Dependent Children (AFDC), 146, 212-13, 215, 218-220, 225-28, 231-32, 235-38, 243-44, 247
Airline discrimination against women, 154-56; see also United Airlines, American Airlines
Albert, Carl, 38, 172, 181
Allan, Virginia, 169, 171
American Airlines, 156; see also Airline discrimination against women
American Association of University Women, 185
American Automobile Insurance Company, 5
American Bankers Association, 80
American Bar Association, 173
American Federation of Labor (AFL), 8-9, 11, 21
American Federation of Labor-Congress of Industrial Organizations (AFL-CIO), 48, 56, 67, 104, 149, 173, 176, 182
American Humane Society, 52
American Medical Association, 80, 102, 105-106
American Newspaper Publishers Association, 154
American Welfare Institute of New York, 52
Ameriplan, 105
Annis, Edward A., 102
Appropriations Committee (House), 81, 214
Area Redevelopment Acts, 44, 55
Army Ordnance Department (Detroit), 5, 9
Automobile excise taxes, 43-44, 94-45, 97

Ball, Robert M., 85, 110, 112, 114, 248
Banking and Currency Committee (House), 23, 36-37, 42, 83
Bayh, Birch E., 169-70, 173-75, 177
Benson, Ezra Taft, 39-40, 52
Berlin Crisis of 1958-59, 49
Blackstone, William, 143, 173
Blue Cross, 106
Boggs, Hale, 81-82, 171
Bolling, Richard, 244
Bolton, Frances P., 150
Bow, Frank T., 214
Boyer, Elizabeth, 158
Brooks, Jack, 178
Bryan, William Jennings, 48

Buchanan, Vera, 37
Bundy, McGeorge, 99
Bureau of Consumer Credit, 187
Burke, Thomas A., 35
Burns, Arthur, 144
Burroughs Corporation, 268
Business and Professional Women Clubs (BPW), 151, 161-71, 179
Byrne, James A., 170
Byrnes, John W., 83, 104, 214

Calloway, Willie, 18
Capitol (Lansing) Peace Corps, 11
Carpenter, Elizabeth ("Liz") E., 151
Carswell, G. Harold, 270
Carter, James ("Jimmy") E. Jr., 269
Celler, Emmanuel, 150, 169-70, 172, 178-79
Census Bureau, 154
Center for Women Policy Studies, 268
Central Intelligence Agency (CIA), 153
Chisholm, Shirley, 172
Christian Crusade (Billy Hargis), 182
Chrysler Corporation, 95, 268
Citizens' Advisory Council on the Status of Women, 169, 175
Citizens Against the ERA, 182
Citizens League (Detroit), 12
<u>Civic Searchlight</u> (Detroit), 9, 21, 55
Civil Defense, 49-50, 55
Civil Rights Act of 1964, 141, 147, 158, 161, 169, 172, 184-85; Title VII, 148-59, 167, 188; <u>see also</u> Equal Employment Opportunity Commission
Civil Rights Commission, 152, 161, 185
Civil Service Code, 146, 160-63
Civil Service Commission, 161
Cobo, Albert E., 12, 21
Cohen, Wilbur J., 85, 105, 248
Commodity Credit Corporation, 37, 41
Common Market, 87-88, 145
Community Facilities Act of 1958, 44
Conable, Barber B. Jr., 80, 83-84, 110, 171, 240
Congress of Industrial Organizations (CIO), 8-9, 12, 16, 19-20, 24, 55
Connolly, John B., 74
Conroy, Sara B., 176
Consumer Power Company, 268
Cook, Marlow W., 174, 177
Cooley, Harold, 40
Corman, James C., 108
Cornell, Robert J., 248
Curtis, Thomas B., 81, 102

Defense Department, 50-51, 70
Defense Supply Agency, 50
de Gaulle, Charles, 223
Democratic National Committee, 9, 12, 14, 21, 269
Democratic Party, see Michigan Democratic Party; see also Democratic National Committee
Department of Civil Defense, see Civil Defense
Department of Defense, see Defense Department
Department of Health, 107
Department of Health, Education and Welfare (HEW), see Health, Education and Welfare
Department of Housing and Urban Development (HUD), see Housing and Urban Development
Department of Justice, see Justice Department
Department of Labor, see Labor Department
Department of State, see State Department
Department of the Treasury, see Treasury Department
Depression of 1929 (Great Depression), 1, 3
Detroit, 4-6, 16-17, 21-23, 35, 37-39, 41-46, 51, 54, 56, 67-68, 74, 88, 222, 225, 267, 269; see also Michigan Democratic Party, Seventeenth District
Detroit Bar Association, 56
Detroit Common Council, 43
Detroit mayoral election of 1949, see Edwards, George
Detroit Recorder's Court, 16-17, 47, 54-56, 67
Dewey, Thomas E., 9
Dingell, John J. Jr., 81, 70
Dingell, John J. Sr., 22, 40, 48, 101
Dirksen, Everett M., 151, 159
"Dixiecrats," 7
Dixon-Yates scandal, 22
Dodge, Anna and Horace, 97, 100
Dole, Robert, 175
Douglas, Paul, 44-45, 70-71, 93
Douglas, William O., 269
Dwyer, Florence, 161

East, Catherine, 169
Economic Growth Council of Detroit, 268
Education Amendments Act of 1972, 185
Education legislation, 22, 41-43
Edelsberg, Herman, 152
Edwards, Don, 178-79
Edwards, George, 12
Edwards, India, 9, 13
Effectiveness of Manpower Training Programs, 229-30
Eisenhower, Dwight D., 14-16, 21-23, 35-36, 41-43, 45-46, 53, 55
Elections of: (1946) 5-6; (1948) 6-10, 12; (1950) 12-13; (1952) 13-16, 18-21, 35, 54, 168; (1954) 14, 18-24,

Elections of:—continued
  (1954)—continued
    35, 45; (1956) 54-55; (1958) 55; (1960) 72; (1964) 102; (1970) 67, 267; (1972) 105, 267
Emory University, 188
Employee Benefit Protection Act, 78
Employee Retirement Income Security Act of 1974 (ERISA), 71, 75-81, 159-60, 215
Equal Credit Opportunity Act of 1974, 187
Equal Employment Opportunity Act of 1972, 163
Equal Employment Opportunity Commission (EEOC), 148-59, 167, 187; see also Civil Rights Act of 1964, Title VII
Equal Pay Act of 1963, 147-48, 150, 185-86, 188
Equal Rights Amendment (ERA), 143, 148, 151, 158, 160-61, 163, 167-85, 221, 268-69
ERAmerica, 176
ERA Ratification Council, 176
Ervin, Sam J. Jr., 173-74, 177, 180-82, 268
Esch, Marvin L., 159

Fair employment practices legislation, 8, 10, 147-49
Fair Labor Standards Act of 1938, 147
Family Assistance Program (FAP), 212-13, 220, 222, 229, 231, 240, 243
Farrell, Lawrence L., 8
Federal Aid to Education, see Education legislation
Federal Bureau of Investigation (FBI), 160, 178
Federal Civil Defense Administration (Department of Defense), 49
Federal Housing Administration, 41, 186
Federal Reserve System, 37
Ferguson, Homer, 35
Fifth Amendment, 113, 161
Filson, Lawrence, 113
Finance Committee (Senate), 73-74, 79, 89
Finch, Robert H., 85
Fiscal Policy Subcommittee (JEC), see Joint Economic Committee, Fiscal Policy Subcommittee
Fitzgerald, George S., 12
Fitzgerald, William E., 39
Fitzsimmons, Frank E., 18
Food and Drug Administration, 51
Food stamp legislation, 38-41, 55, 241-44, 247, 268; see also Sullivan food-stamp bill
Ford Foundation, 99
Ford, Gerald R., 80, 89, 109, 167, 171-72, 269-70
Ford, Henry, 99
Ford, Henry II, 268
Ford Motor Company, 95

Fortas, Abe, 269
Foundations, 97-99
Fourteenth Amendment, 150, 160-61, 167-68, 174-75, 179
Fowler, Henry H., 96
Franco, John R., 7-8, 12, 14
Freedman, Saul, 105
Freund, Paul A., 173
Frontiero, Joseph and Sharron, 163
<u>Frontiero v. Richardson</u> (1973), 163
Fulbright, J. William, 268

Galm, Sharon, 229
General Accounting Office (GAO), 220, 222, 230-34; <u>see also</u> Staats, Elmer B.
General Agreement on Tariffs and Trade, 90
General Motors Corporation, 95, 181
Gibson, John W., 6
Goldstein, Jon H., 228-29
Goldwater, Barry, 72
Goodell, Charles E., 73
Government Operations Committee (House), 36-37, 40, 44, 49-50, 70, 83, 152
Green, Edith, 147-49, 185, 187
Green, William, 48
Gribbs, Roman, 75
Gridiron Club, 176
Griffin, Robert, 46, 175
Griffiths, Hicks G., 1, 3-9, 11-16, 18-20, 36, 38, 54, 156, 265-67
Griffiths, Martha W., family and childhood, 1-3; University of Missouri and marriage to Hicks Griffiths, 3-4; University of Michigan and early law practice, 4-5; first political campaign (1946), 5-6; revitalization of Michigan Democratic Party, 6-9; Michigan State Legislature (1948-52), 9-13; 1952 Congressional campaign, 13-16; Detroit Recorder's Court, 16-19, 54-56; 1954 Congressional election, 19-24, 35-36; Congressional years (1955-60), 36-55; concern for central cities, 37-46, 49-50, 68-69; Joint Economic Committee, 69-81; revenue sharing, 72-75; pension reform, 75-81; Ways and Means Committee, 81-114; trade legislation, 86-91; taxes, 91-101; private foundations, 98-99; national health insurance, 101-109; Social Security legislation, 109-114, 145, 164-66; Equal Pay Act of 1963, 147-48; Civil Rights Act of 1964, 148-59; EEOC, 152-59; fight with the airlines, 154-56; equality for civil service employees, 161-64; ERA, 167-85; credit for women, 186-87; JEC welfare study, 211-244; welfare hearings, 221-23, 225-28; welfare papers, 224-25,

Griffiths, Martha W.—continued
  welfare papers—continued
    228-30, 237-39, 244-46; GAO studies, 230-36; Townsend public-benefit study, 236-38; SSI, 240-42; Tax Credits and Allowances Act, 244-47; retirement, 243, 265-68; post-retirement activities, 268-69

Happiness of Womanhood (HOW), 182
Harris, Robert, 214
Hart, Philip A., 159
Hartke, Vance, 159
Harvard University, 4
Haynsworth, Clement F. 270
Health, Education and Welfare Department (HEW), 69, 165, 185, 188, 217, 221-23, 225, 233-36, 243, 246, 269
Health Security Act, 101-108, 221
Heckler, Margaret, 181
Heller, Walter W., 72, 92-93, 213
Hernandez, Aileen C., 151, 187
Higher Education Act of 1971, 177
Hill-Burton Act, 104
Hoffa, James R., 12, 18, 48
Holcomb, Luther, 152-54
Hoover, Herbert, 2
Housing and Home Finance Administration, 42
Housing and Urban Development Department (HUD), 42, 55, 215, 242, 269
Hoyt v. Florida (1961), 160-61
Humane Slaughter Act of 1958, 52-53, 55
Humane Treatment Act of 1966, 53-54
Humanitarians Opposed to Degrading Our Girls (HOTDOG), 182
Humphrey, Hubert, 52, 70, 73, 159

Ikard, Frank, 82
Income Supplemental Program, 243
Income Transfer Programs, 228-29
Indochinese partition of 1954, see Vietnam War
Indritz, Phineas, 152, 154
Institute for Congress, 268-69
InterAmerican Development Bank, 37
Internal Revenue Service (IRS), 73, 78, 177-78, 226, 247
International Labor Organization, 147
International Women's Year Commission (Homemakers Committee), 269
Ives, Irving M., 46

Japan, 67, 88-90
Javits, Jacob, 52, 78, 105, 159, 175, 214, 248
Jeffrey, Mildred M., 10

Jewish emigration from Soviet Union, 89-90
Job Corps, 229-30
Job Opportunities in the Business Sector (JOBS), 229-30
John Birch Society, 182
Johnson, Claudia ("Lady Bird"), 151
Johnson, Lyndon B., 53, 68-69, 72, 76-77, 88, 95-96,
    102, 149, 151-52, 154, 156, 158, 162, 269; see also
    tax legislation, War on Poverty, Vietnam War
JOIN Plan, 245
Joint Economic Committee (JEC), 44, 50, 54, 69-81, 83,
    88, 92, 95, 101, 114, 159; Economic Problems of
    Women, 187-88, 220, 240; Fiscal Policy Subcommittee,
    71-81, 111, 158; welfare study, 69, 71, 76, 81,
    104, 108, 211-44, 265, 269
Jordan, Barbara, 167
Judiciary Committee (House), 141, 148-50, 169, 177-79, 236
Judiciary Committee (Senate), 168, 177, 180
Justice Department, 155, 169

Kelly, Edna F., 147
Kennedy, Edward M., 107, 175; see also Health Security
    Act
Kennedy, John F., 42, 45-46, 67-68, 76, 81-82, 87, 92,
    94, 96, 107, 147-49
Kennedy, Robert F., 99
Kennedy-Griffiths Health Security Act, see Health
    Security Act
Kennedy-Mills Health Act, see national health insurance
Keogh plan, 80
Kerr-Mills Act, 101-103
Khruschev, Nikita, 67
Kilpatrick, James J., 229, 234
King-Anderson Act, see Medicare
Knebel, Fletcher, 82
Knowles, James F., 72, 76, 214, 221
Knutson, Coya, 40
Koontz, Elizabeth D., 188
Korean War, 16, 37
Ku Klux Klan, 182

Labor Department, 188, 225
Labor legislation, 45-48
Labor-Management Reporting and Disclosure Act of 1959;
    see Landrum-Griffin Act
Labor rackets cases, see Teamsters
Laliberte, Mel L., 6-7
Landrum, Philip, 46
Landrum-Griffin Act (Labor-Management Reporting and Dis-
    closure Act of 1959), 46-48
Lawrence, Margaret, 176

League of Housewives, 182
LeBreton, Edmund, 229
Lerman, Robert L. 245
Lesinski, John, 47-48, 55
Little League Baseball, 185
Long, Russell B., 105, 159
Lowe, Maxwell M., 18

Mackrowicz, Thaddeaus, 48, 81
Macy, John W. Jr., 161
Mahon, George W., 214
Manley, John F., 84
Manpower Development and Training Act (MDTA), 229-30
Marsh, John O, 171
Marshal Plan, 87
Martel, Francis X., 11
Mason, Charles M., 155
May, Catherine, 148
McClellan Teamster probe, 46
McClung, Nelson D., 76, 211
McCormack, John, 44, 48, 69, 81-82, 94, 108
McCulloch, William M., 179
McGovern, George, 39, 47, 245
McNamara, Patrick V., 19, 35, 101, 147
Meany, George, 107
Medicaid, 103, 221, 232
Medicare, 82, 101-105, 232
Medicredit, 105-106
Meyer, Alfred V., 19
Michigan (State), 4-5, 21-22, 35, 38-39, 41, 43-45, 51, 56, 70, 74, 87-88, 94, 102, 147, 150, 217, 222, 269; see also Detroit, Michigan Democratic Party, Recession of 1954, Wayne County
Michigan Democratic Central Committee, 6, 14
Michigan Democratic Club, 6-7
Michigan Democratic Party, 4, 6-9, 11-13, 16, 268; see also Detroit, Seventeenth District
Michigan Efficiency Task Force, 268
Michigan Foundation Conference, 98
Michigan Law Review, 4
Michigan Legislature, 5, 9-11, 13, 15, 17, 73, 104, 266
Michigan Seventeenth Congressional District, see Seventeenth District
Miel, Lucius S., 55
Miller, Emma Guffey, 168
Mills, Wilbur, 71, 74, 78, 81-86, 89-91, 101, 103, 106-109, 214, 267-68; see also Ways and Means Committee
Miriani, Louis, 44
Mondale, Walter F., 100
Moody, Blair, 14, 19

Morris, Frank, 20
Mott, Lucretia, 143
Movie guild swindle, 17
Moynihan, Daniel Patrick, 213
Munnecke, Phoebe, 5
Muskie, Edmund S., 73-74, 181

NAACP, 42
National Association of Women Lawyers (NAWL), 67
National Bank of Detroit, 268
National Commission on Consumer Finance, 187
National Council of Catholic Women, 182
National Federation of Republican Women, 174, 182-83
National Health Care Act, 105
National health insurance, 101-109, 265, 269; see also Health Security Act
National Health Insurance Partnership Act, 105-106
National Labor Relations Act of 1948, 47
National Labor Relations Board, 20, 47
National Organization of Women (NOW), 153-54, 158, 268
National Women's Party, 168-69, 172, 175
Nedzi, Lucien, 172
Neighborhood Youth Corps (NYC), 229-30
New Deal, 8, 148
New Frontier, 67
Nineteenth Amendment, 167
Nossiter, Bernard D., 70
Nixon, Richard M., 69, 73, 78, 88-90, 95, 107, 109, 162, 180, 212, 243, 268-70
Nuclear war, see Civil Defense

Oakman, Charles G., 15-16, 18, 21-23, 35, 45, 54
O'Connor, Don, 54
Office of Child Support Enforcement, 236
Office of Defense Mobilization, 49
Office of Federal Contract Compliance, 188
Office of Price Administration (OPA), 5, 8
O'Hara, James G., 16, 48, 82
Oil depletion allowance, 92, 94, 97, 100
Ozarks, 1-2

Pacific Railroad, 1-2
Panama Canal Zone, 71
Patman, Wright, 214
Paul, Alice, 168
Pechman, Joseph A., 72
Pension legislation, private pensions, 158-60, 164, 215, 238, 265; see also Employee Retirement Income Security Act of 1974; public pensions, 81, 161-62
Perkins, Carl D., 159

Peterson, Esther, 149
Pierce (Peirce) City, Missouri, 1-2, 38
Pinkerton guards, 46
Poindexter, Thomas L., 19-21
Postal pay raise, 23, 45
President's Commission on the Status of Women, 169
Privacy Act of 1974, 236
Protective legislation for women, 151, 156-58, 173, 177, 184-85
Proxmire, William, 159, 211, 214
<u>Public Income Transfer Programs</u>, 224-25

Quillico, John, 48

Rains, Albert, 36
Randolph, Jennings, 77, 159
Rat extermination legislation, 68-69
Rawalt, Marguerite, 169, 171, 173, 175-76
Rayburn, Sam, 38, 52, 70, 82
Reagan, Ronald, 243
Recession of 1954, 22, 36-38
Recession of 1957-58, 43-45
Recycling bill, 100-101
Renegotiation Board, 51
Reston, James, 82
Reuss, Henry S., 73, 80
Reuther, Roy, 24, 41
Reuther, Walter, 37, 44, 78
Revenue Act of 1971, <u>see</u> automobile excise taxes
Revenue sharing, 71-75, 79, 81, 214, 220, 228
Ribicoff, Abraham, 108, 214
Richardson, Elliot L., 105-106
Rockefeller Foundation, 99
Rockefellers, 85, 99-100
Rogers, Paul, 54
Roosa, Robert V., 85
Roosevelt, James, 151
Rostenkowski, Dan, 70, 85
Roth, Russell B., 106
Rules Committee (House), 81, 149, 159, 177
Russia, <u>see</u> Soviet Union
Ryan, Daniel J., 39-41, 268

St. George, Katherine, 148
St. Lawrence Seaway, 21-22
Salk vaccine, 104
Schlafly, Phyllis, 182-84
Schneebeli, Herman T., 80
Scholle, August, 12, 48, 55
Select Committee on The Aging (Senate), 241-42

Seventeenth District (Michigan Congressional), 6, 13-14, 19-24, 35, 45, 55-56, 216, 265-67; see also Detroit
Shanahan, Eileen, 181
Sigler, Kim, 80
Sixteenth Amendment, 246
Small Business Administration, 43
Smith, George E., 55
Smith, Howard K., 150-51
Smith, Margaret Chase, 38, 151
Smith, Neal, 40
Social Security legislation, 84, 96, 101-104, 108-114, 145, 161, 163-67, 169, 174, 177-79, 183, 187, 213, 215-16, 219-20, 223-25, 230, 232-33, 235-38, 240-44, 246, 265; see also Ways and Means Committee
South Central Bell Telephone Company, 157
Soviet Union, 15, 36, 43, 49, 67, 86, 89-90, 158; see also Jewish emigration
Spence, Brent, 37
Spiegel, Arthur, 226-28
Sputnik, 36, 43
Staats, Elmer B., 222-23, 230-31, 234, 236, 248; see also General Accounting Office
Staebler, Neil, 6
Stans, Maurice H., 89
State and Local Fiscal Assistance Act of 1972, 75
State Department, 163
Stein, Herbert, 44, 188
Stevens, Christine, 52-53
Stevenson, Adlai, 52
Stevenson-Sparkman television campaign of 1952, 14
"Stop ERA," see Phyllis Schlafly
Storey, James R., 224-25, 228
Studebaker, 78
Studies in Public Welfare, see JEC welfare study; (also see studies under specific titles)
Sullinger family, 2
Sullivan food-stamp bill, see food stamp legislation
Sullivan, Lenore, 37-40
Supplemental Security Income (SSI), 232, 240-43, 247
Supreme Court (U.S.), 36, 113, 150, 156-57, 160-61, 163, 166-70, 172, 174-75, 177, 179, 184, 188, 269
Swainson, John, 102

Taft, Robert A., 35
Taft-Hartley Act, 22-23, 46
Tax Credits and Allowances Act, 244-47, 264
Tax legislation, (1962) 92; (1964) 71, 92-94, 96; (1969) 97-100, 145; 268
Teamsters, 17-18, 46, 78; see also Hoffa, James R., McClellan Teamster probe

"Teas for Victory," 13
Televising House, 15, 23, 52
Tennessee Valley Authority, 22
Thompson, Clark, W., 82
Thompson, Ruth, 38, 43
Thurmond, J. Strom, 7
Tidelands scandal, 22
Townsend, Alair A., 214-15, 221, 224, 228, 230, 237-39, 240, 245; see also JEC welfare study
Trade Expansion Act of 1962 (TEA), 86-88
Trade Reform Act of 1974, 89-91
Trailer campaign, 14-15, 22
Treasury Department, 94, 98, 100, 103-104, 241, 244, 247
Truman, Harry S., 7, 14-15
Truth, Sojourner, 172

Udall, Stewart, 47
Ullman, Al, 80, 109, 267
Union College, (N.Y.), 3
United Airlines, 155-56; see also Airline discrimination against women
United Auto Workers (UAW), 12-14, 19-24, 41, 45, 55, 104, 107, 268
University of Michigan, 4, 8, 180, 185
University of Missouri, 1, 3
Urban Institute, 243
Urban renewal, 41, 68
U.S.-Canadian Tariff of 1965, 87

Veneman, John J., 223, 228
Vietnam War, 36, 72, 95

Wallace Progressives, 7
War on Poverty, 68-69, 95, 211, 233; see also Johnson, Lyndon B.
Watergate, 91, 109, 187, 234, 243
Watts, 67
Wayne County (Michigan), 6, 9, 12, 19, 22, 39
Ways and Means Committee (House), 54, 69, 74-114, 163-64, 166, 212-20, 228, 240, 266-68; see also Wilbur Mills, Social Security legislation
Weinberger, Casper, 108, 233, 243
Weinberger v. Wiesenfeld (1975), 113, 141
Welfare—An Administrative Nightmare, 225, 229
Welfare study, see JEC welfare study
Wiggins, Charles E. 178-79
Williams, G. Mennen, 5, 8-10, 12-14, 16-17, 19-21, 23, 35, 39, 44, 150
Williams, Harrison A., 78

Williams, Nancy, 13, 36
Wilson, Charles, 35
Wirtz, W. Willard, 76-78
Wolcott, Jessie P., 70
Wolfgang, Myra K,, 151
Women United, 176, 178
Women's Equity Action League (WEAL), 158-59, 175, 185, 268
Women's Lobby, 268
Work Incentive Program (WIN), 229-30
World War I, 3
World War II, 5, 49
Wright, (Charles) Elbridge, 2-3, 41
Wright family, 2
Wright, Jeanettie Hinds, 2
Wright, Martha, 143
Wright, Nelle, 2-3
Wright, Orville, 2-3